Dale Earnhardt

THE FINAL RECORD

John Regruth

MBI Publishing Company

First published in 2001 by MBI Publishing Company, 729 Prospect Avenue, PO Box 1, Osceola, WI 54020-0001 USA

MBI Publishing Company books are also available at discounts in bulk quantity for industrial or sales-promotional use. For details write to Special Sales Manager at Motorbooks International Wholesalers & Distributors, 729 Prospect Avenue, PO Box 1, Osceola, WI 54020-0001 USA.

Library of Congress Cataloging-in-Publication Data Available
ISBN 0-7603-0953-1

On the front cover:
Among Earnhardt's records, none is more impressive than his 10 consecutive Twin 125 victories from 1990 to 1999 at Daytona. The fact that he built such a streak in a short race (50 laps) on a restrictor-plate track—where leaders are regularly shuffled deep into the field, especially late in the race—is remarkable. As unbreakable as Joe DiMaggio's 56, the streak will live long in the memories of NASCAR fans. *Face shot by David Stringer; car shot by Bill Burt*

On the frontispiece:
Earnhardt climbs into his assigned car before the IROC 2000 race at Talladega. As the series leader, Earnhardt started the race from the back of the field. Though he never led a lap, he finished third and retained his points lead. *Bill Burt*

On the title page:
Reminiscent of the scene following his magical win at the Daytona 500 in 1998, crew members of both Richard Childress Racing teams rushed to greet Earnhardt on pit road after his thrilling win in the 1999 DieHard 500 at Talladega. *Bill Burt*

On the back cover:
Earnhardt was one of a handful of drivers who still wore the open-faced helmet. After the untimely deaths of Adam Petty and Kenny Irwin during the 2000 season, Earnhardt defended his career-long helmet choice as being safer than the full-faced helmets worn by most of today's racers, including Irwin and Petty. *David Stringer*

Edited by John Adams-Graf
Designed by Dan Perry

Printed in Hong Kong

Author's Note on Sources & References
To achieve the level of statistical analysis that this book attempts, finding reliable sources of fundamental race data is essential. The core statistics of a race event, i.e., each driver's start, finish, money, laps completed and laps led — must be secured for all races to create an extended, comprehensive look at a driver's career and his standing in stock car racing history. Taken together, the resources on the list above provided that core of statistics. In particular, Fielden's monumental series, *Forty Years of Stock Car Racing*, is the seminal historical research achievement in the world of stock car racing. His work is the foundation for all works that have and will follow, including this book. Any author exploring stock car racing from a historical point of view is automatically indebted to Fielden's incomparable work.

Contents

Preface

In the works for two years, this book was scheduled for release in the summer of 2001 alongside similar books on other drivers. In its original incarnation, it included all Winston Cup races run through the Atlanta event in November of 2000. But at the start of the 2001 season, when Dale Earnhardt's car careened into the wall at Daytona, everything changed. Rather than publish an incomplete look at Earnhardt's career, we chose to step back, sadly, and update every item that was affected by the addition of one more race. With the updates, this book provides a full picture of Earnhardt's racing career at the time his life ended.

Admittedly, when this project started back in 1999, I wasn't much of an Earnhardt admirer. As a committed Jeff Gordon fan, I didn't appreciate the Intimidator's style. Creating this book, however, pushed me to the inescapable conclusion that Earnhardt was the greatest NASCAR driver of all time. The totality of his accomplishments is stunning. As a baseball fan, I find easy analogy on the diamond. Earnhardt's seven championships are equivalent to Babe Ruth's 700-plus home runs. His twin 125-win streak at Daytona—10 straight from 1990 to 1999, perhaps his greatest and most unbreakable mark—resembles DiMaggio's untouchable 56-game hitting streak. On 1,398 separate occasions, Earnhardt fought for and gained the lead in a race—a prolific total akin to Rose and Cobb's 4,000-plus hits. The statistics were so astonishing, his achievements so great, that I sometimes struggled to do them justice. I wanted to continue studying the numbers to find new ways to reveal the extent of his greatness. As the 2001 season began, Earnhardt's chances looked strong. Undoubtedly, he would have added significantly to his records.

Like everyone else, I had selfish reasons for wishing Earnhardt had swerved into the infield rather than into the wall that Sunday afternoon. But after witnessing the strength and courage of Dale Earnhardt Jr. in the weeks following the Daytona 500, it became clear that prolonged sorrow was the wrong choice. With 22 years of Earnhardt memories, why focus on a tragic split second at the end of his career? Earnhardt was doing what he loved, at the track he loved most. This book is a choice to move beyond the sorrow; it acknowledges that last split second, but concentrates on the magic of the preceding 22 years. It is a tribute to an amazing driver and a celebration of his remarkable career.

Quick Facts about Dale Earnhardt's Winston Cup Career

Number of races run before 1st victory	16
Most consecutive victories	4- 1987 (3/29, Darlington; 4/5, North Wilkesboro; 4/12, Bristol; 4/26, Martinsville)
Most consecutive races without a victory	59 (1996/1997)
Most consecutive Top 5 finishes	7 (1996)
Most consecutive Top 10 finishes	12 - twice (1987 & 1995/96)
Fewest points earned in a race	37 - twice (1982 at Riverside, 1989 at Charlotte)
Number times earned maximum 185 points	56 - 1979 (1 time), 1980 (3), 1982 (1), 1983 (2), 1984 (1), 1985 (2), 1986 (3), 1987 (11), 1988 (3), 1989 (5), 1990 (7), 1991 (2), 1993 (6), 1994 (3), 1995 (3), 1996 (1), 1998 (1), 1999 (1)
Most wins in a season	11 - 1987
Most DNFs in a season	18 - 1982
Fewest DNFs in a season	0 - 1997, 2000
Largest single-race prize	$1,080,233 (1998 Daytona 500)
Smallest single-race prize	$1,360 (1976 Dixie 500/Atlanta)
Number of poles	22
Worst starting position	43 (5 times) - (1995 UAW-GM Quality 500/Charlotte, 1997 TranSouth Financial 400/Darlington, 1997 Miller 500/Dover, 1998 California 500, 1998 MBNA Gold 400/Dover)
Worst finish	42 - twice (1982 at Riverside, 1989 at Charlotte)
Lowest position in point standings (after joining series full-time in 1979)	35 (1982, Week 1)
Lowest finish in point standings (after joining series full-time in 1979)	12 (twice) - 1982, 1992
Number of times led the most laps	84 - 1979 (1 time), 1980 (3), 1981 (1), 1982 (4), 1983 (2), 1985 (4), 1986 (7), 1987 (13), 1988 (7), 1989 (6), 1990 (10), 1991 (4), 1993 (9), 1994 (3), 1995 (4), 1996 (3), 1997 (1), 1998 (1), 1999 (1)
Most laps led in a single race	456 of 500 (1989 Budweiser 500/Dover)
Highest percentage of laps led, in a race	91.28 - 335 of 367 (1986 TranSouth Financial 500/Darlington)
Most laps led in a season	3,358 (1987)
Least number of laps completed in a race	3 of 200 (1985 Van Scoy Diamond Mine 500/Pocono)
Tracks where Earnhardt won	Atlanta, Bristol, Charlotte, Darlington, Daytona, Dover, Indianapolis, Martinsville, Michigan, Nashville, North Wilkesboro, Phoenix, Pocono, Richmond, Rockingham, Sears Point, Talladega
Tracks where Earnhardt did not win	California, Homestead, Las Vegas, New Hampshire, Ontario, Riverside, Texas, Texas World, Watkins Glen
Tracks where Earnhardt won a pole	Atlanta, Bristol, Darlington, Daytona, Dover, North Wilkesboro, Richmond, Riverside, Sears Point, Talladega, Watkins Glen
Tracks where Earnhardt did not win a pole	California, Charlotte, Homestead, Indianapolis, Las Vegas, Martinsville, Michigan, Nashville, New Hampshire, Ontario, Phoenix, Pocono, Rockingham, Texas, Texas World
Track where Earnhardt won the most	Talladega (10)
Track where Earnhardt won the most poles	Atlanta (5)
Most lucrative track, career	Daytona - $4,498,565
Worst-to-First: Worst starting spot in an eventual victory	35 (2000 Cracker Barrel 500/Atlanta)
First-to-Worst: Worst finish after starting from the pole	34 (1994 DieHard 500/Talladega)
Favorite starting spot in victories	3rd and 4th (11 victories each)
No. of times won from the pole	5
Consecutive start streak	648

Heart of a Champion

by Dan Markham

That Dale Earnhardt died doing what he loved was the prevailing sentiment following that fateful Daytona 500. Perhaps. But he certainly died doing something for the people he loved.

During the 2001 Daytona 500, Earnhardt had the car to make another run for the checkered flag. Even later, as the reality of Earnhardt's death settled in, it was easy to conjure an alternate ending to the final 500 of his career. Picture the No. 3 car setting up the two leaders, then diving breathtakingly low, into the grass perhaps, ultimately passing the front-runners by simply refusing to give ground, then remaining out front to win his second Daytona 500. Simple, really.

But Earnhardt, for one of the few, if not only, times in his driving career, showed us something else that afternoon. He showed he was not just the most competitive man to ever strap on a helmet. He showed he was a father and a friend and a man with the makings of a damn good boss.

Rather than make a hard charge at the two leaders, Earnhardt elected to hang back. He did so, it appeared, to allow his drivers, luckless friend Michael Waltrip and burgeoning star, and son, Dale Jr., to make it a two-man show. That they did, with Waltrip performing the same kind of exorcism Dale Sr. had done three years earlier—ending a lifetime drought with a Daytona 500 victory. Different droughts, but same euphoria.

Yet the owner would never get to see the Dale Earnhardt, Inc. team earn its one-two finish. The life of NASCAR's greatest driving force—any interpretation of that description is acceptable—would end where so many now-inconsequential "tragedies"

Despite a well-cultivated "Intimidator" image, Earnhardt's wry smile was a familiar sight in the Winston Cup garage area. *Jennifer Regruth*

had happened to him before—the last lap of the Daytona 500.

It was unfathomable to think Earnhardt would have done this 15 years ago, or 5 years ago, or even last year. For the better part of his 49 years, Dale Earnhardt in a race car had one thought in mind, beating all those other son-of-a-guns to the checkered flag, regardless the path he took to get there.

But here he was in the closing laps at Daytona. Friends like Sterling Marlin, Ken Schrader, and Rusty Wallace surrounded him, guys he could certainly use to make a run on those lonesome leaders. And they all would have followed, knowing the quickest way to the front of the pack was in the wake of No. 3.

Instead, he kept them at bay, dueling among them. He performed this previously unexplored technique as skillfully as he had so

Dale Earnhardt settles into his car before the green flag drops at Indianapolis. He performed this ritual 676 times during his Winston Cup career, including a consecutive race streak of 648 races that ended with his fatal accident at the 2001 Daytona 500. Fiercely independent about driver safety, Earnhardt was distinctive in his choice of a open-faced helmet, the low, slouching position of his driver's seat, and the setup of his safety belts. *David Stringer*

many others on a race track. It was Waltrip's and Junior's race; Dale guaranteed it.

This certainly must have surprised Dale Jr., who less than a year earlier had admitted that if Dale Sr. trailed him on the last lap, he expected his father would do whatever it took to finish first. And it surely stunned Waltrip, a veteran whose career was salvaged by Earnhardt, then pushed to this amazing height because of him. But perhaps this was fitting. For this last generous act throws another contradiction, another cause for deeper analysis about Dale Earnhardt, into an already complex mix.

He was the high school dropout who showed remarkable business acumen. He was the shy, humble fellow who could fill a reporter's notebook or television interview with country gems. He was the take-no-prisoners driver who nonetheless commanded the highest respect of the would-be captives. And now, he was the ultimate competitor who yielded a chance at victory to a son and a friend.

We'll never know what he would have said about those last laps at Daytona. This will keep us guessing years after his death, just as he kept us guessing all those marvelous years on the track.

Dale Earnhardt died too soon. But for as long as stock cars are racing on some patch of asphalt for generations to come, there will forever be sentences that begin, "You shoulda seen the time Earnhardt . . ."

That, more than the records, or titles, or money, is the legacy of a champion.

Dale Earnhardt, born on April 29, 1951, inherited numerous traits from his father Ralph: a love of automobiles, a desire to make them go fast, and a fearless attitude inside them were just a few.

Teresa Earnhardt, left, was a familiar sight on pit road before Winston Cup races. Earnhardt called his marriage to Teresa his greatest accomplishment. *David Stringer*

And he also passed down something else: a fitting last name. Earnhardt. Break it down and say it aloud, and you've got "Earn" and "Heart." Two words, a verb and a noun, which serve as fitting adjectives describing just how the man known as the Intimidator forged one of the greatest Winston Cup racing careers in history.

Earn

Ralph Earnhardt was a short-track legend in North Carolina. But his success was mostly limited to those dusty circuits, as he was unable to crash the invite-only world of the highest level of stock car racing.

In those days, access to the best equipment belonged to a scant few drivers. Consequently, the Earnhardt name did not carry the same weight as that of racing families Petty and Allison, or in another circuit, Unser and Andretti. And it certainly didn't carry the same cash.

When Earnhardt teamed permanently with Richard Childress, left, in 1984, his career took off. The two quickly formed one of the most successful teams in NASCAR history. In 17 seasons and 529 races together, they had won 6 championships, 67 races and $39 million. Also picture is former Earnhardt crew chief Larry McReynolds, right. *David Stringer*

Starting his career without those inherited benefits, Dale Earnhardt was required to climb the ladder of racing greatness from the bottom, one rung at a time. And each ascent was made not because of his contacts or his contracts, but because of his undeniable, perhaps unequaled, abilities.

He was never given a dream ride on the circuit's best team. Instead, his talent and tenacity made him too difficult to ignore, and he quickly became one of the best. But even after a phenomenal start to his career, he didn't just join one of the high-dollar teams and coast. With an equally hungry Richard Childress calling the shots, Dale simply made his team the envy of the circuit. He earned his way to the top of the racing world. And when he got there, he earned every victory and championship that followed.

Heart

An anatomical scan of Dale Earnhardt displayed all the required racing equipment. At the top, he had a mind that worked faster than the computers inside today's stock cars. He knew instinctively when to go high or low, when to hold back to avoid the mayhem, and when to push forward and cause some of it. Seven championships are not achieved without a steel-trap brain.

At the bottom, he had a right foot made of gold, a substance heavier than lead and far more valuable. He won 76 times in his career, with many of his best performances coming on the Winston Cup circuit's fastest tracks.

Coursing through his veins was blood a few degrees colder than ice. Throughout his career, Earnhardt went side-by-side with virtually every one of racing's greatest drivers. More often than not, those duels were won by the Intimidator.

His backbone was a steel rod, incapable of folding under even the greatest pressure. Well, since his rookie season when he suffered two broken collarbones in a late-race wreck at Pocono, Earnhardt hadn't missed a start. Even then, Dale came back one week earlier than doctors ordered—and then won the pole in his first two return starts.

All of the rest of Earnhardt's seemingly bionic racing parts, eyes, ears, hands, and legs, suggest the driver was assembled by a mad scientist, or maybe just Ralph while he was tooling around in the garage. But it is the heart that stood above all of them. Dale Earnhardt had, without question, the heart of racer. His career began more than 20 years ago, when force of will and unmistakable talent earned him a place on stock car racing's highest circuit. He won his first championship just one year later.

Two decades after that, when virtually all of his original contemporaries had long since retired (and his one-time chief rival called it quits about a decade past his prime), Earnhardt was still among the most capable drivers on the track. Twenty years after his first title, in an entirely different millennium for crying out loud, Earnhardt was back in the middle of a chase for Winston Cup championship number eight. He didn't get it, but until the moment of his death on February 18, 2001 he was still one of the best bets on the circuit.

Determination like this can't be explained by greed or ego or talent alone. The obvious fact is, while Dale Earnhardt closed in on 50, a number he sadly wouldn't reach, the hunger to win races and championships had not abated a fraction. From his very first races, when he was Ralph's boy, to his most recent successful season, when he became hotshot phenom Dale Jr.'s dad, Dale Earnhardt poured his heart into stock car racing.

The son of hard-working Ralph Earnhardt, Dale was one of the hardest working of all NASCAR drivers. He pulled double duty in the Busch Grand National series for years. Pictured here with fellow driver Tommy Ellis, Earnhardt takes a lunch break in the infield while waiting for Grand National qualifying to begin at Indianapolis Raceway Park. Two of the most successful drivers in Busch series history, Earnhardt and Ellis rank fourth and fifth in all-time career wins, with Earnhardt capturing 23 and Ellis 22 victories. *Don Hamilton*

Driving the No. 3 Wrangler Jeans Chevy for Richard Childress in 1986, Earnhardt steers around the tight turns of Martinsville Speedway. In their third full season together, Earnhardt and Childress won the 1986 Winston Cup championship by 288 points over Darrell Waltrip. *Don Hamilton*

the entire 1979 season. Marcis balked, preferring not to share the attention, and departed the Osterlund team to resume a lengthy career remarkable only in its mediocrity. With Marcis gone, the idea of the multicar team evaporated, leaving Earnhardt as the sole driver for Osterlund. Marcis out, Earnhardt in is the motorsports equivalent of Manhattan for $24 or Babe Ruth for a Broadway flop. This was one lopsided transaction.

Just seven races into his rookie campaign, the North Carolina native recorded his first victory in the Southeastern 500 at Bristol Motor Speedway. And though that was his only victory in the injury-marred year, it was a mere portent of an incredible 1980.

Earnhardt finished second in the season-opening Winston Western 500 at Riverside in 1980 and followed it up with a fourth-place run at Daytona (sadly, another omen). But the

It is interesting, as NASCAR continues to escalate in popularity, how so many of the sport's new followers are oblivious to its past. In 1999, Tony Stewart enjoyed the greatest rookie season in NASCAR history, we were told. One year later, Dale Jr. and Matt Kenseth were threatening to take that honor away. And before that it was Jeff Gordon, who didn't break through during his rookie campaign but quickly established himself as NASCAR's best young driver.

Has there ever been a driver who entered the top circuit so good, so fast? We've been asked that question repeatedly. But none of them, at least not yet, has had as much success in his career's first two seasons as Dale Earnhardt.

Earnhardt had eight Winston Cup races under his belt over the course of four seasons when he was given a shot in Rod Osterlund's second car for the final race of the 1978 season, the Dixie 500 at Atlanta Motor Speedway. He started 10th and finished 4th, a result that opened the upstart owner's eyes to the possibilities for 1979. Osterlund already had Dave Marcis in one car when he brought up the possibility of letting this kid run a second car for

Following the Wrangler sponsorship and its "One Tough Customer" marketing campaign, Earnhardt gained the backing of GM Goodwrench in 1988 and immediately assumed an intimidating black paint scheme. *Bill Burt*

Daytona finish put him at the top of the points chase. And there he would stay. Chalking up victories at Atlanta, a repeat at Bristol, Nashville, Martinsville and his first win in his home state at Charlotte, Earnhardt entered the season finale at Ontario Speedway with a 29-point lead in the championship run. He needed a fifth-place finish to clinch the title, which is precisely where he wound up, holding off the estimable Cale Yarborough.

One year after winning Rookie of the Year honors, Dale Earnhardt was the Winston Cup champion. Gordon didn't do that. Though Stewart (hardly a racing novice when he began his NASCAR career) followed up his rookie year with another solid campaign, he didn't come close either. And the chances of Dale Jr. or Kenseth following Earnhardt's lead during their sophomore campaigns are as likely as Marcis turning up in victory lane again.

Along with a compatible owner and a generous sponsor, much of Earnhardt's success can be attributed to his Goodwrench crew, which quickly gained the reputation as one of the best in NASCAR history. *David Stringer*

By the late 1980s, Earnhardt's "Intimidator" reputation was firmly in place. Here, playing off that image, Earnhardt's crew members dared visitors to approach their stall in the garage area at Indianapolis. *David Stringer*

While a championship season as a second-year racer would indicate Earnhardt could write his own ticket, that wasn't the case. For Earnhardt, lean years would follow, a result more determined by bad luck than misplaced ability. Midway through his first season as defending champion, Earnhardt was devastated by news out of nowhere. Osterlund, the man he credited with giving him the biggest break of his career, announced he was selling the team to J. D. Stacy.

Dale stayed on, but the marriage with Stacy lasted four races. That's when veteran driver Richard Childress, a man whose own driving career was limited by the absence of equal opportunities at the top of the circuit, invited Dale to take the wheel of his Chevrolet. Childress did not step out of the car easily, but he recognized for his team to finally achieve success, he needed to take over car-owning duties full-time.

The Earnhardt-Childress partnership produced few sparks, and Childress realized his team, at that point, was not capable of fielding cars commensurate with his driver's skill. So at season's end, he reluctantly offered Dale the opportunity to find another ride for the 1982 season. Dale, winless in 1981 after his championship season, reluctantly accepted.

As his Winston Cup championships piled higher and his fame increased, Earnhardt took advantage of new opportunities, including providing garage-area commentary for ESPN. Though his uncooperative attitude with the press was legendary, in latter years Earnhardt became one of the most entertaining and informative interviews on the circuit. *Bill Burt*

Georgia, native dominated the superspeedways. Though Earnhardt won twice as many races as the previous year, the Childress team fared poorly in the season standings, finishing well behind champion Darrell Waltrip. But if the team wondered if a championship was indeed in the future, it didn't have long to wait.

In 1986, Earnhardt finally regained the magic of six years earlier, winning five races, earning 16 Top 5s and 23 Top 10s, numbers that added up to a second Winston Cup championship. But that was merely the beginning.

If Earnhardt was good in 1986, in 1987 he was beyond compare. And if there was any hangover from another Daytona disappointment—one year after running out of gas while leading the race, a lengthy pit stop torpedoed his hopes in 1987—it sure didn't show.

Earnhardt won six of the seven races that followed Daytona (curiously finishing 16th in Atlanta, the only race he started from the pole) to build a 220-point cushion. With another three-race winning streak later in the year (Bristol, Darlington, and Richmond), Earnhardt cruised to his second straight championship and third overall. The final numbers

Reminiscent of the scene following his magical win in the Daytona 500 in 1998, crew members of both Richard Childress Racing teams rush to greet Earnhardt on pit road after his thrilling win in the 1999 DieHard 500 at Talladega. *Bill Burt*

So as 1982 began, Dale was driving for his fourth owner in just over a full season. This time, in Bud Moore's No. 15 Ford. And while the team earned a victory in just its sixth race, at Darlington, the lean times of the 1981 season remained the norm. Dale had just seven Top 5 finishes, and only one after the June 13 race at Riverside. The following season was only a little better, with victories at Nashville and Talladega and nine Top 5s. Still, Earnhardt and Moore were clearly not matching his dream 1980 season.

Meanwhile, Childress was enjoying some success with the driver he signed to replace Earnhardt, Ricky Rudd. But Childress clamored to be reunited with Earnhardt, and fortunately

for both, the opportunity presented itself: Rudd would take over Earnhardt's slot on the Bud Moore team, and Earnhardt would rejoin Childress' organization. This time, the conditions were right for the close friends to join forces. Dale Earnhardt had finally found a home.

The partnership clicked immediately, with Earnhardt placing second in the Daytona 500, a theme that would recur for the next 13 years. But it was not until the second half of the season at Talladega that Earnhardt reached victory lane for Childress. A second victory at Atlanta in the penultimate race of the season, followed.

The wins doubled in 1985, all on some of NASCAR's shorter tracks. That was Bill Elliott's million-dollar season, when the Dawsonville,

Proof of the respect Earnhardt commanded on the Winston Cup circuit was the reaction to his victories, especially later in his career. Here, an elated Earnhardt shakes hands with well-wishers following his win at Talladega in the spring of 1999. The win broke a prolonged nine-race losing streak for Earnhardt at the track. *Bill Burt*

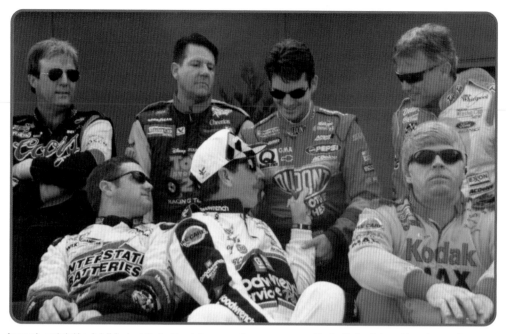

Apparently not intimidated, Jeff Gordon jokingly attempts to cover up the sponsor name on Earnhardt's hat during a driver photo session at Daytona. Reminding the young driver who's boss, Earnhardt grabs and pulls Gordon toward him, promising to get his revenge on the track. The two biggest stars in NASCAR, Earnhardt and Gordon combined to win 10 Winston Cup championships (7 for Earnhardt, 3 for Gordon). Gordon is viewed by many observers as one of the drivers who will have to help NASCAR fill the void left by Earnhardt's passing. *Sean Stringer*

included 11 victories and 21 Top 5 finishes—in just 29 races. Only five times did he finish outside the Top 10 and only twice out of the Top 20.

A painful 12-point loss to Rusty Wallace in the 1989 title chase was quickly forgotten one year later, perhaps the only time Earnhardt was the recipient of truly good fortune. Earnhardt overtook Mark Martin in the second-to-last race to claim the championship. For Martin, still searching for his first Cup title, 1990 was the year the championship was lost not on the track, but in NASCAR's offices. After the season's second race at Richmond, where Martin beat Earnhardt to the finish line, NASCAR inspectors discovered an illegal carburetor spacer on his Jack Roush Ford. Cup officials fined Martin $40,000 and penalized him 46 points, more than the difference between first-place Earnhardt and second-place Martin, 26 points, at season's end.

There would be no such drama in 1991. Posting 4 victories and 21 Top 10s, Earnhardt shook off a midseason challenge from Rudd and coasted to his fifth championship. The race for the title was essentially decided in the fifth-to-last race of the season, at North Wilkesboro,

when Earnhardt won and nearly doubled his margin (to 112 points) en route to a comfortable season victory. It was the second time Earnhardt collected back-to-back titles, a feat he would repeat in the 1993 and 1994 seasons.

The last title was a testament to consistency. Despite winning just four times, Earnhardt manhandled the competition in the points chase, beating runner-up Martin by 444 points. The 1994 championship was built on 20 Top 5 finishes and 25 Top 10s. But that title was more important for what it meant than how it was crafted. With his seventh championship, Earnhardt matched the previously considered unreachable total of the King, Richard Petty. The eighth title, which Earnhardt chased in 1995 before losing to the newcomer Gordon by 34 points, would elude him until the end. But the 2000 season confirmed it was still a possi-

bility, making his tragic death in the 2001 season opener all the more painful. While King Richard's 200 career victories are out of reach for everyone barring an inexplicable return by NASCAR to its days of equipment monopolies, an eighth championship would have allowed the millions of Earnhardt fans to say, with incontrovertible evidence to back it up, "There goes the greatest stock car driver who ever lived."

Even stuck on seven forever, they can make a pretty strong case.

In 1998, 20 years after his first Daytona 500, the greatest driver of the final 20 years of the twentieth century finally achieved what had eluded him so often. Dale Earnhardt was the Daytona 500 champion. There are many words that can be used to describe Dale's victory: overdue, popular, spectacular,

Earnhardt called the ascendancy of his son, Dale Jr., to Winston Cup stardom one of his proudest moments. Junior didn't disappoint his father. Like Dale Sr., Junior won the seventh race of his rookie season (at Texas Motor Speedway). Dale Sr.'s first victory came at Bristol. *Bill Burt*

The Earnhardts were the most prominent father-son combination on the Winston Cup circuit since Bobby and Davey Allison competed during the late 1980s. At Talladega, Earnhardt started fourth and his son lined up directly behind him in sixth for the 2000 DieHard 500. *Bill Burt*

surprising, deserved, etc. But a word that cannot is 'validating'.

Had Dale Earnhardt never won the Daytona 500, it would not have in any way diminished his career. With 7 championships and 70 victories under his belt at the time, Earnhardt owed no apologies for his inability to win the circuit's biggest race. If anything, the Daytona International Speedway owed him its condolences. It may be one thing if Earnhardt's failures in the 500 had been the result of the track simply having his number. But the opposite was true. Earnhardt owned Daytona. His record at the Speedway exceeded imagination, with a track-record number of victories in shootouts, 125s, IROC races, and the summer race, plus hardware from the events on the Grand National series. Only the 500 escaped him, where bad pit stops, cut tires, and fuel miscalculations seemed to leave the hunter haunted.

But if Dale's 19-year run of misfortune in the 500 was mystifying, it paled next to his mark in the Twin 125s, which may be the most marvelous record in motorsports. For 10 straight years, drivers checking the line-up of the Twin 125s had to scan for just one name. If Earnhardt was in their flight, they knew they were fighting for second. From 1990 through 1999, Earnhardt won his 125. This mark, as much as any, defined Dale Earnhardt's unparalleled skill. The run came to an end in 2000, and perhaps only because his Chevrolet was seriously underequipped against the Fords, a fact NASCAR quickly rectified.

The 125-mile race, one of many Speed Weeks activities at Daytona International Speedway, is perhaps the best identifier of the best at Daytona. The race is long enough to allow the fastest drivers time to get to the front, but not too long where cut tires spoil the day of a dominating car. Look at it this way: Derrick Cope has never won a 125. And for 10 straight years, and 12 overall, Dale Earnhardt beat more than half of the field for the 500 to the flag. Yes, Daytona owed him one. But after all those near misses in the 500, 1998 was hardly the year most observers expected Earnhardt to end his drought. He was coming off his first winless season since a one-year run in a Pontiac in 1981. Moreover, it had been just a few months since his unexplainable blackout during the Southern 500, when he passed out during the race and ran straight into the wall. Earnhardt, many were saying and writing, was done as a threat in Winston Cup racing.

But all those fears, and all those years, were erased after 200 laps at Daytona in the winter of 1998. The man who couldn't win Daytona did just that. There was no black cloud hanging over the Man in Black that day. A crash on Lap 199 prevented a final-lap dogfight, and Earnhardt took the white and yellow flags simultaneously, a color combination that added to black and white.

The victory could not have been more popular. After his victory lap, Earnhardt came down pit road to the most moving spectacle of all. Drivers and crew members from every team, men, who had silently and not-so-silently cursed Earnhardt over the years when Dale's damn-the-torpedoes racing style had left them bruised and beaten, lined pit road to offer heartfelt congratulations.

No, that victory didn't validate Earnhardt as one of the greatest. But it did demonstrate he was as well respected as he was feared, as liked as he was loathed. It was justice being served.

For nearly two decades, the signature image of stock car racing was the slouching profile of Dale Earnhardt, wearing an open-faced helmet, in his famous black Chevrolet. *Bill Burt*

Career Statistics

Chapter 1

A Statistical Breakdown of Dale Earnhardt's Career Performance

"Finishing second," race car drivers often say, "just means you're the first loser." Winston Cup racing may be the most austere of all sports. Winning is everything. Few drivers thrived in this hypercompetitive environment as well as the no-nonsense Earnhardt. The following section offers the bottom-line statistical view of Earnhardt's career.

A peek under the hood of Dale Earnhardt's career reveals his amazing talent. In 676 starts, he won 76 times (sixth all-time) on 17 different Winston Cup tracks. His $41.6 million in career earnings is an all-time record. *Bill Burt*

Year	Final Standing	Races Run	Wins	Top 5s	Top 10s	Poles	Avg. Start	Avg. Finish	DNF's	Total Points	Bonus Points	Points per Race	Total Winnings	Races Led	Laps Led	Pct. Led	On Lead Lap	Miles Driven
1975	—	1	0	0	0	0	33.00	22.00	0	97	0	97.0	$1,925	0	0	0.0	0	533
1976	—	2	0	0	0	0	20.50	25.00	3	225	0	112.5	3,085	0	0	0.0	0	558
1977	—	1	0	0	0	0	36.00	38.00	1	49	0	49.0	1,375	0	0	0.0	0	38
1978	41st	5	0	1	2	0	21.40	11.20	0	660	0	132.0	20,145	0	0	0.0	0	2,366
1979	7th	27	1	11	17	4	7.74	10.67	4	3,749	85	138.9	264,086	16	604	6.5	6	9,357
1980	1st	31	5	19	24	0	9.06	8.19	4	4,661	140	150.4	588,926	25	1,185	11.5	13	11,136
1981	7th	31	0	9	17	0	7.97	13.55	10	3,975	65	128.2	347,113	12	300	2.9	7	10,062
1982	12th	30	1	7	12	1	10.60	18.80	18	3,402	110	113.4	375,325	18	1,062	10.5	6	7,787
1983	8th	30	2	9	14	0	9.20	15.33	13	3,732	105	124.4	446,272	19	1,027	10.1	8	8,946
1984	4th	30	2	12	22	0	10.83	9.63	2	4,265	80	142.2	616,788	16	446	4.3	10	10,850
1985	8th	28	4	10	16	1	9.54	14.68	9	3,561	105	127.2	546,596	17	1,237	13.1	9	9,149
1986	1st	29	5	16	23	1	6.90	7.38	4	4,468	165	154.1	1,783,880	26	2,127	22.4	15	11,164
1987	1st	29	11	21	24	1	7.28	5.93	2	4,696	200	161.9	2,099,243	27	3,358	35.8	23	10,898
1988	3rd	29	3	13	19	0	10.17	8.83	1	4,256	135	146.8	1,214,089	20	1,808	18.6	17	11,314
1989	2nd	29	5	14	19	0	8.03	10.28	2	4,164	140	143.6	1,435,730	22	2,735	28.1	19	10,796
1990	1st	29	9	18	23	4	5.86	8.03	1	4,430	160	152.8	3,083,056	22	2,438	25.1	20	10,955
1991	1st	29	4	14	21	0	11.10	8.62	2	4,287	120	147.8	2,396,685	20	1,125	11.6	17	11,435
1992	12th	29	1	6	15	1	14.69	14.86	4	3,574	45	123.2	915,463	9	483	5.0	9	10,198
1993	1st	30	6	17	21	2	9.70	8.20	2	4,526	150	150.9	3,353,789	21	1,475	14.7	21	11,808
1994	1st	31	4	20	25	2	15.26	8.03	3	4,694	130	151.4	3,300,733	23	1,014	10.0	22	11,409
1995	2nd	31	5	19	23	3	13.81	9.23	2	4,580	140	147.7	3,154,241	24	1,583	16.0	22	11,714
1996	4th	31	2	13	17	2	14.61	10.65	2	4,327	105	139.6	2,285,926	18	614	6.4	21	11,523
1997	5th	32	0	7	16	0	19.97	12.13	0	4,216	55	131.8	2,151,909	10	220	2.2	21	12,509
1998	8th	33	1	5	13	0	26.45	16.15	3	3,928	75	119.0	2,990,749	14	273	2.7	16	12,278
1999	7th	34	3	7	21	0	24.79	12.03	3	4,492	45	132.1	3,048,236	8	230	2.3	22	12,762
2000	2nd	34	2	13	24	0	21.09	9.38	0	4,865	85	143.1	4,918,886	17	353	3.5	28	13,184
2001	—	1	0	0	0	0	7.00	12.00	1	132	5	132.0	296,833	1	16	8.0	0	499.5
Totals		**676**	**76**	**281**	**428**	**22**	**12.90**	**11.06**	**96**	**94,011**	**2,445**	**139.1**	**$41,641,084**	**405**	**25,713**	**11.77**	**352**	**245,227**

Earnhardt's first career Winston Cup victory came in 1979 at Bristol Motor Speedway. That race was Earnhardt's 16th career start and the seventh race of his official rookie season. Only Davey Allison won earlier, taking the sixth race he started during his 1987 rookie campaign. *Bill Burt*

Career Start / Finish Breakdown

Career Start Breakdown

Pos.	No. of Starts	Pct.
Pole*	26	3.85
2	32	4.73
3	38	5.62
4	39	5.77
5	51	7.54
6	26	3.85
7	36	5.33
8	40	5.92
9	27	3.99
10	30	4.44
11	33	4.88
12	21	3.11
13	24	3.55
14	24	3.55
15	21	3.11
16	19	2.81
17	17	2.51
18	14	2.07
19	14	2.07
20	13	1.92
21	7	1.04
22	11	1.63
23	8	1.18
24	9	1.33
25	7	1.04
26	8	1.18
27	7	1.04
28	7	1.04
29	6	0.89
30	7	1.04
31	4	0.59
32	2	0.30
33	8	1.18
34	8	1.18
35	2	0.30
36	3	0.44
37	13	1.92
38	6	0.89
39	2	0.30
40	0	—
41	1	0.15
42	0	—
43	5	0.74

Career Start Statistics

Total Starts	676
Average Start	12.90
Front Row (Pct.)	58 (8.6)
Top 5	186 (27.5)
Top 10	345 (51)
Top 20	545 (80.6)
Top 30	622 (92)
Pos. 31 – 43	54 (8)

Career Finish Breakdown

Pos.	No. of Finishes	Pct.
Win	76	11.24
2	70	10.36
3	59	8.73
4	43	6.36
5	33	4.88
6	28	4.14
7	28	4.14
8	34	5.03
9	35	5.18
10	22	3.25
11	18	2.66
12	20	2.96
13	10	1.48
14	12	1.78
15	9	1.33
16	12	1.78
17	11	1.63
18	7	1.04
19	6	0.89
20	12	1.78
21	8	1.18
22	9	1.33
23	5	0.74
24	7	1.04
25	16	2.37
26	6	0.89
27	6	0.89
28	5	0.74
29	14	2.07
30	6	0.89
31	6	0.89
32	3	0.44
33	5	0.74
34	5	0.74
35	8	1.18
36	3	0.44
37	1	0.15
38	4	0.59
39	5	0.74
40	6	0.89
41	1	0.15
42	2	0.30
43	0	—

Career Finish Statistics

Average Finish	11.06
Top 2 (Pct.)	146 (21.6)
Top 5	281 (41.6)
Top 10	428 (63.3)
Top 20	545 (80.6)
Top 30	627 (92.8)
Pos. 31 – 43	49 (7.2)
DNFs	96 (14.2)

*Indicates number of starts from pole position, not number of poles won.
See Listing of Pole Starts for more detail.

Year	Career Race	Pole No.	Track - Race	Speed	Fin.
1979	24	1	Riverside: NAPA Riverside 400	113.089	13
	29	2	Richmond: Capital City 400	92.605	4
	30	3	Dover: CRC Chemicals 500	135.726	9
	33	4	North Wilkesboro: Holly Farms 400	112.783	4
1982	102	5	Atlanta: Coca-Cola 500	163.774	28
1985	207	6	Bristol: Busch 500	113.586	1
1986	220	7	Atlanta: Motorcraft 500	170.713	2
1987	249	8	Atlanta: Motorcraft Quality Parts 500	175.497	16
1989	327	*	Martinsville: Goody's 500	91.913[1]	9
	329	*	North Wilkesboro: Holly Farms 400	Field set by points	10
1990	336	*	Atlanta: Motorcraft Quality Parts 500	Field set by points	1
	349	9	Talladega: DieHard 500	192.513	1
	350	10	Watkins Glen: The Bud at the Glen	121.190	7
	352	11	Bristol: Busch 500	115.604	8
	353	12	Darlington: Heinz Southern 500	158.448	1
1992	408	13	Watkins Glen: The Bud at the Glen	116.882	9
1993	424	*	Darlington: TranSouth 500	Field set by points	1
	428	14	Talladega: Winston 500	192.355	4
	429	15	Sears Point: Save Mart Supermarkets 300k	91.838	6
1994	464	16	Daytona: Pepsi 400	191.339	3
	467	17	Talladega: DieHard 500	193.470	34
1995	484	18	Atlanta: Purolator 500	185.077	4
	495	19	Daytona: Pepsi 400	191.355	3
	504	20	Richmond: Miller Genuine Draft 400	122.543	3
1996	512	21	Daytona: Daytona 500	189.510	2
	531	22	Watkins Glen: The Bud at the Glen	120.733	6

[1]Jimmy Hensley won the pole in Earnhardt's car. Earnhardt drove the race, but Hensley given credit for winning the pole.

Pole Statistics

No. of Poles	22
Avg. Finished after Pole Starts	7.27
Wins from the Pole	5
No. of Track Records	0
Fastest Pole Speed	193.470
Slowest Pole Speed	91.838

Thanks to his efforts on the track, Earnhardt drew a crowd wherever he went. Humpy Wheeler, president of Lowe's Motor Speedway in Charlotte, called Earnhardt a "resurrected Confederate soldier" and theorized that Earnhardt's independent rebel personality appealed to NASCAR's blue-collar fan base and made him even more popular than stock car racing's "King," Richard Petty. *David Stringer*

Year	Career Race	Win No.	Track – Race	Start Pos.	Laps/	Led	Pct. Led	Money
1979	16	1	Bristol: Southeastern 500	9	500 /	164	32.80	$19,800
1980*	41	2	Atlanta: Atlanta 500	31	328 /	50	15.24	36,200
	42	3	Bristol: Valleydale Southeastern 500	4	500 /	208	41.60	20,625
	54	4	Nashville: Busch Nashville 420	7	420 /	103	24.52	14,600
	63	5	Martinsville: Old Dominion 500	7	500 /	174	34.80	25,375
	64	6	Charlotte: National 500	4	334 /	148	44.31	49,050
1982	104	7	Darlington: CRC Chemicals Rebel 500	5	367 /	181	49.32	31,450
1983	145	8	Nashville: Busch Nashville 420	3	420 /	212	50.48	23,125
	147	9	Talladega: Talladega 500	4	188 /	41	21.81	46,950
1984	177	10	Talladega: Talladega 500	3	188 /	40	21.28	47,100
	187	11	Atlanta: Atlanta Journal 500	10	328 /	48	14.63	40,610
1985	190	12	Richmond: Miller High Life 400	4	400 /	95	23.75	33,625
	193	13	Bristol: Valleydale 500	12	500 /	214	42.80	31,525
	207	14	Bristol: Busch 500	1	500 /	343	68.60	34,675
	211	15	Martinsville: Goody's 500	11	500 /	58	11.60	37,725
1986*	222	16	Darlington: TranSouth 500	4	367 /	335	91.28	52,250
	223	17	North Wilkesboro: First Union 400	5	400 /	195	48.75	38,550
	227	18	Charlotte: Coca-Cola 600	3	400 /	26	6.50	98,150
	242	19	Charlotte: Oakwood Homes 500	3	334 /	80	23.95	82,050
	244	20	Atlanta: Atlanta Journal 500	4	328 /	162	49.39	67,950
1987*	247	21	Rockingham: Goodwrench 500	14	492 /	319	64.84	53,900
	248	22	Richmond: Miller High Life 400	3	400 /	235	58.75	49,150
	250	23	Darlington: TranSouth 500	2	367 /	239	65.12	52,985
	251	24	North Wilkesboro: First Union 400	3	400 /	219	54.75	44,675
	252	25	Bristol: Valleydale Meats 500	3	500 /	134	26.80	43,850
	253	26	Martinsville: Sovran Bank 500	4	500 /	156	31.20	50,850
	259	27	Michigan: Miller American 400	5	200 /	152	76.00	60,250
	261	28	Pocono: Summer 500	16	200 /	85	42.50	55,875
	265	29	Bristol: Busch 500	6	500 /	314	62.80	47,175
	266	30	Darlington: Southern 500	5	202 /	108	53.47	64,650
	267	31	Richmond: Wrangler Jeans Indigo 400	8	400 /	220	55.00	44,950
1988	278	32	Atlanta: Motorcraft Quality Parts 500	2	328 /	270	82.32	67,950
	282	33	Martinsville: Pannill Sweatshirts 500	14	500 /	181	36.20	53,550
	294	34	Bristol: Busch 500	5	500 /	220	44.00	48,500
1989	310	35	North Wilkesboro: First Union 400	3	400 /	296	74.00	51,225
	314	36	Dover: Budweiser 500	2	500 /	456	91.20	59,350
	324	37	Darlington: Heinz Southern 500	10	367 /	153	41.69	71,150
	326	38	Dover: Peak Performance 500	15	500 /	375	75.00	59,950
	332	39	Atlanta: Atlanta Journal 500	3	328 /	249	75.91	81,700
1990*	336	40	Atlanta: Motorcraft Quality Parts 500	1	328 /	216	65.85	85,000
	337	41	Darlington: TranSouth 500	15	367 /	129	35.15	61,985
	341	42	Talladega: Winston 500	5	188 /	107	56.91	98,975
	346	43	Michigan: Miller Genuine Draft 400	5	200 /	22	11.00	72,950
	347	44	Daytona: Pepsi 400	3	160 /	127	79.38	72,850
	349	45	Talladega: DieHard 500	1	200 /	134	67.00	152,975
	353	46	Darlington: Heinz Southern 500	1	367 /	99	26.98	205,350
	354	47	Richmond: Miller Genuine Draft 400	6	400 /	173	43.25	59,225

Year	No.	Win	Race	Start	Laps / Led	Pct	Earnings
	360	48	Phoenix: Checker 500	3	312 / 262	83.97	72,100
1991*	363	49	Richmond: Pontiac Excitement 400	19	400 / 150	37.50	67,950
	369	50	Martinsville: Hanes 500	10	500 / 251	50.20	63,600
	378	51	Talladega: DieHard 500	4	188 / 101	53.72	88,670
	386	52	North Wilkesboro: Tyson/Holly Farms 400	16	400 / 9	2.25	69,350
1992	400	53	Charlotte: Coca-Cola 600	13	400 / 54	13.50	125,100
1993*	424	54	Darlington: TranSouth 500	1	367 / 212	57.77	64,815
	430	55	Charlotte: Coca-Cola 600	14	400 / 151	37.75	156,650
	431	56	Dover: Budweiser 500	8	500 / 224	44.80	68,030
	434	57	Daytona: Pepsi 400	5	160 / 110	68.75	75,940
	436	58	Pocono: Miller Genuine Draft 500	11	200 / 71	35.50	66,795
	437	59	Talladega: DieHard 500	11	188 / 59	31.38	87,315
1994*	454	60	Darlington: TranSouth Financial 400	9	293 / 176	60.07	70,190
	455	61	Bristol: Food City 500	24	500 / 183	36.60	72,570
	458	62	Talladega: Winston Select 500	4	188 / 64	34.04	94,865
	478	63	Rockingham: AC Delco 500	20	492 / 109	22.15	60,600
1995	487	64	North Wilkesboro: First Union 400	5	400 / 198	49.50	77,400
	490	65	Sears Point: SaveMart Supermarkets 300	4	74 / 2	2.70	74,860
	499	66	Indianapolis: Brickyard 400	13	160 / 28	17.50	565,600
	506	67	Martinsville: Goody's 500	2	500 / 253	50.60	78,150
	511	68	Atlanta: NAPA 500	11	328 / 268	81.71	141,850
1996	513	69	Rockingham: Goodwrench Service 400	18	393 / 95	24.17	83,840
	515	70	Atlanta: Purolator 500	18	328 / 136	41.46	91,050
1998	575	71	Daytona: Daytona 500	4	200 / 107	53.50	1,080,233
1999	616	72	Talladega: DieHard 500	17	188 / 70	37.23	147,795
	630	73	Bristol: Goody's Headache Powder 500	26	500 / 46	9.20	89,880
	637	74	Talladega: Winston 500	27	188 / 18	9.57	120,290
2000	645	75	Atlanta: Cracker Barrel 500	35	325 / 34	10.46	123,100
	671	76	Talladega: Winston 500	20	188 / 34	18.09	135,900

*Denotes won Winston Cup championship

Victory Statistics

No. of Victories	76
Avg. Starting Pos.	8.76
Favorite Starting Spot in Victories	3 & 4 (11 times)
Total Victory Earnings	$6,816,868
Laps Led (Pct.) in victories	11,740 (43.71)
Fewest Laps Led in a Win	2
Most Laps Led in a Win	456
Highest Pct. Led	91.28
Lowest Pct. Led	2.25

A master of aerodynamic disruption on drafting tracks and an artist with his bumper on crowded short tracks, Earnhardt took regular advantage of the respect—and fear—the No. 3 car produced in his Winston Cup competitors. Only Darrell Waltrip won more races during NASCAR's modern era. *David Stringer*

Dale Earnhardt's Career Performance on Current and Former Winston Cup Tracks

Tracks	Track Length	No. of Races	Wins	Win Pct.	Top 5s	Top 10s	Poles	Avg. Start	Avg. Finish	DNFs	Total Winnings	Races Led	Laps Led	Pct. Led	Total Points	Points/ Race
Short Tracks																
Bristol	.533	43	9	20.9	20	30	2	13.2	9.3	2	$1,278,381	30	3,758	17.7	6,303	146.6
Martinsville	.526	44	6	13.6	18	24	0	12.2	11.9	11	$1,211,455	22	1,947	8.9	5,984	136
Nashville	.596	12	2	16.7	5	9	0	8.3	8.9	1	$109,820	4	375	7.4	1,733	144.4
North Wilkesboro	.626	36	5	13.9	21	32	1	9.8	6.3	2	$853,685	24	2,680	18.6	5,630	156.4
Richmond	.750	44	5	11.4	25	33	2	13.2	8.3	2	$1,272,235	24	1,976	11.3	6,546	148.8
Short Track Totals		**179**	**27**	**15.1**	**89**	**128**	**5**	**11.9**	**9.0**	**18**	**$4,725,576**	**104**	**10,736**	**13.4**	**26,196**	**146.3**
1-mile Ovals																
Dover	1.000	44	3	6.8	19	25	1	16.4	12.1	7	$1,273,660	26	2,150	10.1	5,953	135.3
New Hampshire	1.058	12	0	0.0	2	6	0	21.7	11.5	0	$632,325	3	65	1.8	1,596	133
Phoenix	1.000	13	1	7.7	5	9	0	14.6	9.5	1	$494,480	5	337	8.4	1,840	141.5
Rockingham	1.017	44	3	6.8	13	28	0	14.2	11.4	7	$1,160,755	29	1,415	6.9	6,016	136.7
1-mile Oval Totals		**113**	**7**	**6.2**	**39**	**68**	**1**	**15.9**	**11.5**	**15**	**$3,561,220**	**63**	**3,967**	**8.0**	**15,405**	**136.3**
Speedways (1 - 2 miles)																
Atlanta	1.540	46	9	19.6	26	30	4	12.1	9.6	7	$1,796,825	32	2,647	17.7	6,715	146
Charlotte	1.500	48	5	10.4	16	22	0	17.3	14.8	11	$1,933,533	30	1,522	8.6	6,093	126.9
Darlington	1.336	44	9	20.5	19	24	1	12.4	11.4	6	$1,597,990	27	2,648	17.7	6,109	138.8
Homestead	1.500	2	0	0.0	0	1	0	30.0	14.0	0	$126,275	0	0	0.0	245	122.5
Las Vegas	1.500	3	0	0.0	0	3	0	32.3	7.7	0	$270,750	1	1	0.1	435	145
Texas	1.500	4	0	0.0	0	3	0	26.0	14.0	0	$373,925	0	0	0.0	496	124
Speedway Totals		**147**	**23**	**15.6**	**61**	**83**	**5**	**14.9**	**12.2**	**24**	**$6,099,298**	**90**	**6,818**	**13.8**	**20,093**	**136.69**
SuperSpeedways (greater than 2 miles)																
California	2.000	4	0	0.0	0	1	0	25.3	13.5	0	$210,275	1	2	0.2	497	124.3
Daytona	2.500	46	3	6.5	22	34	3	9.4	10.7	9	$4,498,656	36	1,285	15.6	6,507	141.5
Indianapolis	2.500	7	1	14.3	3	5	0	12.3	10.4	0	$1,296,305	4	37	3.3	975	139.3
Michigan	2.000	43	2	4.7	12	25	0	14.7	12.6	5	$1,151,680	19	597	6.9	5,663	131.7
Ontario (Calif.)	2.000	2	0	0.0	1	2	0	4.0	7.0	0	$18,335	2	11	2.8	303	151.5
Pocono	2.500	41	2	4.9	10	22	0	11.6	14.1	9	$1,089,420	24	455	5.6	5,230	127.6
Talladega	2.660	44	10	22.7	23	27	3	10.2	12.4	11	$3,081,045	38	1,377	16.8	6,085	138.3
Texas World	2.000	3	0	0.0	1	2	0	4.3	7.7	1	$33,850	3	191	31.8	455	151.7
SuperSpeedway Totals		**190**	**18**	**9.5**	**72**	**118**	**6**	**11.6**	**12.2**	**35**	**$11,379,566**	**127**	**3,955**	**10.9**	**25,715**	**135.3**
Road Courses																
Sears Point	1.949	12	1	8.3	4	9	1	11.9	8.6	0	$450,205	4	45	4.5	1,737	144.8
Riverside	2.620	20	0	0.0	13	14	1	6.8	10.7	3	$255,165	9	58	2.7	2,793	139.7
Watkins Glen	2.454	15	0	0.0	3	8	3	8.2	11.5	0	$449,515	8	134	10.2	2,023	134.9
Road Course Totals		**47**	**1**	**2.1**	**20**	**31**	**5**	**8.5**	**10.4**	**3**	**$1,154,885**	**21**	**237**	**5.3**	**6,553**	**139.4**

Earnhardt on the Short Tracks

Daytona and Talladega made him famous, but Dale Earnhardt built his legend on NASCAR's short tracks. He had more wins (27) and laps led (10,736) on Winston Cup bullrings than on any other track type in his career.

In the beginning, there was Bristol Motor Speedway, which gave birth to Earnhardt's reputation for toughness and uncommon skill. He won his first two starts at the .533-mile Tennessee track, remarkable considering its renown for chewing up rookie drivers. The legend grew at Martinsville in the fall of 1980 when Earnhardt outlasted Cale Yarborough and somehow managed to win a caution-filled race. That improbable victory boosted him to his first Winston Cup championship. At Nashville and North Wilkesboro, Earnhardt proved he belonged with the sport's short-track greats. He broke the Yarborough-Waltrip stranglehold at Nashville to claim two victories. Defining dominance, he finished in the Top 10 in 90 percent of his 36 North Wilkesboro starts—a track record.

The short tracks also solidified Earnhardt's win-at-all-costs "Intimidator" image. At Richmond in 1986, he wrecked race leader Waltrip with three laps to go. NASCAR reacted by fining Earnhardt $5,000, placing him under $10,000 bond and putting him on probation. At Bristol in 1999, Earnhardt tapped and spun race leader Terry Labonte on the final lap, clearing the way for victory and igniting a thundering chorus of boos from the crowd of 150,000.

In short, without short tracks, there would have been no Earnhardt. His father Ralph, a legend of North Carolina's dirt tracks, would have been proud.

Short Track Record Book – Modern Era
(minimum 10 starts)

Category	Earnhardt's Total	Earnhardt's Rank	Modern Era Short Track Leader*
Career Starts	179	6th	Darrell Waltrip – 225
Total Points[1]	26,196	2nd	Darrell Waltrip – 31,149
Avg. Start	11.9	21st	Cale Yarborough – 4.1
Avg. Finish	9.0	3rd	Cale Yarborough – 6.4
Wins	27	3rd	Darrell Waltrip – 47
Winning Pct.	15.1	4th	Cale Yarborough – 35.4
Top 5s	89	2nd	Darrell Waltrip – 113
Top 10s	128	2nd	Darrell Waltrip – 141
DNFs	18	38th	J.D. McDuffie – 61
Poles	5	16th	Darrell Waltrip – 35
Front Row Starts	15	14th	Darrell Waltrip – 57
Laps Led	10,736	3rd	Darrell Waltrip – 14,840
Pct. Led	13.4	5th	Cale Yarborough – 37.6
Races Led	104	2nd	Darrell Waltrip – 133
Times Led	285	2nd	Darrell Waltrip – 343
Times Led Most Laps	28	3rd	Darrell Waltrip – 37
Bonus Points	660	2nd	Darrell Waltrip – 850
Laps Completed	74,537	3rd	Darrell Waltrip – 92,033
Pct. of Laps Completed	93.2	10th	Johnny Benson – 95.8
Points per Race[1]	146.3	2nd	Cale Yarborough – 157.9
Lead Lap Finishes	89	2nd	Darrell Waltrip – 101

*2nd-place driver or co-leader listed in parentheses if Earnhardt is track leader.
[1]Since the institution of the current Winston Cup point system in 1975

What is a short track?
A short track is any track measuring less than one mile in length.

Which tracks are short tracks?
There are five modern era short tracks:
- Bristol*
- Martinsville*
- Nashville
- North Wilkesboro
- Richmond*

*still active

One secret to Earnhardt's success was a thorough knowledge of his race car. He turned wrenches in his dad's garage for years before getting his chance to race. Living on a shoestring budget during his early pre-NASCAR years, he was forced to act as his own crew chief. Even after gaining success, he was known as a hands-on driver. Here, he helps his crew push the No. 3 Chevy to its starting spot on pit road at Rockingham. *Bill Burt*

NASCAR's one-mile ovals mostly escaped Earnhardt's mastery. He tolerated the tracks, knowing a trip to Atlanta or Darlington or Talladega or Bristol couldn't be far away. While he consistently produced victories elsewhere, Earnhardt finished with just seven wins in 113 starts on the one-milers. Only road courses were stingier in his career.

However, while not his most successful track type, Earnhardt made history on one-mile racetracks. His most dominating performance ever came in Dover's two races in 1989 when he led 831 of a possible 1,000 competitive laps. That effort is the most in track history and the third best at a track in the modern era. Earnhardt generated similar dominance at Phoenix in 1990. In a timely championship-winning effort, he led the final 262 laps to win the Checker 500 and assumed the points lead over Mark Martin – a lead he maintained a week later at Atlanta to clinch his fourth Winston Cup title.

While Rockingham was a consistent friend—offering comfort (three wins, 28 Top 10s) after all of those disappointing Daytona 500s—he never found a consistent groove there. New Hampshire, meanwhile, was one of those open-wheel tracks NASCAR insisted on adding to the schedule. Like the other recently added tracks, Earnhardt never warmed to NHIS; his career ended with no wins in 12 New England starts.

One-Mile Oval Record Book – Modern Era
(min. 10 starts)

Category	Earnhardt's Total	Earnhardt's Rank	Modern Era 1-Mile Oval Leader*
Career Starts	113	4th	Darrell Waltrip – 133
Total Points[1]	15,405	1st	(Darrell Waltrip – 15,011)
Avg. Start	15.9	27th	David Pearson – 5.1
Avg. Finish	11.5	5th	Tony Stewart – 6.7
Wins	7	8th	J. Gordon, R. Petty, R. Wallace – 10
Winning Pct.	6.2	9th	David Pearson – 31.0
Top 5s	38	1st	(Mark Martin – 38)
Top 10s	68	1st	(Darrell Waltrip – 57)
DNFs	15	34th	J.D. McDuffie – 43
Poles	1	27th	M. Martin, R. Wallace – 11
Front Row Starts	6	18th	Mark Martin – 18
Laps Led	3,967	2nd	Cale Yarborough – 4,951
Pct. Led	8.0	10th	David Pearson – 25.9
Races Led	63	1st	(Mark Martin – 50)
Times Led	181	1st	(Cale Yarborough –152)
Times Led Most Laps	7	7th	Cale Yarborough – 15
Bonus Points	350	1st	(Mark Martin – 280)
Laps Completed	45,703	3rd	Darrell Waltrip – 53,580
Pct. of Laps Completed	92.5	15th	Tony Stewart – 99.9
Points per Race[1]	136.3	5th	Tony Stewart – 156.0
Lead Lap Finishes	45	2nd	Mark Martin – 46

*2nd-place driver or co-leader listed in parentheses if Earnhardt is track leader.
[1]Since the institution of the current Winston Cup point system in 1975

Which tracks are one-mile ovals?

There are four modern era one-mile ovals:
- Dover*
- New Hampshire*
- Phoenix*
- Rockingham*

*still active

During Dale Earnhardt's career, there was one sure thing on race day: he would get the loudest ovation during driver introductions. Despite Bill Elliott's stranglehold on the official Most Popular Driver award, a trip to the track quickly confirmed that Earnhardt commanded the largest legion of fans. *Bill Burt*

Earnhardt on the Speedways

NASCAR's six speedways can be broken into two groups: the new and the venerable. Earnhardt accelerated his career on the venerable tracks and struggled on the new ones. At Atlanta, Earnhardt's career is literally without equal. He is the track's greatest modern-era driver, whether measured by wins, Top 5s, Top 10s, laps led, races led, total points, average finish, lead-lap finishes or money won. Similarly, at Darlington, only the great David Pearson has more wins all-time on the egg-shaped track. Charlotte, meanwhile, was considered Earnhardt's home track. He won five times there and ran his first Winston Cup race in the 1975 World 600; 24 years later, his son, Dale Jr., launched his career at Charlotte in the Coca-Cola 600.

At the newer speedways, Earnhardt struggled to make his mark. He did not win in his nine starts at Homestead, Las Vegas and Texas and, incredibly, led just one of more than 2,500 competitive laps. Considering his greatness at Atlanta, Earnhardt's record at Texas will forever baffle his fans. Despite being similar to Atlanta in size, shape and banking, Earnhardt never led a lap or finished higher than sixth. Texas did produce one special moment, however: his son's first Winston Cup victory.

Speedway Record Book – Modern Era
(min. 10 starts)

Category	Earnhardt's Total	Earnhardt's Rank	Modern Era Speedway Leader*
Career Starts	147	5th	Darrell Waltrip – 175
Total Points[1]	20,093	1st	(Bill Elliott – 18,990)
Avg. Start	14.9	22nd	David Pearson – 4.4
Avg. Finish	11.9	1st	(Tony Stewart – 12.5)
Wins	23	1st	(D. Pearson, D. Waltrip – 14)
Winning Pct.	15.6	3rd	Jeff Gordon – 20.7
Top 5s	61	1st	(Darrell Waltrip – 55)
Top 10s	83	1st	(Darrell Waltrip – 80)
DNFs	24	30th	Dave Marcis – 68
Poles	5	12th	David Pearson – 25
Front Row Starts	15	7th	David Pearson – 35
Laps Led	6,818	1st	Cale Yarborough – 4,930
Pct. Led	13.6	3rd	David Pearson – 15.1
Races Led	90	1st	(Darrell Waltrip – 85)
Times Led	362	1st	(Darrell Waltrip – 287)
Times Led Most Laps	24	1st	(B. Allison, D. Pearson – 15)
Bonus Points	570	1st	(Darrell Waltrip – 470)
Laps Completed	45,634	4th	Darrell Waltrip – 51,148
Pct. of Laps Completed	91.2	8th	Dale Earnhardt, Jr. – 96.9
Points per Race[1]	136.7	1st	(Bobby Labonte – 134.6)
Lead Lap Finishes	68	1st	Mark Martin – 51

*2nd-place driver or co-leader listed in parentheses if Earnhardt is track leader.
[1]Since the institution of the current Winston Cup point system in 1975

What is a speedway?
A speedway is any track longer than one mile, but shorter than two miles.

Which tracks are speedways?
There are six modern era speedways:
- Atlanta*
- Charlotte*
- Darlington*
- Homestead*
- Las Vegas*
- Texas*

*still active

While Earnhardt battled many of the greats in NASCAR history – from Richard Petty to Cale Yarborough to Darrell Waltrip to Bill Elliott to Jeff Gordon – his rivalry with Rusty Wallace was arguably the most intense of his career. Their on-track jostling created distinct camps among NASCAR fans, those pulling for the No. 2 car and those partial to the No. 3. Here, Earnhardt battles Wallace during the 1999 Brickyard 400. *Bill Burt*

Coupled with his short track bullying, NASCAR's superspeedways defined Dale Earnhardt as a racer. His reputation for toughness and fearlessness was born on the Winston Cup series' longest and fastest racetracks. Earnhardt's ability to thrive under the pressure of high-speed, nose-to-tail racing and his ability to walk away from spectacular wrecks gave him an aura of invincibility.

In particular, the advent of restrictor-plate racing in 1988 created stages (at Daytona and Talladega) on which Earnhardt gave command performances. The famous Earnhardt myth—that he could see the air, that he could see the draft—took hold on these tracks; he did nothing—in interviews or in his car—to discourage the legend.

On modern era superspeedways, no driver has won more, finished in the Top 5 or Top 10 more often, or led races as frequently as Earnhardt. Without question, his best all-time track was Talladega, bettering even Bristol, Atlanta and Darlington. He won on the 2.66-mile track 10 times, more than twice as many times as anyone else. Daytona, especially the preseason Speed Weeks events, produced huge successes in his career.

The other superspeedways also contributed to Earnhardt's greatness. His 1979 wreck at Pocono knocked him out of racing for a month—then established his toughness when he returned earlier than advised. Earnhardt's 1995 victory in the Brickyard 400 at the open-wheel Mecca—Indianapolis—was another milestone. The old Ontario, Calif., track didn't contribute to his win column, but it was the track where he clinched his rookie-of-the-year title in 1979 and his first Winston Cup title in 1980.

SuperSpeedway Record Book – Modern Era
(min. 10 starts)

Category	Earnhardt's Total	Earnhardt's Rank	Modern Era SuperSpeedway Leader*
Career Starts	190	4th	Darrell Waltrip – 223
Total Points[1]	25,715	1st	(Darrell Waltrip – 24,921)
Avg. Start	11.6	11th	Bobby Isaac – 4.4
Avg. Finish	12.2	2nd	Jeff Gordon – 11.0
Wins	18	T-1st	(D. Pearson, R. Petty – 18)
Winning Pct.	9.5	8th	David Pearson – 22.0
Top 5s	72	1st	(D. Waltrip, C. Yarborough – 61)
Top 10s	118	1st	(Bill Elliott – 98)
DNFs	35	23rd	Dave Marcis – 67
Poles	6	11th	Bill Elliott – 23
Front Row Starts	16	10th	Bill Elliott – 39
Laps Led	3,955	1st	(Cale Yarborough – 3,203)
Pct. Led	10.9	6th	Jeff Gordon – 16.3
Races Led	127	1st	(Darrell Waltrip – 114)
Times Led	532	1st	(Cale Yarborough – 516)
Times Led Most Laps	23	1st	(Buddy Baker – 21)
Bonus Points	750	1st	(Darrell Waltrip – 630)
Laps Completed	32,808	5th	Darrell Waltrip – 36,268
Pct. of Laps Completed	90.4	22nd	Matt Kenseth – 99.7
Points per Race[1]	135.3	2nd	Jeff Gordon – 141.8
Lead Lap Finishes	110	1st	(Bill Elliott – 97)

*2nd-place driver or co-leader listed in parentheses if Earnhardt is track leader.
[1]Since the institution of the current Winston Cup point system in 1975

What is a superspeedway?
A superspeedway is any track measuring two miles or greater in length.

Which tracks are superspeedways?
There are eight modern era superspeedways:
California*
Daytona*
Indianapolis*
Michigan*
Ontario, CA
Pocono*
Talladega*
Texas World
*still active

Earnhardt's ability to remain competitive in the championship points race year after year was remarkable. In 21 full Winston Cup seasons, he finished outside of the Top 10 in points just twice (and he didn't drop far, falling to 12th in 1982 and 1992). He finished 1st or 2nd 10 times and 14 times in the Top 5. *Don Hamilton*

Earnhardt on the Road Courses

One of the great quests of Earnhardt's career came on NASCAR's road courses. Like the Daytona 500, he excelled for many seasons before finally getting a well-deserved victory. Not until his 36th road course start—the 1995 Sears Point race—did he finally claim that coveted victory. But if Earnhardt was not great on the road courses, he was consistently good. He finished with 31 Top 10s in 47 starts – tops in the modern era. On the series' current road courses—Sears Point and Watkins Glen—he completed 99.6 percent of all possible laps, finishing off the lead lap only one time.

Though qualifying was never his strength anywhere, the road courses were relatively fertile ground for Earnhardt poles. Percentage-wise, he won more of his 22 career poles on road courses than any other track type. Two of his road-course qualifying feats were memorable: his 1979 pole at Riverside was the first of his career. In 1996, he won the pole at Watkins Glen just 14 days after his terrible Talladega wreck.

Road Course Record Book – Modern Era
(min. 10 starts)

Category	Earnhardt's Total	Earnhardt's Rank	Modern Era Road Course Leader*
Career Starts	47	3rd	Darrell Waltrip – 53
Total Points[1]	6,553	2nd	Darrell Waltrip – 6,598
Avg. Start	8.5	9th	Cale Yarborough – 3.8
Avg. Finish	10.4	5th	Mark Martin – 7.2
Wins	1	14th	J. Gordon, R. Wallace – 6
Winning Pct.	2.1	21st	Jeff Gordon – 37.5
Top 5s	20	2nd	Ricky Rudd – 21
Top 10s	31	1st	(M. Martin, R. Petty – 25)
DNFs	3	74th	Hershel McGriff – 23
Poles	5	4th	Darrell Waltrip – 9
Front Row Starts	6	8th	Darrell Waltrip – 16
Laps Led	237	13th	Bobby Allison – 820
Pct. Led	5.3	14th	Cale Yarborough – 33.6
Races Led	21	3rd	Darrell Waltrip – 23
Times Led	33	7th	Bobby Allison – 69
Times Led Most Laps	2	11th	Bobby Allison – 8
Bonus Points	115	5th	Bobby Allison – 150
Laps Completed	4,206	3rd	Darrell Waltrip – 4,743
Pct. of Laps Completed	94.5	15th	Johnny Benson – 99.5
Points per Race[1]	139.4	5th	Cale Yarborough – 163
Lead Lap Finishes	40	1st	(Darrell Waltrip – 34)

*2nd-place driver or co-leader listed in parentheses if Earnhardt is track leader.
[1]Since the institution of the current Winston Cup point system in 1975

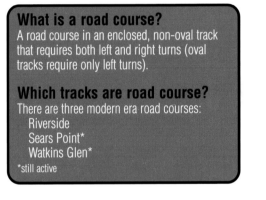

What is a road course?
A road course in an enclosed, non-oval track that requires both left and right turns (oval tracks require only left turns).

Which tracks are road course?
There are three modern era road courses:
Riverside
Sears Point*
Watkins Glen*

*still active

Earnhardt became one of the first NASCAR stars to convert his on-track success into off-track appeal, developing the broadest fan base in the sport. He copyrighted his signature and created a collectibles empire that regularly landed him on *Fortune* magazine's annual list of the richest sport's figures. *Bill Burt*

The Record Book

Chapter 2

Dale Earnhardt's Standing in Winston Cup history—
All-Time & the Modern Era

In 1972, NASCAR history—in evolutionary terms—shifted abruptly to a new plateau. A series sponsorship deal with the R. J. Reynolds tobacco company ushered in the series' "Modern Era," fundamentally changing the NASCAR world. The most important of these changes was a significant reduction in the number of races staged on a reduced number of racetracks. Accompanied by the 1975 introduction of the current point system—which rewards making the race and consistency more than victories—the result has been a steady increase in the series' competitiveness. Today, more teams show up every weekend with more race knowledge about fewer racetracks and with better funding from a more diverse set of sponsors than ever before.

From a statistical point of view, the 1972 demarcation makes historical comparison a tap dance. Judging Earnhardt's modern-era career in light of the cross-era career of a racer such as Richard Petty is fruitless. In 1967, Petty won 27 times in 48 starts. Often, he was one of just a few Grand National regulars to enter a race, giving him an enormous advantage over the local Saturday night racers against whom he competed. Today's drivers face better competition in fewer events.

In recognition of these distinct eras and their fundamental differences, this section puts Earnhardt's career in both contexts, All-Time and Modern Era. All-time records include all drivers who have competed since NASCAR's inception in 1949; the Modern Era includes only results from 1972 to the present.

*Records through February 18, 2001

All-Time Records	29-31
Modern Era Records	32-35

Earnhardt's ability to lead races, as he is doing here at Talladega, was historic. He led 25,713 laps, second only to Cale Yarborough in the modern era. Earnhardt led 405 of the 676 races he started, a modern-era record. *Bill Burt*

Championships

1	**Dale Earnhardt**	**7**
	Richard Petty	7
3	Jeff Gordon	3
	David Pearson	3
	Lee Petty	3
	Darrell Waltrip	3
	Cale Yarborough	3
8	Buck Baker	2
	Tim Flock	2
	Ned Jarrett	2
	Terry Labonte	2
	Herb Thomas	2
	Joe Weatherly	2
14	Bobby Allison	1
	Red Byron	1
	Bill Elliott	1
	Bobby Isaac	1
	Dale Jarrett	1
	Alan Kulwicki	1
	Bobby Labonte	1
	Benny Parsons	1
	Bill Rexford	1
	Rusty Wallace	1
	Rex White	1

Career Starts

1	Richard Petty	1,184
2	Dave Marcis	878
3	Darrell Waltrip	809
4	Bobby Allison	718
5	Buddy Baker	699
6	Ricky Rudd	696
7	**Dale Earnhardt**	**676**
8	Terry Labonte	674
9	J.D. McDuffie	653
10	Buck Baker	636
11	Bill Elliott	624
12	James Hylton	601
13	Kyle Petty	586
14	David Pearson	574
15	Buddy Arrington	560
16	Cale Yarborough	559
17	Geoffrey Bodine	552
18	Elmo Langley	536
19	Rusty Wallace	527
20	Benny Parsons	526
21	Sterling Marlin	504
22	Neil Castles	497
23	Wendell Scott	495
24	Ken Schrader	493
25	Morgan Shepherd	481
26	Harry Gant	474
27	Michael Waltrip	463
28	Mark Martin	459
29	Jimmy Means	455
30	Cecil Gordon	450
31	Lee Petty	427
32	Dale Jarrett	424
33	Jim Paschal	422
34	G.C. Spencer	415
35	Brett Bodine	407
36	Lake Speed	402
37	Frank Warren	396
38	Henley Gray	374
39	Neil Bonnett	363
40	Dick Brooks	358
41	Derrike Cope	354
42	Ned Jarrett	352
43	Ed Negre	338
	Rick Mast	338
45	Jimmy Spencer	335
46	Bobby Hillin Jr.	334
47	Jabe Thomas	322
48	John Sears	318
49	Junior Johnson	313
	Ernie Irvan	313

Career Wins

1	Richard Petty	200
2	David Pearson	105
3	Bobby Allison	85
4	Darrell Waltrip	84
5	Cale Yarborough	83
6	**Dale Earnhardt**	**76**
7	Lee Petty	54
8	Rusty Wallace	53
9	Jeff Gordon	52
10	Junior Johnson	50
	Ned Jarrett	50
12	Herb Thomas	48
13	Buck Baker	46
14	Bill Elliott	40
15	Tim Flock	39
16	Bobby Isaac	37
17	Fireball Roberts	33
18	Mark Martin	32
19	Rex White	28
20	Fred Lorenzen	26
21	Jim Paschal	25
	Joe Weatherly	25
23	Dale Jarrett	24
24	Benny Parsons	21
	Jack Smith	21
	Terry Labonte	21
27	Ricky Rudd	20
	Speedy Thompson	20
29	Buddy Baker	19
	Davey Allison	19
	Fonty Flock	19
32	Geoffrey Bodine	18
	Harry Gant	18
	Neil Bonnett	18
35	Curtis Turner	17
	Marvin Panch	17
37	Bobby Labonte	16
38	Ernie Irvan	15
	Jeff Burton	15
40	Dick Hutcherson	14
	LeeRoy Yarbrough	14
42	Dick Rathmann	13
	Tim Richmond	13
44	Donnie Allison	10
45	Bob Welborn	9
	Cotton Owens	9
	Paul Goldsmith	9
	Tony Stewart	9
49	Kyle Petty	8
50	A.J. Foyt	7
	Darel Dieringer	7
	Jim Reed	7
	Marshall Teague	7

Winning Pct.

1	Herb Thomas	20.87
2	Tim Flock	20.86
3	Jeff Gordon	20.16
4	David Pearson	18.29
5	Richard Petty	16.89
6	Fred Lorenzen	16.46
7	Fireball Roberts	16.02
8	Junior Johnson	15.97
9	Cale Yarborough	14.85
10	Ned Jarrett	14.20
11	Dick Hutcherson	13.59
12	Lee Petty	12.65
13	Fonty Flock	12.34
14	Rex White	12.02
15	Bobby Isaac	12.01
16	Bobby Allison	11.84
17	**Dale Earnhardt**	**11.24**
18	Joe Weatherly	10.87
19	Darrell Waltrip	10.38
20	Dick Rathmann	10.16
21	Speedy Thompson	10.10
22	Rusty Wallace	10.06
23	Davey Allison	9.95
24	Curtis Turner	9.24
25	Jack Smith	7.98
26	Marvin Panch	7.87
27	Buck Baker	7.23
28	Paul Goldsmith	7.09
29	LeeRoy Yarbrough	7.07
30	Tim Richmond	7.03
31	Mark Martin	6.97
32	Jeff Burton	6.70
33	Jim Reed	6.60
34	Bill Elliott	6.41
35	Bobby Labonte	6.18
36	Jim Paschal	5.92
37	Dale Jarrett	5.66
38	Cotton Owens	5.63
39	A.J. Foyt	5.47
40	Neil Bonnett	4.96
41	Bob Welborn	4.92
42	Ernie Irvan	4.81
43	Donnie Allison	4.13
44	Benny Parsons	3.99
45	Darel Dieringer	3.87
46	Harry Gant	3.80
47	Geoffrey Bodine	3.26
48	Charlie Glotzbach	3.23
49	Terry Labonte	3.12
50	Ricky Rudd	2.87

Earnhardt benefited throughout his career from a top-notch race crew. Here, during the 1998 Brickyard 400, his crew regroups following a pit. The Goodwrench crew proved to be effective all day, helping Earnhardt overcome a poor starting position (28th) en route to a Top 5 finish, one of three Top 5s in his career at Indy. *David Stringer*

Career Money

1	**Dale Earnhardt**	**41,641,084**
2	Jeff Gordon	35,070,956
3	Dale Jarrett	28,110,523
4	Rusty Wallace	25,598,013
5	Mark Martin	25,567,723
6	Bill Elliott	24,063,426
7	Terry Labonte	23,694,880
8	Darrell Waltrip	22,493,879
9	Bobby Labonte	21,370,578
10	Ricky Rudd	20,207,749
11	Jeff Burton	18,927,368
12	Ken Schrader	15,862,664
13	Sterling Marlin	15,637,402
14	Geoff Bodine	14,747,014
15	Kyle Petty	12,448,558
16	Ernie Irvan	11,624,617
17	Michael Waltrip	11,238,037
18	Bobby Hamilton	10,652,008
19	Jimmy Spencer	10,214,378
20	Ward Burton	9,604,637
21	Jeremy Mayfield	9,191,112
22	John Andretti	8,873,362
23	Morgan Shepherd	8,565,265
24	Richard Petty	8,541,218
25	Brett Bodine	8,536,763
26	Harry Gant	8,524,844
27	Ted Musgrave	8,390,905
28	Rick Mast	8,079,728
29	Bobby Allison	7,673,808
30	Joe Nemechek	7,557,205
31	Mike Skinner	7,357,540
32	Tony Stewart	7,170,228
33	Johnny Benson	7,089,023
34	Dave Marcis	7,059,562
35	Davey Allison	6,689,154
36	Kenny Wallace	6,462,615
37	Wally Dallenbach Jr	6,080,578
38	Derrike Cope	6,022,678
39	Chad Little	5,792,830
40	Cale Yarborough	5,645,887
41	Lake Speed	5,452,187
42	Robert Pressley	5,281,323
43	Dick Trickle	5,233,624
44	Alan Kulwicki	5,059,052
45	Ricky Craven	4,943,069
46	Hut Stricklin	4,810,644
47	Steve Park	4,776,011
48	Jerry Nadeau	4,633,694
49	Kenny Irwin	4,606,943
50	Benny Parsons	4,426,287

Top 5s

1	Richard Petty	555
2	Bobby Allison	336
3	David Pearson	301
4	**Dale Earnhardt**	**281**
5	Darrell Waltrip	276
6	Cale Yarborough	255
7	Buck Baker	246
8	Lee Petty	231
9	Buddy Baker	202
10	Benny Parsons	199
11	Mark Martin	185
	Ned Jarrett	185
13	Terry Labonte	175
	Rusty Wallace	175
15	Ricky Rudd	166
16	Bill Elliott	156
17	Jim Paschal	149
18	James Hylton	140
19	Bobby Isaac	134
20	Dale Jarrett	129
	Jeff Gordon	129
22	Harry Gant	123
23	Herb Thomas	122
24	Junior Johnson	121
25	Rex White	110
26	Joe Weatherly	105
27	Tim Flock	102
28	Geoffrey Bodine	99
29	Marvin Panch	96
30	Dave Marcis	94
	Jack Smith	94
32	Fireball Roberts	93
33	Neil Bonnett	83
34	Donnie Allison	78
	Speedy Thompson	78
36	Bobby Labonte	75
	Fred Lorenzen	75
38	Jeff Burton	73
39	Fonty Flock	72
40	Dick Rathmann	69
41	Ernie Irvan	68
42	Davey Allison	66
43	LeeRoy Yarbrough	65
44	Dick Hutcherson	64
	Ken Schrader	64
46	Elmo Langley	63
47	Morgan Shepherd	62
48	Sterling Marlin	59
49	Bob Welborn	58
50	Dick Brooks	57

Career Top 5 Pct

1	Dick Hutcherson	62.14
2	Tim Flock	54.55
3	Lee Petty	54.10
4	Dick Rathmann	53.91
5	Herb Thomas	53.04
6	Ned Jarrett	52.56
7	David Pearson	52.44
8	Jeff Gordon	50.00
9	Fred Lorenzen	47.47
10	Rex White	47.21
11	Richard Petty	46.88
12	Bobby Allison	46.80
13	Fonty Flock	46.75
14	Joe Weatherly	45.65
15	Cale Yarborough	45.62
16	Fireball Roberts	45.15
17	Marvin Panch	44.44
18	Bobby Isaac	43.51
19	**Dale Earnhardt**	**41.57**
20	Mark Martin	40.31
21	Speedy Thompson	39.39
22	Buck Baker	38.68
23	Junior Johnson	38.66
24	Benny Parsons	37.83
25	Jim Reed	35.85
26	Jack Smith	35.74
27	Jim Paschal	35.31
28	Paul Goldsmith	34.65
29	Davey Allison	34.55
30	Darrell Waltrip	34.12
31	Rusty Wallace	33.21
32	LeeRoy Yarbrough	32.83
33	Jeff Burton	32.59
34	Cotton Owens	32.50
35	Donnie Allison	32.23
36	Bob Welborn	31.69
37	Charlie Glotzbach	30.65
38	Dale Jarrett	30.42
39	Curtis Turner	29.35
40	Bobby Labonte	28.96
41	Buddy Baker	28.90
42	Terry Labonte	25.96
43	Harry Gant	25.95
44	Bill Elliott	25.00
45	Darel Dieringer	24.86
46	Bill Blair	24.39
47	Ricky Rudd	23.85
48	James Hylton	23.29
49	Joe Eubanks	23.27
50	Neil Bonnett	22.87

Top 10s

1	Richard Petty	712
2	Bobby Allison	446
3	**Dale Earnhardt**	**428**
4	Darrell Waltrip	390
5	Buck Baker	372
6	David Pearson	366
7	Mike Bliss	340
8	Terry Labonte	337
9	Lee Petty	332
10	Ricky Rudd	323
11	Cale Yarborough	318
12	Buddy Baker	311
13	James Hylton	301
14	Bill Elliott	286
15	Benny Parsons	283
16	Rusty Wallace	279
17	Mark Martin	278
18	Ned Jarrett	239
19	Jim Paschal	230
20	Dave Marcis	222
21	Harry Gant	208
22	Elmo Langley	193
23	Dale Jarrett	191
24	Geoffrey Bodine	188
25	Neil Castles	178
26	Ken Schrader	171
27	Bobby Isaac	170
28	Kyle Petty	167
29	Jeff Gordon	166
30	Morgan Shepherd	165
31	Rex White	163
32	Sterling Marlin	159
33	Herb Thomas	156
	Neil Bonnett	156
35	Joe Weatherly	153
36	Dick Brooks	150
37	Junior Johnson	148
38	Wendell Scott	147
39	Jack Smith	141
40	G.C. Spencer	138
41	Tim Flock	129
42	John Sears	127
43	Marvin Panch	126
44	Bobby Labonte	122
	Fireball Roberts	122
46	Tiny Lund	119
47	Donnie Allison	115
48	Cecil Gordon	111
49	J.D. McDuffie	106
	Speedy Thompson	106

All-Time Records

Career Poles

1	Richard Petty	126
2	David Pearson	113
3	Cale Yarborough	70
4	Bobby Allison	59
4	Darrell Waltrip	59
6	Bobby Isaac	50
	Bill Elliott	50
8	Junior Johnson	47
9	Buck Baker	44
10	Buddy Baker	40
11	Mark Martin	39
	Tim Flock	39
13	Herb Thomas	38
14	Geoff Bodine	37
15	Rex White	36
16	Fireball Roberts	35
	Ned Jarrett	35
	Rusty Wallace	35
19	Fonty Flock	33
	Fred Lorenzen	33
	Jeff Gordon	33
22	Ricky Rudd	26
	Terry Labonte	26
24	Alan Kulwicki	24
	Jack Smith	24
26	Ken Schrader	23
27	**Dale Earnhardt**	**22**
	Dick Hutcherson	22
29	Bobby Labonte	21
	Marvin Panch	21
31	Benny Parsons	20
	Neil Bonnett	20
33	Ernie Irvan	19
	Joe Weatherly	19
35	Donnie Allison	18
	Lee Petty	18
	Speedy Thompson	18
38	Curtis Turner	17
	Harry Gant	17
40	Dave Marcis	14
	Davey Allison	14
	Glen Wood	14
	Tim Richmond	14
44	Charlie Glotzbach	12
	Jim Paschal	12
46	Cotton Owens	11
	Dale Jarrett	11
	Darel Dieringer	11
49	A.J. Foyt	10
	Dick Rathmann	10
	LeeRoy Yarbrough	10
	Sterling Marlin	10

Laps Led

1	Richard Petty	52,194
2	Cale Yarborough	31,776
3	Bobby Allison	27,539
4	**Dale Earnhardt**	**25,713**
5	David Pearson	25,425
6	Darrell Waltrip	23,130
7	Rusty Wallace	17,719
8	Bobby Isaac	13,229
9	Junior Johnson	12,651
10	Jeff Gordon	10,709
11	Bill Elliott	10,325
12	Buddy Baker	9,748
13	Mark Martin	9,571
14	Ned Jarrett	9,468
15	Geoffrey Bodine	8,680
16	Harry Gant	8,445
17	Fred Lorenzen	8,131
18	Tim Flock	6,937
19	Ricky Rudd	6,872
20	Benny Parsons	6,860
21	Terry Labonte	6,807
22	Neil Bonnett	6,383
23	Herb Thomas	6,197
24	Dale Jarrett	6,005
25	Fireball Roberts	5,970
26	Buck Baker	5,662
27	Ernie Irvan	5,484
28	Davey Allison	4,991
29	Lee Petty	4,787
30	Curtis Turner	4,771
31	Fonty Flock	4,682
32	Donnie Allison	4,642
33	Jim Paschal	4,591
34	Rex White	4,583
35	Jeff Burton	4,169
36	Dick Hutcherson	3,995
37	Kyle Petty	3,847
38	Speedy Thompson	3,667
39	Joe Weatherly	3,487
40	LeeRoy Yarbrough	3,421
41	Jack Smith	3,228
42	Marvin Panch	3,089
43	Bobby Labonte	2,977
44	Sterling Marlin	2,839
45	Dave Marcis	2,699
46	Alan Kulwicki	2,686
47	Tim Richmond	2,537
48	Darel Dieringer	2,517
49	Tony Stewart	2,439
50	Ken Schrader	2,370

Races Led

1	Richard Petty	599
2	Bobby Allison	414
3	**Dale Earnhardt**	**405**
4	Darrell Waltrip	402
5	Cale Yarborough	340
6	David Pearson	329
7	Rusty Wallace	244
8	Buddy Baker	242
9	Terry Labonte	237
10	Bill Elliott	233
11	Mark Martin	228
12	Geoffrey Bodine	220
13	Ricky Rudd	196
14	Dave Marcis	195
15	Benny Parsons	192
	Harry Gant	192
17	Jeff Gordon	177
18	Bobby Isaac	155
	Neil Bonnett	155
20	Dale Jarrett	155
21	Junior Johnson	138
22	Ken Schrader	134
23	Ernie Irvan	123
24	Sterling Marlin	121
25	Bobby Labonte	114
26	Ned Jarrett	111
27	Donnie Allison	105
28	Morgan Shepherd	104
29	Buck Baker	103
30	Kyle Petty	98
31	Davey Allison	97
32	Lee Petty	93
33	Fireball Roberts	90
34	Herb Thomas	84
	Jeff Burton	84
36	Fred Lorenzen	83
37	Tim Flock	82
38	Michael Waltrip	78
39	Alan Kulwicki	77
40	Jim Paschal	76
	Tim Richmond	76
42	Curtis Turner	69
43	Joe Weatherly	67
44	LeeRoy Yarbrough	66
	Rex White	66
46	James Hylton	65
47	Jimmy Spencer	63
47	Marvin Panch	63
49	Brett Bodine	62
50	Fonty Flock	56

Modern Era Records

Championships

1	**Dale Earnhardt**	**7**
2	Richard Petty	4
3	Jeff Gordon	3
	Darrell Waltrip	3
	Cale Yarborough	3
6	Terry Labonte	2
7	Bobby Allison	1
	Bill Elliott	1
	Dale Jarrett	1
	Alan Kulwicki	1
	Bobby Labonte	1
	Benny Parsons	1
	Rusty Wallace	1

Starts

1	Darrell Waltrip	809
2	Dave Marcis	756
3	Ricky Rudd	696
4	**Dale Earnhardt**	**676**
5	Terry Labonte	674
6	Bill Elliott	624
7	Richard Petty	619
8	Kyle Petty	586
9	Geoffrey Bodine	552
10	Rusty Wallace	527
11	Sterling Marlin	504
12	Ken Schrader	493
13	Morgan Shepherd	478
14	Bobby Allison	476
15	Harry Gant	474
16	Michael Waltrip	463
17	Mark Martin	459
18	Jimmy Means	455
19	J.D. McDuffie	443
20	Benny Parsons	441
21	Buddy Arrington	426
22	Dale Jarrett	424
23	Brett Bodine	407
24	Lake Speed	402
25	Buddy Baker	391
26	Cale Yarborough	366
27	Neil Bonnett	363
28	Derrike Cope	354
29	Rick Mast	338
30	Jimmy Spencer	335
31	Bobby Hillin Jr	334
32	James Hylton	325
33	Ernie Irvan	313
34	Bobby Hamilton	302
35	Cecil Gordon	300
36	Ted Musgrave	298
37	Dick Trickle	297
38	Hut Stricklin	284
39	Dick Brooks	276
40	Richard Childress	272
41	D.K. Ulrich	261
42	Bobby Labonte	259
43	Greg Sacks	258
	Jeff Gordon	258
45	Frank Warren	239
46	Lennie Pond	232
47	Tommy Gale	229
48	John Andretti	228
49	Wally Dallenbach Jr	225
50	Jeff Burton	224

Victories

1	Darrell Waltrip	84
2	**Dale Earnhardt**	**76**
3	Cale Yarborough	69
4	Richard Petty	60
5	Bobby Allison	55
6	Rusty Wallace	53
7	Jeff Gordon	52
8	David Pearson	45
9	Bill Elliott	40
10	Mark Martin	32
11	Dale Jarrett	24
12	Terry Labonte	21
13	Ricky Rudd	20
	Benny Parsons	20
15	Davey Allison	19
16	Neil Bonnett	18
	Geoffrey Bodine	18
	Harry Gant	18
19	Bobby Labonte	16
20	Buddy Baker	15
	Ernie Irvan	15
	Jeff Burton	15
23	Tim Richmond	13
24	Tony Stewart	9
25	Kyle Petty	8
26	Sterling Marlin	6
27	Alan Kulwicki	5
	Dave Marcis	5
29	Morgan Shepherd	4
	Donnie Allison	4
	Ken Schrader	4
32	Bobby Hamilton	3
	Jeremy Mayfield	3
34	A.J. Foyt	2
	John Andretti	2
	Ward Burton	2
	Derrike Cope	2
	Jimmy Spencer	2
	Dale Earnhardt Jr	2

Winning Pct.

1	David Pearson	21.84
2	Jeff Gordon	20.16
3	Cale Yarborough	18.85
4	Mark Donohue	16.67
5	Tony Stewart	13.04
6	Bobby Allison	11.55
7	**Dale Earnhardt**	**11.24**
8	Darrell Waltrip	10.38
9	Rusty Wallace	10.06
10	Davey Allison	9.95
11	Richard Petty	9.69
12	Tim Richmond	7.03
13	Mark Martin	6.97
14	Jeff Burton	6.70
15	Bill Elliott	6.41
16	Bobby Labonte	6.18
17	Ray Elder	5.88
18	Dale Jarrett	5.66
19	Dale Earnhardt Jr	5.00
20	Neil Bonnett	4.96
21	Ernie Irvan	4.79
22	Benny Parsons	4.54
23	Earl Ross	3.85
24	Buddy Baker	3.84
25	Harry Gant	3.80
26	Geoffrey Bodine	3.26
27	Terry Labonte	3.12
28	Ricky Rudd	2.87
29	Donnie Allison	2.52
30	Matt Kenseth	2.44
31	Alan Kulwicki	2.42
32	A.J. Foyt	2.38
33	Bobby Isaac	1.54
34	Jeremy Mayfield	1.43
35	Kyle Petty	1.37
36	Sterling Marlin	1.19
37	Steve Park	1.10
38	Bobby Hamilton	0.99
39	Jerry Nadeau	0.96
40	Ward Burton	0.93
41	John Andretti	0.88
42	Morgan Shepherd	0.84
43	Ken Schrader	0.81
44	Jody Ridley	0.71
45	Dave Marcis	0.66
46	Ron Bouchard	0.63
47	Jimmy Spencer	0.60
48	Derrike Cope	0.56
49	Phil Parsons	0.50
50	Joe Nemechek	0.45

The former pilot of the No. 3 Chevrolet, Richard Childress, gave up his driving career in 1981 without a win in 285 starts. He and Earnhardt teamed briefly during the 1981 season, running 11 races together and scoring 2 Top-5 finishes. When they reunited in 1984, they created one of NASCAR's greatest teams. *David Stringer*

Modern Era Records

Money Won

1	**Dale Earnhardt**	**41,641,084**
2	Jeff Gordon	35,070,956
3	Dale Jarrett	28,110,523
4	Rusty Wallace	25,598,013
5	Mark Martin	25,567,723
6	Bill Elliott	24,063,426
7	Terry Labonte	23,694,880
8	Darrell Waltrip	22,493,879
9	Bobby Labonte	21,370,578
10	Ricky Rudd	20,207,749
11	Jeff Burton	18,927,368
12	Ken Schrader	15,862,664
13	Sterling Marlin	15,637,402
14	Geoff Bodine	14,747,014
15	Kyle Petty	12,448,558
16	Ernie Irvan	11,624,617
17	Michael Waltrip	11,238,037
18	Bobby Hamilton	10,652,008
19	Jimmy Spencer	10,214,378
20	Ward Burton	9,604,637
21	Jeremy Mayfield	9,191,112
22	John Andretti	8,873,362
23	Morgan Shepherd	8,565,265
24	Brett Bodine	8,536,763
25	Harry Gant	8,524,844
26	Ted Musgrave	8,390,905
27	Rick Mast	8,079,728
28	Joe Nemechek	7,557,205
29	Mike Skinner	7,357,540
30	Tony Stewart	7,170,228
31	Johnny Benson	7,089,023
32	Davey Allison	6,689,154
33	Kenny Wallace	6,462,615
34	Wally Dallenbach Jr	6,080,578
35	Derrike Cope	6,022,678
36	Chad Little	5,792,830
37	Lake Speed	5,452,187
38	Robert Pressley	5,281,323
39	Dick Trickle	5,233,624
40	Alan Kulwicki	5,059,052
41	Ricky Craven	4,943,069
42	Hut Stricklin	4,810,644
43	Steve Park	4,776,011
44	Jerry Nadeau	4,633,694
45	Kenny Irwin	4,606,943

Top 5s

1	**Dale Earnhardt**	**281**
2	Darrell Waltrip	276
3	Richard Petty	221
4	Bobby Allison	217
5	Cale Yarborough	197
6	Mark Martin	185
7	Terry Labonte	175
	Rusty Wallace	175
9	Benny Parsons	172
10	Ricky Rudd	166
11	Bill Elliott	156
12	Dale Jarrett	129
	Jeff Gordon	129
14	Buddy Baker	128
15	Harry Gant	123
16	David Pearson	108
17	Geoffrey Bodine	99
18	Neil Bonnett	83
19	Bobby Labonte	75
	Dave Marcis	75
21	Jeff Burton	73
22	Ernie Irvan	68
23	Davey Allison	66
24	Ken Schrader	64
25	Morgan Shepherd	63
26	Sterling Marlin	59
27	Kyle Petty	51
28	Donnie Allison	42
	Tim Richmond	42
30	Lennie Pond	39
31	Alan Kulwicki	38
32	Dick Brooks	30
33	Jeremy Mayfield	28
34	Tony Stewart	24
35	Jimmy Spencer	22
36	Ted Musgrave	20
	Cecil Gordon	20
38	Ron Bouchard	19
	Joe Ruttman	19
40	Michael Waltrip	19
41	Bobby Hamilton	17
42	Lake Speed	16
	Bobby Isaac	16
	Brett Bodine	16
45	Ward Burton	15
	Dick Trickle	15
	James Hylton	15
48	A.J. Foyt	14
49	John Andretti	12
50	Mike Skinner	10
	Joe Millikan	10
	Phil Parsons	10

Top 5 Pct.

1	Cale Yarborough	53.83
2	David Pearson	52.43
3	Jeff Gordon	50.00
	Bobby Unser	50.00
5	Bobby Allison	45.59
6	**Dale Earnhardt**	**41.57**
7	Ray Elder	41.18
8	Mark Martin	40.31
9	Benny Parsons	39.00
10	Fred Lorenzen	37.50
11	Richard Petty	35.70
12	Tony Stewart	34.78
13	Davey Allison	34.55
14	Darrell Waltrip	34.12
15	Rusty Wallace	33.21
16	Buddy Baker	32.74
17	Jeff Burton	32.59
18	Dale Jarrett	30.42
19	Bobby Labonte	28.96
20	LeeRoy Yarbrough	27.78
21	Donnie Allison	26.42
22	Terry Labonte	25.96
23	Harry Gant	25.95
24	Bill Elliott	25.00
25	Bobby Isaac	24.62
26	Ricky Rudd	23.85
27	Neil Bonnett	22.87
28	Tim Richmond	22.70
29	Ernie Irvan	21.73
30	Gary Bettenhausen	20.00
	Ron Fellows	20.00
32	Earl Ross	19.23
33	Alan Kulwicki	18.36
34	Geoffrey Bodine	17.93
35	Ramo Stott	17.39
36	Lennie Pond	16.81
37	A.J. Foyt	16.67
	Charlie Glotzbach	16.67
	Jim Insolo	16.67
	Mark Donohue	16.67
41	George Follmer	15.00
42	Carl Joiner	14.29
	Jackie Oliver	14.29
	Pete Hamilton	14.29
45	Jeremy Mayfield	13.33
46	Morgan Shepherd	13.18
47	Ken Schrader	12.98
48	Joe Millikan	12.50
48	Matt Kenseth	12.20
50	Ron Bouchard	11.88

Top 10s

1	**Dale Earnhardt**	**428**
2	Darrell Waltrip	390
3	Terry Labonte	337
4	Ricky Rudd	323
5	Richard Petty	311
6	Bobby Allison	300
7	Bill Elliott	286
8	Rusty Wallace	279
9	Mark Martin	278
10	Benny Parsons	239
11	Cale Yarborough	231
12	Harry Gant	208
13	Buddy Baker	199
14	Dale Jarrett	191
15	Geoffrey Bodine	188
16	Dave Marcis	180
17	Ken Schrader	171
18	Morgan Shepherd	168
19	Kyle Petty	167
20	Jeff Gordon	166
21	Sterling Marlin	159
22	Neil Bonnett	156
23	Ernie Irvan	124
	David Pearson	124
25	Bobby Labonte	122
26	Dick Brooks	108
27	Jeff Burton	103
28	Davey Allison	92
29	Lennie Pond	88
30	James Hylton	87
31	Michael Waltrip	83
32	Tim Richmond	78
33	Richard Childress	76
34	Lake Speed	75
34	Alan Kulwicki	75
36	Cecil Gordon	71
37	Buddy Arrington	68
38	Donnie Allison	67
39	Jimmy Spencer	62
40	Ron Bouchard	60
41	Brett Bodine	59
	Joe Ruttman	59
43	Bobby Hamilton	58
44	Ward Burton	57
45	Jody Ridley	56
46	Ted Musgrave	55
	J.D. McDuffie	55
48	Jeremy Mayfield	52
49	Tony Stewart	44
	Coo Coo Marlin	44

Modern Era Records

Poles

1	Darrell Waltrip	59
2	David Pearson	57
3	Cale Yarborough	51
4	Bill Elliott	50
5	Mark Martin	39
6	Geoffrey Bodine	37
7	Bobby Allison	36
8	Rusty Wallace	35
9	Jeff Gordon	33
10	Buddy Baker	30
11	Terry Labonte	26
	Ricky Rudd	26
13	Alan Kulwicki	24
14	Richard Petty	23
	Ken Schrader	23
16	**Dale Earnhardt**	**22**
	Ernie Irvan	22
18	Bobby Labonte	21
19	Neil Bonnett	20
20	Benny Parsons	19
21	Harry Gant	17
22	Tim Richmond	14
	Davey Allison	14
24	Dave Marcis	12
25	Dale Jarrett	11
26	Sterling Marlin	10
27	Donnie Allison	9
28	Bobby Isaac	8
	Kyle Petty	8
30	Morgan Shepherd	7
31	Jeremy Mayfield	6
	Joe Nemechek	6
	Ward Burton	6
34	Mike Skinner	5
	Brett Bodine	5
	Lennie Pond	5
	Ted Musgrave	5
	A.J. Foyt	5
	Bobby Hamilton	5
40	Tony Stewart	4
	Rick Mast	4
	John Andretti	4
43	Jeff Burton	3
	Joe Ruttman	3
	Kenny Irwin	3
	Loy Allen	3
	Ricky Craven	3
	Ron Bouchard	3
49	Greg Sacks	2
	Johnny Benson Jr	2
	Dale Earnhardt Jr	2
	Michael Waltrip	2
	Steve Park	2
	Kenny Wallace	2

Laps Led

1	Cale Yarborough	27,260
2	**Dale Earnhardt**	**25,713**
3	Darrell Waltrip	23,130
4	Bobby Allison	18,502
5	Rusty Wallace	17,719
6	Richard Petty	16,902
7	Jeff Gordon	10,709
8	Bill Elliott	10,325
9	David Pearson	10,079
10	Mark Martin	9,571
11	Geoffrey Bodine	8,680
12	Harry Gant	8,445
13	Ricky Rudd	6,872
14	Terry Labonte	6,807
15	Buddy Baker	6,580
16	Benny Parsons	6,552
17	Neil Bonnett	6,383
18	Dale Jarrett	6,005
19	Ernie Irvan	5,484
20	Davey Allison	4,991
21	Jeff Burton	4,169
22	Kyle Petty	3,847
23	Bobby Labonte	2,977
24	Sterling Marlin	2,839
25	Alan Kulwicki	2,686
26	Tim Richmond	2,537
27	Tony Stewart	2,439
28	Ken Schrader	2,370
29	Dave Marcis	2,332
30	Donnie Allison	2,297
31	Morgan Shepherd	2,141
32	Bobby Hamilton	1,736
33	Jeremy Mayfield	1,637
34	Bobby Isaac	1,399
35	Ward Burton	1,366
36	Brett Bodine	1,035
37	Mike Skinner	994
38	Lennie Pond	926
39	Jimmy Spencer	886
40	Joe Ruttman	807
41	A.J. Foyt	730
42	John Andretti	668
43	Lake Speed	632
44	Michael Waltrip	546
45	Ricky Craven	506
46	Rick Mast	478
47	Hut Stricklin	471
48	Steve Park	457
49	Dick Brooks	453
50	Dale Earnhardt Jr	440

Races Led

1	**Dale Earnhardt**	**405**
2	Darrell Waltrip	402
3	Bobby Allison	306
4	Richard Petty	289
5	Cale Yarborough	271
6	Rusty Wallace	244
7	Terry Labonte	237
8	Bill Elliott	233
9	Mark Martin	228
10	Geoffrey Bodine	220
11	Ricky Rudd	196
12	Harry Gant	192
13	Dave Marcis	183
14	Benny Parsons	182
15	Buddy Baker	178
16	Jeff Gordon	177
17	Neil Bonnett	155
	Dale Jarrett	155
19	David Pearson	140
20	Ken Schrader	134
21	Ernie Irvan	124
22	Sterling Marlin	121
23	Bobby Labonte	114
24	Morgan Shepherd	104
25	Kyle Petty	98
26	Davey Allison	97
27	Jeff Burton	84
28	Michael Waltrip	78
29	Alan Kulwicki	77
30	Tim Richmond	76
31	Donnie Allison	69
32	Jimmy Spencer	63
33	Brett Bodine	62
34	Lennie Pond	53
35	Ward Burton	49
36	Bobby Hamilton	47
37	Jeremy Mayfield	46
38	John Andretti	44
39	Mike Skinner	41
40	Lake Speed	39
41	Ted Musgrave	38
42	Joe Ruttman	34
43	A.J. Foyt	33
	Tony Stewart	33
45	Bobby Isaac	31
46	James Hylton	29
	Johnny Benson Jr	29
	Rick Mast	29
49	Ricky Craven	28
	Dick Brooks	28

Average Start

1	David Pearson	5.58
2	Cale Yarborough	7.15
3	Bobby Allison	8.44
4	Jeff Gordon	8.82
5	Benny Parsons	9.05
6	Mark Martin	9.40
7	Donnie Allison	9.97
8	Buddy Baker	10.73
9	Neil Bonnett	11.93
10	Alan Kulwicki	12.00
11	Davey Allison	12.38
12	Rusty Wallace	12.43
13	Tim Richmond	12.46
14	Harry Gant	12.51
15	**Dale Earnhardt**	**12.90**
16	Bill Elliott	13.07
17	Geoffrey Bodine	13.29
18	Richard Petty	13.40
19	Ricky Rudd	13.63
20	Darrell Waltrip	13.71
21	Bobby Labonte	14.31
22	Terry Labonte	14.55
23	Ken Schrader	14.84
24	Coo Coo Marlin	15.04
25	Ron Bouchard	15.12
26	Lennie Pond	15.43
27	Dick Brooks	15.92
28	Ernie Irvan	16.21
29	Dale Jarrett	16.92
30	Joe Ruttman	17.39
31	Morgan Shepherd	17.96
	Mike Skinner	17.96
33	Sterling Marlin	18.11
34	Richard Childress	18.43
35	Jody Ridley	18.53
36	Ward Burton	18.51
37	Joe Nemechek	19.04
38	Brett Bodine	19.62
39	Rick Wilson	19.74
40	Kyle Petty	20.03
41	Jerry Nadeau	20.49
42	Jeff Burton	20.60
43	John Andretti	20.90
44	Walter Ballard	21.02
45	Lake Speed	21.13
46	Rick Mast	21.16
47	Michael Waltrip	21.31
48	Phil Parsons	21.35
49	Dave Marcis	21.60
50	Jeremy Mayfield	21.84

Modern Era Records

Average Finish

1	**Dale Earnhardt**	**11.06**
2	Cale Yarborough	11.45
3	Bobby Allison	11.58
4	Jeff Gordon	11.79
5	Mark Martin	12.38
6	David Pearson	13.45
7	Rusty Wallace	14.01
8	Richard Petty	14.15
9	Terry Labonte	14.24
10	Davey Allison	14.25
11	Benny Parsons	14.39
12	Bill Elliott	14.44
13	Bobby Labonte	14.97
14	Darrell Waltrip	15.12
15	Tim Richmond	15.18
16	Ricky Rudd	15.47
17	Buddy Baker	15.52
18	Dale Jarrett	15.66
19	Jeff Burton	15.84
20	Harry Gant	15.87
21	Alan Kulwicki	16.41
22	Neil Bonnett	16.52
23	Jody Ridley	16.58
24	Ken Schrader	16.87
25	Richard Childress	17.21
26	Ron Bouchard	17.23
27	James Hylton	17.34
28	Ernie Irvan	17.35
29	Lennie Pond	17.78
30	Dick Brooks	17.80
31	Buddy Arrington	17.84
32	Cecil Gordon	17.84
33	Sterling Marlin	17.89
34	Geoffrey Bodine	18.03
35	Elmo Langley	18.12
36	Morgan Shepherd	18.24
37	David Sisco	18.53
38	Donnie Allison	18.67
39	Kyle Petty	18.71
40	Walter Ballard	18.88
41	Coo Coo Marlin	19.05
42	Ted Musgrave	20.02
43	Frank Warren	20.08
44	Phil Parsons	20.12
45	Joe Ruttman	20.18
46	Jeremy Mayfield	20.39
47	Michael Waltrip	20.43
48	D.K. Ulrich	20.49
49	Dave Marcis	20.52
50	Mike Skinner	20.62

Open-wheel great and four-time Indianapolis 500 winner A. J. Foyt looks in on the Goodwrench team's preparations for the Brickyard 400. Foyt, who won seven Winston Cup Grand National races (including the 1972 Daytona 500), qualified 40th for the inaugural Brickyard. He finished 30th. *David Stringer*

When his career came to an end abruptly in 2001, Earnhardt was the leading money winner at 12 of the 26 tracks at which he competed as a Winston Cup driver. His $41.6 million in winnings is an all-time NASCAR record. *Don Hamilton*

The Seasons

This section gets into the details of Earnhardt's career, season-by-season. Every race in Earnhardt's career is listed, presenting his start, finish, total laps, laps completed, race-ending condition and money won. Earnhardt's championship performance is also charted, including championship and bonus points earned for each race, his position in the points standings, and how far he trailed the points leader. If Earnhardt is the points leader at any point, the second place driver in the standings is listed in parentheses along with the margin of Earnhardt's lead. The context of each race is also available with the "Career Race" column, which indicates the number of races in which Earnhardt had competed in at any point in his career.

Each season is put into historical context with the inclusion of full statistics and a season summary. For each season, 20 statistical categories are cataloged. Earnhardt's total for each category is listed, along with his rank and that category's leader. If Earnhardt is the leader in a category, the second-place driver is listed in parentheses with his total. The season summary explores Earnhardt's accomplishments or details memorable moments and is often accompanied by tables that allow greater insight into his career.

Before the first running of the Brickyard 400, Jeff Gordon, Dale Earnhardt and pole winner Rick Mast gather at the famed "yard of bricks" at the start-finish line of the Indianapolis Motor Speedway. *David Stringer*

1975-78: Getting Started

Dale Earnhardt took a unique route in preparing for his 1979 rookie season on the Winston Cup Grand National circuit. Unlike modern-day rookie hopefuls who look to test stock-car racing's top series on their home tracks or on track configurations they've grown comfortable with, Earnhardt first starts came in some of the biggest Grand National events on the series' biggest and fastest tracks. By the time he began his career in earnest, Earnhardt had run in three World 600s at Charlotte, a Southern 500 at Darlington and had logged valuable miles at Atlanta, Daytona and Talladega.

Earnhardt opened his career at Charlotte in the 1975 World 600, the longest, most grueling event on the Grand National schedule. He drove the No. 8 Dodge owned by Ed Negre. Twenty-four years later, his son, Dale Jr., would open his career in the No. 8 Chevy, owned by Dale Sr., in the 1999 Coca-Cola 600.

There was a trade off to Earnhardt's strategy, however. By choosing the toughest races on the toughest tracks, he had to suffer through poor performances and look to learn rather than win. Indeed, he never got close to the front in his first five races. Then success began to creep in to his efforts: a Top 10 in his first Daytona race, followed by solid runs at Talladega and Darlington. Finally, in his final tune up for his 1979 rookie campaign, Earnhardt finished in the Top 5 at Atlanta in his first start for Rod Osterlund. With 11 races under his belt and a solid ride locked up with Osterlund, Earnhardt was ready to launch one of the most successful careers in NASCAR history.

Earnhardt in 1975-78

Races Run	9
Victories	0
Winning Pct.	0
Total Winnings	$26,530
Poles	0
Top 5s	1
Top 10s	2
DNF's	3
Average Start	24.1
Average Finish	18.4
Races Led	0
Laps Led (Pct.)	0 (0)
Laps Completed (Pct.)	2,155 (74.2)
Total Points	982
Points per Race	109.1
Total Bonus Points	0

Year	Career Race	Race No.	Date	Race	St.	Fin.	Total Laps	Laps Completed	Laps Led	Condition	Money	Pts.	Bonus Pts.
1975	1	13	May 25	Charlotte: World 600[1]	33	22	400	355	0	Running	1,925	97	0
1976	2	13	May 30	Charlotte: World 600[2]	25	31	400	156	0	DNF - Engine	1,725	70	0
	3	29	Nov 7	Atlanta: Dixie 500[3]	16	19	328	260	0	DNF - Crash	1,360	106	0
1977	4	27	Oct 9	Charlotte: NAPA National 500[4]	36	38	334	25	0	DNF - Rear End	1,375	49	0
1978*	5	12	May 28	Charlotte: World 600[5]	28	17	400	382	0	Running	3,415	112	0
	6	16	July 4	Daytona: Firecracker 400	28	7	160	157	0	Running	3,990	146	0
	7	19	Aug 6	Talladega: Talladega 500	27	12	188	180	0	Running	2,740	127	0
	8	22	Sep 4	Darlington: Southern 500	14	16	367	313	0	Running	3,100	115	0
	9	29	Nov 5	Atlanta: Dixie 500[6]	10	4	328	327	0	Running	7,500	160	0

* Also participated in fall race at Charlotte and at Ontario as a relief driver.

[1]Drove No. 8 Ed Negre Dodge
[2]Drove No. 30 Katy Ballard Chevrolet
[3]Drove No. 77 Johnny Ray Chevrolet
[4]Drove No. 19 Johnny Ray Chevrolet
[5]Began driving No. 96 Will Cronkite Ford; At Charlotte, relieved by Harry Gant
[6]Drove No. 98 Rod Osterlund Chevrolet

"I don't think anyone really likes racing next to Dale. But you've got to appreciate his aggressiveness and competitive nature."
—Bill Elliott

1979: Rookie Sensation

Few drivers in NASCAR history made as big an impact in their rookie seasons as Dale Earnhardt. The Kannapolis, N.C., native showed his hand early, offering not-so-subtle clues as to the kind of driver he would soon become. In just the seventh race of 1979, he won the Southeastern 500 at Bristol. Besides Davey Allison, who won his sixth race in 1987, no rookie has won earlier in his rookie season. Earnhardt's early win was wonderfully prescient: In 2000, his son, Dale Jr., won the seventh race of his 2000 rookie year at Texas.

Another telling sign in Earnhardt's rookie season was his toughness. The only races Earnhardt ever failed to start in his Winston Cup career came in 1979 after a vicious, tumbling wreck at Pocono. He broke both collarbones and a leg in the crash and missed four races as a result.

But Earnhardt demonstrated his trademark toughness when he returned just six weeks later and won the pole in each of his first two post-injury starts. His amazing effort was yet another prescient turn of events: in 1996, he accomplished a similar feat after a wreck at Talladega, during which he suffered a broken sternum and collarbone. After the 1996 crash, Earnhardt qualified for and started the Brickyard 400 just six days later. Then, in the second race after the wreck, he won the pole at Watkins Glen.

After returning from his Pocono mishap, from 1979 until the tragic 2001 Daytona 500, Earnhardt didn't miss a race. His life-ending accident at Daytona ended a consecutive start streak of 648 races—second all-time in NASCAR history, just seven races shy of Terry Labonte's record.

The juiciest coincidence in Earnhardt's rookie campaign was the fact that his introduction to the Winston Cup world came during Richard Petty's final championship season. NASCAR's King Richard wrapped up his seventh title in '79, more than a thousand points ahead of the seventh-place driver in the standings—Earnhardt. Within 14 seasons, Earnhardt tied Petty's title total.

From a historical point of view, it can safely be argued that Tony Stewart and Davey Allison exceeded Earnhardt's performance in their rookie seasons. Earnhardt's son, Dale Jr., also can claim a greater first season in terms of victories (though inconsistency cost Little E the mantle of 'greatest rookie'). Still, Earnhardt's first full season was one of the best ever—and he backed it up with a championship in his second year.

Earnhardt in 1979

Category	Earnhardt's Total	Earnhardt's Rank	1979 Leader
Money	$264,086	7th	Richard Petty – 561,934
Total Points	3,749	7th	Richard Petty – 4,830
Avg. Start	7.7	9th	Buddy Baker – 4.76
Avg. Finish	10.7	5th	Richard Petty – 6.4
Wins	1	8th	Buddy Baker – 7
Top 5s	11	7th	Richard Petty – 23
Top 10s	17	7th	Richard Petty – 27
DNFs	4	34th	Dick May – 16
Poles	4	3rd	Buddy Baker – 7
Front Row Starts	4	7th	Buddy Baker – 11
Laps Led	604	7th	Darrell Waltrip – 2,128
Races Led	16	5th	Darrell Waltrip – 26
Times Led	55	7th	Darrell Waltrip – 119
Miles Led	775	7th	Darrell Waltrip – 2,629
Times Led Most Laps	1	8th	Darrell Waltrip – 8
Bonus Points	85	6th	Darrell Waltrip – 170
Laps Completed	8,340	14th	Darrell Waltrip – 9,994
Miles Completed	9,357	15th	Darrell Waltrip – 11,768
Points per Race	138.9	5th	Richard Petty – 155.8
Fin. on Lead Lap	6	7th	Richard Petty – 15

Rookie Season Comparison

Driver	Year	Wins	Top 5s	Top 10s	Poles	Laps Led	Points Ranking	Money
Tony Stewart	1999	3	12	21	2	1,227	4th	$3,190,149
Davey Allison*	1987	2	9	10	5	710	21st	361,060
Dale Earnhardt Jr	2000	2	3	5	2	426	16th	2,793,596
Dale Earnhardt	1979	1	11	17	4	604	7th	274,810
Morgan Shepherd	1981	1	3	7	1	518	13th	170,473
Matt Kenseth	2000	1	4	11	0	162	14th	2,345,564
Jeff Gordon	1993	0	7	11	1	230	14th	765,168

*Allison competed in 22 of 29 races in 1987

1979 Performance Chart

No. 2 Rod Osterlund Chevrolet

Career Race	Season Race	Date	Race	St.	Fin.	Total Laps	Laps Completed	Laps Led	Condition	Money	Pts.	Bonus Pts.	Point Standing	Behind Leader	Points Leader
10	1	Jan 14	Riverside: Winston Western 500	10	21	119	103	0	Running	$2,230	100	0	21	-85	D. Waltrip
11	2	Feb 18	Daytona: Daytona 500	10	8	200	199	10	Running	22,845	147	5	4	-113	D. Waltrip
12	3	Mar 4	Rockingham: Carolina 500	5	12	492	460	0	Running	3,250	127	0	8	-98	D. Waltrip
13	4	Mar 11	Richmond: Richmond 400	4	13	400	390	0	Running	2,015	124	0	7	-139	D. Waltrip
14	5	Mar 18	Atlanta: Atlanta 500	17	12	328	321	0	Running	4,835	127	0	8	-182	D. Waltrip
15	6	Mar 25	North Wilkesboro: Northwestern Bank 400	5	4	400	400	9	Running	4,275	165	5	7	-181	B. Allison
16	7	Apr 1	Bristol: Southeastern 500	9	1	500	500	163	Running	19,800	185	10	5	-171	B. Allison
17	8	Apr 8	Darlington: CRC Chemicals Rebel 500	13	23	367	300	4	Running	5,600	99	5	8	-243	D. Waltrip
18	9	Apr 22	Martinsville: Virginia 500	11	8	500	495	0	Running	4,200	142	0	8	-271	D. Waltrip
19	10	May 6	Talladega: Winston 500	14	36	188	4	0	DNF - Crash	5,075	55	0	8	-391	D. Waltrip
20	11	May 12	Nashville: Sun-Drop Music City USA 420	7	4	420	419	0	Running	5,350	160	0	7	-336	D. Waltrip
21	12	May 20	Dover: Mason-Dixon 500	6	5	500	497	0	Running	7,750	155	0	5	-325	B. Allison
22	13	May 27	Charlotte: World 600	15	3	400	400	121	Running	27,100	170	5	5	-310	D. Waltrip
23	14	June 3	Texas World: Texas 400	3	12	200	189	41	DNF - Crash	6,400	132	5	5	-363	D. Waltrip
24	15	June 10	Riverside: NAPA Riverside 400	1	13	95	87	2	Running	7,250	129	5	5	-409	D. Waltrip
25	16	June 17	Michigan: Gabriel 400	13	6	200	200	1	Running	7,540	155	5	5	-383	D. Waltrip
26	17	July 4	Daytona: Firecracker 400	21	3	160	160	1	Running	14,980	170	5	5	-378	D. Waltrip
27	18	July 14	Nashville: Busch Nashville 420	3	3	420	417	0	Running	7,200	165	0	5	-398	D. Waltrip
28	19	July 30	Pocono: Coca-Cola 500[1]	3	29	200	98	43	DNF - Crash	4,680	81	5	5	-473	D. Waltrip
*	20	Aug 5	Talladega: Talladega 500	Did Not Start due to Injury									6	-658	D. Waltrip
*	21	Aug 19	Michigan: Champion Spark Plug 400	Did Not Start due to Injury									7	-764	D. Waltrip
*	22	Aug 25	Bristol: Volunteer 500	Did Not Start due to Injury									9	-944	D. Waltrip
*	23	Sep 3	Darlington: Southern 500	Did Not Start due to Injury									12	-1,084	D. Waltrip
29	24	Sep 9	Richmond: Capital City 400[2]	1	4	400	399	19	Running	7,250	165	5	11	-1,094	D. Waltrip
30	25	Sep 16	Dover: CRC Chemicals 500[3]	1	9	500	495	46	Running	7,000	143	5	9	-1,027	D. Waltrip
31	26	Sep 23	Martinsville: Old Dominion 500	5	29	500	67	0	DNF - Crash	3,510	76	0	13	-1,086	D. Waltrip
32	27	Oct 7	Charlotte: NAPA National 500	8	10	334	327	55	Running	14,515	139	5	10	-1,117	D. Waltrip
33	28	Oct 14	North Wilkesboro: Holly Farms 400	1	4	400	398	12	Running	10,425	165	5	9	-1,081	D. Waltrip
34	29	Oct 21	Rockingham: American 500	10	5	492	488	0	Running	8,300	155	0	8	-1,089	R. Petty
35	30	Nov 4	Atlanta: Dixie 500	7	2	328	328	69	Running	16,700	175	5	8	-1,066	D. Waltrip
36	31	Nov 18	Ontario: Los Angeles Times 500	6	9	200	199	8	Running	7,500	143	5	7	-1,081	R. Petty

[1]Injured in crash
[2]Relieved by Lennie Pond
[3]Relieved by Bill Elliott

1980: The First Championship

Though he arrived on the scene with a winning reputation and then exceeded expectations with a tremendously successful rookie season, nothing prepared the NASCAR world for Dale Earnhardt's championship run in 1980. In just his second full season, the 29-year-old driver constructed a dominant season that saw him lead the championship points battle for all but one race. In NASCAR history, since the circuit matured in the mid-1950s, no driver has won a championship title as quickly as Earnhardt.

Driving the No. 2 Rod Osterlund Pontiac, Earnhardt took on—and stared down—the biggest names in NASCAR history. Richard Petty, Cale Yarborough, Bobby Allison and Darrell Waltrip all took whacks at the young driver sitting atop the Winston Cup point standings. Each was turned away.

Earnhardt assumed the points lead with a fourth-place finish in the season's second race at Daytona and never relinquished his advantage. For nine months, he maintained a sometimes-tenuous lead. After the May race at Talladega, Earnhardt held a plush 148-point lead over Yarborough. By the June Michigan race, Petty had trimmed the edge to a mere 13 points. By August, Earnhardt rebuilt his lead to 150 points over Yarborough, only to see his cushion deflate to 23 points two races later.

The turning point—and another indication of his steely determination—came when Earnhardt won back-to-back fall races at Martinsville and Charlotte. Those wins opened the lead back to 115 points and enabled Earnhardt to hold off a furious comeback attempt by Yarborough. At season's end, Earnhardt won by 19 points, the fifth-closest points race in Winston Cup history. In addition to winning the title, Earnhardt began developing his prowess on short tracks, with wins at Bristol, Nashville and Martinsville, and on high-banked speedways, winning at Atlanta and Charlotte.

Earnhardt in 1980

Category	Earnhardt's Total	Earnhardt's Rank	1980 Leader*
Money	$588,926	1st	(C. Yarborough – 567,891)
Total Points	4,661	1st	(C. Yarborough – 4,642)
Avg. Start	9.1	9th	Cale Yarborough – 3.1
Avg. Finish	8.2	1st	(C. Yarborough – 9.0)
Wins	5	2nd	Cale Yarborough – 6
Top 5s	19	T-1st	(Cale Yarborough – 19)
Top 10s	24	1st	(Cale Yarborough – 22)
DNFs	4	36th	J.D. McDuffie – 15
Poles	0	—	Cale Yarborough – 14
Front Row Starts	1	10th	Cale Yarborough – 20
Laps Led	1,185	3rd	Cale Yarborough – 2,810
Races Led	25	3rd	Yarborough, Waltrip – 28
Times Led	103	3rd	Cale Yarborough – 118
Miles Led	1,426	3rd	Cale Yarborough – 3,155
Times Led Most Laps	3	4th	D. Waltrip, Yarborough – 9
Bonus Points	140	3rd	Yarborough, Waltrip – 185
Laps Completed	9,615	1st	(Jody Ridley – 9,579)
Miles Completed	11,136	1st	(Cale Yarborough – 11,015)
Points per Race	150.4	1st	(Cale Yarborough – 149.7)
Fin. on Lead Lap	13	2nd	Cale Yarborough – 16

* 2nd-place driver listed in parentheses if Earnhardt is category leader.

Fastest Champions
Number of seasons before first Winston Cup/Grand National title

Driver	Year	No. of Seasons
Dale Earnhardt	1980	2
Jeff Gordon	1995	3
Ned Jarrett	1961	3
Benny Parsons	1973	4
Rex White	1960	5
Lee Petty	1954	5
Richard Petty	1964	6
Terry Labonte	1984	6
Rusty Wallace	1989	6

1980 Performance Chart

No. 2 Rod Osterlund Chevrolet

Career Race	Season Race	Date	Race	St.	Fin.	Total Laps	Laps Completed	Laps Led	Condition	Money	Pts.	Bonus Pts.	Point Standing	Behind Leader	Points Leader
37	1	Jan 19	Riverside: Winston Western 500	5	2	119	119	0	Running	$19,400	170	0	2	-15	D. Waltrip
38	2	Feb 17	Daytona: Daytona 500	32	4	200	199	10	Running	36,350	165	5	1	+39	(T. Labonte)
39	3	Feb 24	Richmond: Richmond 400	13	5	400	398	0	Running	6,550	155	0	1	+31	(B. Allison)
40	4	Mar 9	Rockingham: Carolina 500	7	3	492	491	6	Running	14,420	170	5	1	+52	(R. Petty)
41	5	Mar 16	Atlanta: Atlanta 500	31	1	328	328	50	Running	36,200	180	5	1	+65	(B. Allison)
42	6	Mar 30	Bristol: Valleydale Southeastern 500	4	1	500	500	208	Running	20,625	185	10	1	+85	(B. Allison)
43	7	Apr 13	Darlington: CRC Chemicals Rebel 500	5	29	189	104	15	DNF - Engine	6,640	81	5	1	+93	(B. Allison)
44	8	Apr 20	North Wilkesboro: Northwestern Bank 400	4	6	400	395	0	Running	6,525	150	0	1	+73	(B. Allison)
45	9	Apr 27	Martinsville: Virginia 500	11	13	500	484	0	Running	5,400	124	0	1	+61	(D. Waltrip)
46	10	May 4	Talladega: Winston 500	4	2	188	188	55	Running	28,700	175	5	1	+148	(Yarborough)
47	11	May 10	Nashville: Music City USA 420	7	6	420	418	27	Running	5,825	155	5	1	+128	(Yarborough)
48	12	May 18	Dover: Mason-Dixon 500	16	10	500	475	0	DNF - Engine	7,675	134	0	1	+102	(R. Petty)
49	13	May 25	Charlotte: World 600	4	20	400	367	105	Running	13,690	108	5	1	+45	(R. Petty)
50	14	June 1	Texas World: NASCAR 400	7	9	200	191	54	Running	8,800	143	5	1	+18	(R. Petty)
51	15	June 8	Riverside: Warner W. Hodgdon 400	5	5	95	95	21	Running	9,100	160	5	1	+36	(R. Petty)
52	16	June 15	Michigan: Gabriel 400	3	12	200	197	55	Running	7,825	132	5	1	+13	(R. Petty)
53	17	July 4	Daytona: Firecracker 400	7	3	160	160	44	Running	16,580	170	5	1	+28	(R. Petty)
54	18	July 12	Nashville: Busch Nashville 420	7	1	420	420	103	Running	14,600	180	5	1	+48	(R. Petty)
55	19	Jul y27	Pocono: Coca-Cola 500	11	4	200	200	6	Running	11,415	165	5	1	+144	(R. Petty)
56	20	Aug 3	Talladega: Talladega 500	16	3	188	188	3	Running	16,975	170	5	1	+150	(Yarborough)
57	21	Aug 17	Michigan: Champion Spark Plug 400	8	35	200	79	1	DNF - Engine	6,410	63	5	1	+33	(Yarborough)
58	22	Aug 23	Bristol: Busch Volunteer 500	7	2	500	500	24	Running	11,450	175	5	1	+23	(Yarborough)
59	23	Sep 1	Darlington: Southern 500	8	7	367	366	27	Running	11,125	151	5	1	+98	(Yarborough)
60	24	Sep 7	Richmond: Capital City 400	5	4	400	399	39	Running	7,575	165	5	1	+111	(R. Petty)
61	25	Sep 14	Dover: CRC Chemicals 500	9	34	500	151	1	DNF - Engine	6,210	66	5	1	+60	(R. Petty)
62	26	Sep 21	North Wilkesboro: Holly Farms 400	8	5	400	399	0	Running	6,925	155	0	1	+90	(Yarborough)
63	27	Sep 28	Martinsville: Old Dominion 500	7	1	500	500	176	Running	25,375	185	10	1	+105	(Yarborough)
64	28	Oct 5	Charlotte: National 500	4	1	334	334	148	Running	49,050	185	10	1	+115	(Yarborough)
65	29	Oct 19	Rockingham: American 500	11	18	492	443	3	Running	6,650	114	5	1	+44	(Yarborough)
66	30	Nov 2	Atlanta: Atlanta Journal 500	13	3	328	327	1	Running	14,700	170	5	1	+29	(Yarborough)
67	31	Nov 15	Ontario: Los Angeles Times 500	2	5	200	200	3	Running	10,835	160	5	1	+19	(Yarborough)

*2nd-place driver listed in parentheses if Earnhardt is current points leader

1981: Post-Championship Hangover

After stringing together the most successful first two seasons in NASCAR history, Dale Earnhardt got a taste of "racin' luck" in 1981—on and off the track. Off the track, Earnhardt played musical owners, finding himself in the employ of three different car owners. Sixteen races into the 1981 season, Earnhardt's first owner, Rod Osterlund, vacated the sport and sold his team and equipment to J.D. Stacy. Together, Osterlund and Earnhardt won a championship, a Rookie of the Year award, six races and four poles.

Faced with new ownership, Earnhardt quickly decided against driving for the financially unstable Stacy. The 30-year-old drove just four races with his new owner before jumping to the No. 3 Pontiac owned by Richard Childress. Though the Childress-Earnhardt team would later prove to be nearly invincible, in 1981 they were together only for 11 races.

In those 11 races, Earnhardt and Childress combined for two Top 5s, six Top 10s and $69,905 in winnings. Inconsistency resulting from mechanical problems, however, marred the team's effort. Earnhardt suffered through engine problems in three of the final six races of the season and finished just two of his Childress-backed races on the lead lap.

The off-track chaos was reflected in Earnhardt's on-track performance. Where in 1980 he displayed the consistency necessary to hold the points lead for nine months, in 1981 Earnhardt never collected four straight Top 10 finishes. His DNFs (i.e., races he did not finish) increased to a then-career-high 10 and his Top 5 finishes dropped by more than half to nine from the previous season.Similarly, while in his first two seasons Earnhardt showed enough muscle to lead often and win regularly, in 1981 he led fewer laps than as a rookie and, more startling, did not win a race—one of just two seasons in which he failed to win.

In the end, Earnhardt dropped back to seventh in the point standings, more than 900 points behind '81 champion Darrell Waltrip. Unfortunately for Earnhardt, he was entering the "Dark Years" of his NASCAR career, a stretch from 1981 through 1983 during which he never seriously contended for the championship and rarely contended for a win.

Earnhardt in 1981

Category	Earnhardt's Total	Earnhardt's Rank	1981 Leader
Money	$347,113	6th	Darrell Waltrip – 799,134
Total Points	3,975	7th	Darrell Waltrip – 4,880
Avg. Start	8.0	6th	Darrell Waltrip – 5.3
Avg. Finish	13.5	7th	Bobby Allison – 6.8
Wins	0	—	Darrell Waltrip – 12
Top 5s	9	7th	B. Allison, Waltrip – 21
Top 10s	17	5th	Bobby Allison – 26
DNFs	10	9th	Kyle Petty – 18
Poles	0	—	Darrell Waltrip – 11
Front Row Starts	3	6th	Darrell Waltrip – 15
Laps Led	300	10th	Darrell Waltrip – 2,517
Races Led	12	9th	Darrell Waltrip – 27
Times Led	41	7th	Bobby Allison – 121
Miles Led	479	8th	Darrell Waltrip – 2,330
Times Led Most Laps	1	6th	Darrell Waltrip – 11
Bonus Points	65	9th	Darrell Waltrip – 190
Laps Completed	8,134	11th	Bobby Allison – 10,098
Miles Completed	10,062	6th	Bobby Allison – 11,609
Points per Race	128.2	9th	Darrell Waltrip – 157.4
Fin. on Lead Lap	7	5th	Darrell Waltrip – 22

"He's from the old school and I am, too. The old school taught you to take care of yourself."
—Dave Marcis,
former Winston Cup driver

1981 Performance Chart

No. 2 Rod Osterlund Pontiac

Career Race	Season Race	Date	Race	St.	Fin.	Total Laps	Laps Completed	Laps Led	Condition	Money	Pts.	Bonus Pts.	Point Standing	Behind Leader	Points Leader
68	1	Jan 11	Riverside: Winston Western 500	6	3	119	119	0	Running	$16,325	165	0	3	-20	B. Allison
69	2	Feb 15	Daytona: Daytona 500	7	5	200	200	4	Running	37,365	160	5	4	-40	B. Allison
70	3	Feb 22	Richmond: Richmond 400	6	7	400	397	0	Running	7,550	146	0	2	-39	R. Petty
71	4	Mar 1	Rockingham: Carolina 500	11	26	492	285	0	DNF - Crash	8,250	85	0	3	-124	R. Petty
72	5	Mar 15	Atlanta: Coca-Cola 500	5	3	328	327	0	Running	19,400	165	0	3	-58	B. Allison
73	6	Mar 29	Bristol: Valleydale 500[1]	2	28	500	140	65	DNF - Crash	7,270	84	5	4	-139	B. Allison
74	7	Apr 5	North Wilkesboro: Northwestern Bank 400	2	10	400	395	0	Running	8,800	134	0	6	-185	B. Allison
75	8	Apr 12	Darlington: CRC Chemicals Rebel 500	5	17	367	346	0	Running	9,150	112	0	7	-211	B. Allison
76	9	Apr 26	Martinsville: Virginia 500	10	25	500	155	0	DNF - Engine	6,600	88	0	6	-247	B. Allison
77	10	May 3	Talladega: Winston 500	4	8	188	183	5	Running	14,775	147	5	6	-280	B. Allison
78	11	May 9	Nashville: Melling Tool 420	12	20	420	379	0	Running	6,500	103	0	5	-342	B. Allison
79	12	May 17	Dover: Mason-Dixon 500	14	3	500	499	0	Running	15,125	165	0	6	-347	B. Allison
80	13	May 24	Charlotte: World 600	5	18	400	362	54	DNF - Engine	13,675	114	5	5	-418	B. Allison
81	14	June 7	Texas World: Budweiser NASCAR 400	3	2	200	200	96	Running	18,650	180	10	5	-408	B. Allison
82	15	June 14	Riverside: Warner W. Hodgdon 400	2	2	95	95	11	Running	18,725	175	5	4	-309	B. Allison
83	16	June 21	Michigan: Gabriel 400	7	5	200	200	37	Running	11,925	160	5	4	-329	B. Allison
84	17	July 4	Daytona: Firecracker 400[2]	3	35	160	71	1	DNF - Vibration	8,360	63	5	5	-350	B. Allison
85	18	July 11	Nashville: Busch Nashville 420	7	7	420	418	0	Running	7,375	146	0	5	-379	B. Allison
86	19	July 26	Pocono: Mountain Dew 500	8	11	200	198	4	Running	9,190	135	5	5	-337	B. Allison
87	20	Aug 2	Talladega: Talladega 500	3	29	188	83	5	DNF - Transmission	9,375	81	5	5	-421	B. Allison
88	21	Aug 16	Michigan: Champion Spark Plug 400[3]	10	9	200	200	0	Running	7,955	138	0	6	-434	B. Allison
89	22	Aug 22	Bristol: Busch 500	14	27	500	31	0	DNF - Crash	2,620	82	0	7	-517	B. Allison
90	23	Sep 7	Darlington: Southern 500	10	6	367	366	0	Running	10,695	150	0	6	-510	B. Allison
91	24	Sep 13	Richmond: Wrangler Sanfor-Set 400	11	6	400	398	0	Running	6,270	150	0	6	-520	B. Allison
92	25	Sep 20	Dover: CRC Chemicals 500	22	15	500	490	0	Running	5,275	118	0	6	-574	D. Waltrip
93	26	Sep 27	Martinsville: Old Dominion 500	7	26	500	148	0	DNF - Engine	2,690	85	0	6	-669	D. Waltrip
94	27	Oct 4	North Wilkesboro: Holly Farms 400	10	4	400	399	0	Running	7,270	160	0	5	-694	D. Waltrip
95	28	Oct 11	Charlotte: National 500	24	25	334	220	2	DNF - Ignition	4,920	93	5	6	-781	D. Waltrip
96	29	Nov 1	Rockingham: American 500	5	9	492	489	16	Running	7,360	143	5	6	-823	D. Waltrip
97	30	Nov 8	Atlanta: Atlanta Journal 500	9	25	328	222	0	DNF - Engine	4,290	88	0	7	-910	D. Waltrip
98	31	Nov 22	Riverside: Winston Western 500	3	4	119	119	0	Running	10,560	160	0	7	-905	D. Waltrip

[1]After crash, relieved Terry Labonte (finished 7th)
[2]Osterlund sold team to JD Stacy
[3]Switched to No. 3 Richard Childress Pontiac

1982: Hitting a Career Low

After the off-track instability and on-track inconsistency of 1981, Dale Earnhardt sought a steady, reliable hand in his choice of owner in 1982. He signed on with Bud Moore to drive the No. 15 Ford (yes, Chevy fans, he drove a Ford).

Moore, a highly respected car owner, first became involved in NASCAR ownership during the association's second year in 1950 and became a full-time owner in 1961. On the impressive list of drivers who drove for Moore before Earnhardt joined him were seven Grand National or Winston Cup champions, including Joe Weatherly, David Pearson, Cale Yarborough, Bobby Allison, Darrell Waltrip and Benny Parsons. Moore and his drivers had produced 73 victories by the time Earnhardt arrived. In other words, if Earnhardt was gun-shy about car owners following his chaotic '81 season – during which he drove for three separate owners and won zero races—Bud Moore seemed the perfect remedy.

Unfortunately, Earnhardt's decision had the exact opposite effect. The Bud Moore-Dale Earnhardt team never clicked. The 1982 season turned out to be the worst of Earnhardt's career. The once-promising star finished the year a career-low 12th in the point standings, more than 1,000 points behind repeat champion Darrell Waltrip.

The most glaring statistic in Earnhardt's 1982 performance is his 18 DNFs. The inability to finish races destroyed the competitive racer's chances at his two favorite things, wins and championships. The DNFs piled up quickly; only once did Earnhardt enjoy a run of three consecutive races in which he was running at the end. In the season's final 13 events, Earnhardt pulled behind the wall early 11 times, including the final eight races consecutively.

Not surprisingly, Earnhardt's Top 5 and Top 10 finishes dropped to below-rookie-season levels and his average finish for the season was a career-worst 18.8. Despite the disappointment and increased sideline time, Earnhardt showed signs of strength. He broke a then-career-high 39-race winless streak in the Darlington spring race, the first of nine career Darlington victories for Earnhardt. Moore's team also helped Earnhardt to his first qualifying pole in three seasons (at Atlanta).

Another positive sign for Earnhardt was his ability to charge to the front of the pack. Though he didn't complete many laps in 1982 (a career-low 7,208), he managed to lead a lot while on the track. He led the most laps in four races and led a total of 1,062 laps, both third best in the series in 1982.

Earnhardt in 1982

Category	Earnhardt's Total	Earnhardt's Rank	1982 Leader
Money	$375,325	6th	Darrell Waltrip – 923,151
Total Points	3,402	12th	Darrell Waltrip – 4,489
Avg. Start	10.6	10th	Darrell Waltrip – 3.8
Avg. Finish	18.8	24th	Darrell Waltrip – 9.1
Wins	1	6th	Darrell Waltrip – 12
Top 5s	7	9th	T. Labonte, Waltrip – 17
Top 10s	12	11th	Terry Labonte – 21
DNFs	18	2nd	Lake Speed – 19
Poles	1	9th	Darrell Waltrip – 7
Front Row Starts	1	13th	Darrell Waltrip – 14
Laps Led	1,062	3rd	Darrell Waltrip – 3,027
Races Led	18	3rd	Darrell Waltrip – 27
Times Led	78	3rd	Bobby Allison – 125
Miles Led	1,176	3rd	Bobby Allison – 3,217
Times Led Most Laps	4	3rd	Bobby Allison – 10
Bonus Points	110	3rd	Darrell Waltrip – 175
Laps Completed	7,208	16th	Darrell Waltrip – 9,455
Miles Completed	7,787	21st	Bobby Allison – 10,860
Points per Race	113.4	19th	Darrell Waltrip – 149.6
Fin. on Lead Lap	6	6th	Darrell Waltrip – 15

"Earnhardt puts everyone on the defensive because of the way he drives. The drivers have a choice— they can either compete with him or let him get away with it."
—*Junior Johnson*

1982 Performance Chart

No. 15 Bud Moore Ford

Career Race	Season Race	Date	Race	St.	Fin.	Total Laps	Laps Completed	Laps Led	Condition	Money	Pts.	Bonus Pts.	Point Standing	Behind Leader	Points Leader
99	1	Feb 14	Daytona: Daytona 500	10	36	200	44	6	DNF - Engine	$14,700	60	5	35	-125	B. Allison
100	2	Feb 21	Richmond: Richmond 400	8	4	250	250	1	Running	10,960	165	5	13	-102	B. Allison
101	3	Mar 14	Bristol: Valleydale 500	9	2	500	500	255	Running	18,480	180	10	7	-80	T. Labonte
102	4	Mar 21	Atlanta: Coca-Cola 500	1	28	287	211	155	DNF - Engine	21,375	89	10	9	-133	T. Labonte
103	5	Mar 28	Rockingham: Warner W. Hodgdon Carolina 500	6	25	492	191	30	DNF - Overheating	8,660	93	5	11	-215	T. Labonte
104	6	Apr 4	Darlington: CRC Chemicals Rebel 500	5	1	367	367	181	Running	31,450	185	10	7	-180	T. Labonte
105	7	Apr 18	North Wilkesboro: Northwestern Bank 400	14	3	400	400	10	Running	12,425	170	5	6	-185	T. Labonte
106	8	Apr 25	Martinsville: Virginia National Bank 500	15	23	500	100	0	DNF - Overheating	7,170	94	0	6	-199	T. Labonte
107	9	May 2	Talladega: Winston 500	20	8	188	186	3	Running	14,850	147	5	7	-227	T. Labonte
108	10	May 8	Nashville: Cracker Barrel 420	12	10	420	415	0	Running	7,735	134	0	6	-263	T. Labonte
109	11	May 16	Dover: Mason-Dixon 500	10	3	500	497	11	Running	15,700	170	5	5	-253	T. Labonte
110	12	May 30	Charlotte: World 600	15	30	400	279	122	DNF - Gasket	18,470	83	10	4	-236	T. Labonte
111	13	June 6	Pocono: Van Scoy Diamond Mine 500	4	34	200	45	8	DNF - Ball Joint	8,575	66	5	7	-330	T. Labonte
112	14	June 13	Riverside: Budweiser 400	5	4	95	95	5	Running	11,935	165	5	5	-345	T. Labonte
113	15	June 20	Michigan: Gabriel 400	11	7	200	199	0	Running	13,550	146	0	4	-283	T. Labonte
114	16	July 4	Daytona: Firecracker 400	13	29	160	89	0	DNF - Engine	9,265	76	0	5	-329	B. Allison
115	17	July 10	Nashville: Busch Nashville 420	13	9	420	417	0	Running	7,635	138	0	4	-326	T. Labonte
116	18	July 25	Pocono: Mountain Dew 500	7	25	200	134	9	DNF - Crash	9,700	93	5	5	-398	T. Labonte
117	19	Aug 1	Talladega: Talladega 500	18	35	188	29	0	DNF - Crash	9,290	58	0	7	-500	T. Labonte
118	20	Aug 22	Michigan: Champion Spark Plug 400	18	30	200	76	0	DNF - Brakes	8,750	73	0	9	-577	B. Allison
119	21	Aug 28	Bristol: Busch 500	12	6	500	499	74	Running	9,600	155	5	8	-602	B. Allison
120	22	Sep 6	Darlington: Southern 500	5	3	367	367	36	Running	21,225	170	5	8	-540	B. Allison
121	23	Sep 12	Richmond: Wrangler Sanfor-Set 4001	6	27	400	158	0	DNF - Engine	7,105	82	0	8	-643	B. Allison
122	24	Sep 19	Dover: CRC Chemicals 500	16	20	500	402	101	DNF - Battery	8,825	108	5	8	-674	B. Allison
123	25	Oct 3	North Wilkesboro: Holly Farms 400	15	20	400	365	0	DNF - Brakes	7,235	103	0	9	-670	B. Allison
124	26	Oct 10	Charlotte: National 500	15	25	334	237	0	DNF - Ball Joint	9,565	88	0	8	-730	B. Allison
125	27	Oct 17	Martinsville: Old Dominion 500	12	27	500	118	0	DNF - Brakes	7,230	82	0	9	-796	D. Waltrip
126	28	Oct 31	Rockingham: Warner W. Hodgdon American 500	8	14	492	445	52	DNF - Engine	9,300	126	5	9	-850	D. Waltrip
127	29	Nov 7	Atlanta: Atlanta Journal 500	8	34	328	85	3	DNF - Crash	8,385	66	5	10	-954	D. Waltrip
128	30	Nov 21	Riverside: Winston Western 500	7	42	119	8	0	DNF - Oil Leak	8,125	37	0	12	-1,087	D. Waltrip

[1] After engine failure, relieved Morgan Shepherd (finished 12th)

1983: First Talladega Win

In his second season in Bud Moore's Ford, Dale Earnhardt must have had difficulty understanding where 1982 ended and 1983 began. After failing to finish his final eight races in 1982, Earnhardt suffered a similar fate in eight of his first nine events of the ensuing season. Engine difficulty was a culprit five times, while two accidents and brake problems forced him to quit the other races early. The only time he went the distance was in Week 2 at Richmond, when he started eighth and finished second.

While the season improved, it would have been nearly impossible for Earnhardt's fortune to get worse. Dale went the distance in eight straight races, culminating with his second victory for Moore in the Busch Nashville 420. Another victory followed two events later, as Dale posted the first of his 10 career triumphs at Talladega. That mid-season three-week span proved to be the zenith of Earnhardt's two-year tenure with Moore. The same problems from 1982 and early 1983 resurfaced down the stretch. DNFs were logged in four of the last eight races, surrounding a runner-up showing at North Wilkesboro and a pair of Top 5s at Martinsville and Riverside. Earnhardt closed the season in eighth place in the points, 935 points behind champion Bobby Allison. When the season ended, Earnhardt was looking for a way out of his deal with Moore. An old friend—Richard Childress—supplied the answer.

Earnhardt in 1983

Category	Earnhardt's Total	Earnhardt's Rank	1983 Leader
Money	$446,272	6th	Bobby Allison – 883,010
Total Points	3,732	8th	Bobby Allison – 4,667
Avg. Start	9.2	9th	Ricky Rudd – 6.6
Avg. Finish	15.3	10th	Bobby Allison – 7.7
Wins	2	5th	B. Allison, Waltrip – 6
Top 5s	9	8th	Darrell Waltrip – 22
Top 10s	14	9th	B. Allison, Waltrip – 25
DNFs	13	3rd	G. Bodine, T. Gale – 15
Poles	0	—	Darrell Waltrip – 7
Front Row Starts	1	12th	Darrell Waltrip – 10
Laps Led	1,027	3rd	Darrell Waltrip – 2,363
Races Led	19	3rd	Bobby Allison – 25
Times Led	56	3rd	Bobby Allison – 88
Miles Led	876	4th	Bobby Allison – 2,093
Times Led Most Laps	2	4th	Bobby Allison – 8
Bonus Points	105	3rd	Bobby Allison – 165
Laps Completed	7,701	16th	Bobby Allison – 10,038
Miles Completed	8,946	14th	Bobby Allison – 11,526
Points per Race	124.4	8th	Bobby Allison – 155.6
Fin. on Lead Lap	8	6th	Darrell Waltrip – 20

Restrictor-plate races defined Earnhardt's career, especially at Talladega. His first victory at Talladega came in 1983, before NASCAR instituted the plates as a way to slow the cars on the circuit's longest tracks. Earnhardt went on to win nine more races at Talladega, eight with restrictor plates. Here he takes the middle line en route to winning the 1999 Winston 500. *Bill Burt*

1983 Performance Chart

No. 15 Bud Moore Ford

Career Race	Season Race	Date	Race	St.	Fin.	Total Laps	Laps Completed	Laps Led	Condition	Money	Pts.	Bonus Pts.	Point Standing	Behind Leader	Points Leader
129	1	Feb 20	Daytona: Daytona 500	3	35	200	63	2	DNF - Engine	$37,011	63	5	34	-117	Yarborough
130	2	Feb 27	Richmond: Richmond 400	8	2	400	400	81	Running	16,575	175	5	9	-88	Ruttman
131	3	Mar 13	Rockingham: Warner W. Hodgdon Carolina 500	4	33	492	73	6	DNF - Crash	8,000	69	5	18	-193	Elliott
132	4	Mar 27	Atlanta: Coca-Cola 500	8	33	328	246	34	DNF - Engine	8,075	69	5	21	-210	Brooks
133	5	Apr 10	Darlington: TranSouth 500	17	13	367	348	2	DNF - Engine	7,890	129	5	19	-230	Bonnett
134	6	Apr 17	North Wilkesboro: Northwestern Bank 400	11	29	400	40	0	DNF - Engine	6,450	76	0	22	-319	Bonnett
135	7	Apr 24	Martinsville: Virginia National Bank 500	11	26	500	351	0	DNF - Crash	7,240	85	0	23	-371	B. Allison
136	8	May 1	Talladega: Winston 500	17	24	188	120	1	DNF - Brakes	10,035	96	5	20	-425	Gant
137	9	May 7	Nashville: Marty Robbins 420	7	24	420	258	0	DNF - Engine	6,450	91	0	22	-499	Gant
138	10	May 15	Dover: Mason-Dixon 500	17	8	500	491	28	Running	10,500	147	5	17	-531	B. Allison
139	11	May 21	Bristol: Valleydale 500	5	9	500	495	116	Running	7,930	143	5	16	-563	B. Allison
140	12	May 29	Charlotte: World 600	3	5	400	399	55	Running	28,700	160	5	15	-578	B. Allison
141	13	June 5	Riverside: Budweiser 400	15	4	95	95	0	Running	11,475	160	0	12	-515	B. Allison
142	14	June 12	Pocono: Van Scoy Diamond Mine 500	9	8	200	199	0	Running	11,200	142	0	11	-558	B. Allison
143	15	June 19	Michigan: Gabriel 400	15	15	200	198	0	Running	10,125	118	0	11	-615	B. Allison
144	16	July 4	Daytona: Firecracker 400	7	9	160	158	19	Running	11,900	143	5	10	-598	B. Allison
145	17	July 16	Nashville: Busch Nashville 420	3	1	420	420	212	Running	23,125	185	10	9	-578	B. Allison
146	18	July 24	Pocono: Like Cola 500	10	30	200	71	0	DNF - Engine	8,500	73	0	10	-680	B. Allison
147	19	July 31	Talladega: Talladega 500	4	1	188	188	41	Running	46,950	185	10	8	-638	B. Allison
148	20	Aug 21	Michigan: Champion Spark Plug 400	13	7	200	200	0	Running	12,140	146	0	8	-558	B. Allison
149	21	Aug 27	Bristol: Busch 500	6	2	419	419	194	Running	15,725	175	5	7	-548	B. Allison
150	22	Sep 5	Darlington: Southern 500	17	11	367	363	0	Running	11,855	130	0	8	-603	B. Allison
151	23	Sep 11	Richmond: Wrangler Sanfor-Set 400	9	22	400	181	0	DNF - Rear End	6,850	97	0	8	-691	B. Allison
152	24	Sep 18	Dover: Budweiser 500[1]	3	35	500	90	59	DNF - Gasket	7,890	63	5	8	-813	B. Allison
153	25	Sep 25	Martinsville: Goody's 500	5	4	500	499	0	Running	11,200	160	0	9	-828	B. Allison
154	26	Oct 2	North Wilkesboro: Holly Farms 400	6	2	400	400	134	Running	15,500	175	5	8	-823	B. Allison
155	27	Oct 9	Charlotte: Miller High Life 500	16	14	334	332	6	Running	11,650	126	5	8	-848	B. Allison
156	28	Oct 30	Rockingham: Warner W. Hodgdon American 500	16	17	492	436	14	DNF - Engine	9,330	117	5	9	-851	B. Allison
157	29	Nov 6	Atlanta: Atlanta Journal 500	2	33	328	49	19	DNF - Clutch	7,995	69	5	9	-957	B. Allison
158	30	Nov 20	Riverside: Winston Western 500	9	4	119	119	4	Running	13,725	165	5	8	-935	B. Allison

[1] After mechanical problems, relieved Kyle Petty (finished 26th)

Earnhardt's "Dark Years" – 1981-1983

A comparison

Seasons	Races	Wins	Winning Pct.	DNFs	DNF Pct.
1981 – 1983	91	3	3.3	41	45.1
Rest of Career	585	73	12.5	55	9.4

1984: Earnhardt Joins Childress

After two frustrating seasons in a Ford, Earnhardt was optimistic about his second go-around in Richard Childress' Chevrolet. The two were an instant near-success. In the season-opening Daytona 500, Dale ran second to Cale Yarborough, his best finish in six tries at the Great American Race.

For the next 17 races, second-best was the best the No. 3 car could manage, as Earnhardt added runner-up efforts at Atlanta, Charlotte and Michigan. Finally, the team broke through at the Talladega 500, leading 40 of 188 laps en route to victory. Another win would come in the season's second-to-last race, the Atlanta Journal 500. Together, the Earnhardt-Childress combination generated 67 wins.

Though not winning regularly, Earnhardt's consistent efforts were good enough to grab the points lead after the Fourth of July Pepsi Firecracker 400 at Daytona. He held that lead for five more races, through the second Michigan race in August, before Terry Labonte overtook him. Engine failures at Darlington and Charlotte doomed Earnhardt's title hopes; he finished fourth in the standings, 243 points behind Labonte.

After two years of early exits with Moore, the 1984 season was a refreshing change for Earnhardt. He was running at the end of all but two races. But if he thought his DNF problems were a thing of the past, he was due for another dose in 1985.

Earnhardt's Car Owners (1979 – 2000)

Owner	Races	W. C. Titles	Wins	Top 5s	Poles	Money
Richard Childress	529	6	67	227	17	$39,662,737
Rod Osterlund	74	1	6	37	4	1,072,097
Bud Moore	60	0	3	16	1	821,597
J.D. Stacy	4	0	0	0	0	34,300

Earnhardt in 1984

Category	Earnhardt's Total	Earnhardt's Rank	1984 Leader
Money	$616,788	6th	Terry Labonte – 767,716
Total Points	4,265	4th	Terry Labonte – 4,508
Avg. Start	10.8	11th	Bill Elliott – 5.2
Avg. Finish	9.6	5th	Cale Yarborough – 7.4
Wins	2	6th	Darrell Waltrip – 7
Top 5s	12	6th	Terry Labonte – 17
Top 10s	22	4th	Elliott, T. Labonte – 24
DNFs	2	45th	J. Ruttman, G. Sacks – 14
Poles	0	—	Four tied with 4
Front Row Starts	2	10th	Bill Elliott – 11
Laps Led	446	10th	Darrell Waltrip – 2,030
Races Led	16	6th	Terry Labonte – 26
Times Led	60	4th	Cale Yarborough – 77
Miles Led	663	8th	Darrell Waltrip – 1,577
Times Led Most Laps	0	—	Darrell Waltrip – 7
Bonus Points	80	6th	T. Labonte, Waltrip – 145
Laps Completed	9,584	4th	Harry Gant – 9,899
Miles Completed	10,850	4th	Harry Gant – 11,395
Points per Race	142.2	5th	Cale Yarborough – 153.0
Fin. on Lead Lap	10	6th	Gant, Labonte, Waltrip – 15

1984 Performance Chart

No. 3 RCR Enterprises Chevrolet

Career Race	Season Race	Date	Race	St.	Fin.	Total Laps	Laps Completed	Laps Led	Condition	Money	Pts.	Bonus Pts.	Point Standing	Behind Leader	Points Leader
159	1	Feb 19	Daytona: Daytona 500	29	2	200	200	19	Running	$81,825	175	5	2	-10	Yarborough
160	2	Feb 26	Richmond: Miller High Life 400	17	6	400	399	0	Running	8,675	150	0	3	-25	D. Waltrip
161	3	Mar 4	Rockingham: Warner W. Hodgdon Carolina 500[1]	8	14	492	470	0	Running	9,335	121	0	5	-38	D. Waltrip
162	4	Mar 18	Atlanta: Coca-Cola 500	9	2	328	328	26	Running	26,935	175	5	2	-2	T. Labonte
163	5	Apr 1	Bristol: Valleydale 500	17	7	500	498	2	Running	7,530	151	5	3	-31	D. Waltrip
164	6	Apr 8	North Wilkesboro: Northwestern Bank 400	10	8	400	399	0	Running	7,260	142	0	4	-49	T. Labonte
165	7	Apr 15	Darlington: TranSouth 500	14	5	367	366	24	Running	12,825	160	5	4	-64	T. Labonte
166	8	Apr 29	Martinsville: Sovran Bank 500	15	9	500	497	0	Running	7,345	138	0	3	-96	D. Waltrip
167	9	May 6	Talladega: Winston 500	5	27	188	149	3	Running	10,475	87	5	4	-58	D. Waltrip
168	10	May 12	Nashville: Coors 420	5	19	420	410	0	Running	7,250	106	0	5	-132	D. Waltrip
169	11	May 20	Dover: Budweiser 500	11	5	500	499	0	Running	11,600	155	0	5	-127	D. Waltrip
170	12	May 27	Charlotte: World 600	19	2	400	400	91	Running	49,625	175	5	2	-42	D. Waltrip
171	13	June 3	Riverside: Budweiser 400	3	5	95	95	0	Running	10,950	155	0	3	-22	D. Waltrip
172	14	June 10	Pocono: Van Scoy Diamond Mine 500	8	8	200	199	34	Running	11,360	147	5	3	-30	D. Waltrip
173	15	June 17	Michigan: Miller High Life 400	15	2	200	200	0	Running	28,175	170	0	2	-30	D. Waltrip
174	16	July 4	Daytona: Pepsi Firecracker 400	2	8	160	159	5	Running	13,600	147	5	1	+47	(D. Waltrip)
175	17	July 14	Nashville: Pepsi 420	16	3	420	419	33	Running	10,775	170	5	1	+42	(D. Waltrip)
176	18	July 22	Pocono: Like Cola 500	5	10	200	198	9	Running	11,300	139	5	1	+55	(Elliott)
177	19	July 29	Talladega: Talladega 500	3	1	188	188	40	Running	47,100	180	5	1	+65	(T. Labonte)
178	20	Aug 12	Michigan: Champion Spark Plug 400	14	7	200	199	0	Running	12,700	146	0	1	+31	(T. Labonte)
179	21	Aug 25	Bristol: Busch 500	9	10	500	478	64	Running	7,800	139	5	2	-15	T. Labonte
180	22	Sep 2	Darlington: Southern 500	20	38	367	57	0	DNF - Engine	7,860	49	0	4	-113	T. Labonte
181	23	Sep 9	Richmond: Wrangler Sanfor-Set 400	13	3	400	400	9	Running	13,450	170	5	2	-90	T. Labonte
182	24	Sep 16	Dover: Delaware 500	2	5	500	497	35	Running	11,710	160	5	3	-105	T. Labonte
183	25	Sep 23	Martinsville: Goody's 500	11	12	500	489	0	Running	7,865	127	0	3	-153	T. Labonte
184	26	Oct 7	Charlotte: Miller High Life 500	16	39	334	74	0	DNF - Engine	8,010	46	0	4	-267	T. Labonte
185	27	Oct 14	North Wilkesboro: Holly Farms 400	9	7	400	400	0	Running	8,150	146	0	5	-264	T. Labonte
186	28	Oct 21	Rockingham: Warner W. Hodgdon American 500	6	13	492	470	4	Running	8,710	129	5	5	-305	T. Labonte
187	29	Nov 11	Atlanta: Atlanta Journal 500	10	1	328	328	48	Running	40,610	180	5	5	-203	T. Labonte
188	30	Nov 18	Riverside: Winston Western 500	4	11	119	119	0	Running	9,000	130	0	4	-243	T. Labonte

*2nd-place driver listed in parentheses if Earnhardt is current points leader
[1]Relieved by Connie Saylor

1985: Prelude to a Championship

The second season of the Earnhardt-Childress reunion could adequately be described as one step forward, one step back. In 1985, the Childress team gave Earnhardt a ride that was considerably more potent, enabling Dale to move to his rightful place at the front of the field with greater frequency. But the engine powering the Chevy was not the most stable piece of machinery in the Winston Cup garage area.

After completing all but two races in 1984, Earnhardt's day ended early on nine occasions in the follow-up campaign. In each case, engine trouble was the reason for the early trip behind the wall. His season effectively ended during a seven-race stretch from Darlington in mid-April to Pocono in early June. In all but two races, Earnhardt parked his car before race's end. In consecutive races at Riverside and Pocono, Dale managed to complete a combined 22 laps before engine failures hit, resulting in 40th and 39th place finishes, the worst back-to-back showings of his career.

But Earnhardt ran up front more often in 1985, including early-season wins at Richmond and Bristol. He led 1,237 laps that season, an increase of almost 800 from 1984. And though his competitive hopes for the season were gone before summer, Earnhardt and Childress delivered a foreshadowing of the seasons to come during the campaign's final 10 races (see chart). Only once over that stretch did Earnhardt fail to finish, while he and his team earned checkered flags at Bristol and Martinsville. Seven Top 10s in the final eight races were an encouraging building block for 1986, when the pieces would finally come together again.

Earnhardt & Childress Put the Pieces Together

The Final 10 Races of 1985

Driver	Points	Wins	Top 10s	Laps Led
Darrell Waltrip	1,599	2	8	380
Dale Earnhardt	1,527	2	8	647
Harry Gant	1,523	2	8	756
Ricky Rudd	1,447	1	8	135
Geoffrey Bodine	1,378	0	6	254

Earnhardt in 1985

Category	Earnhardt's Total	Earnhardt's Rank	1985 Leader
Money	$546,596	7th	Bill Elliott – 2,433,187
Total Points	3,561	8th	Darrell Waltrip – 4,292
Avg. Start	9.5	9th	Bill Elliott – 4.9
Avg. Finish	14.7	10th	Darrell Waltrip – 7.4
Wins	4	2nd	Bill Elliott – 11
Top 5s	10	6th	Darrell Waltrip – 18
Top 10s	16	7th	Darrell Waltrip – 21
DNFs	9	16th	J.D. McDuffie – 15
Poles	1	6th	Bill Elliott – 12
Front Row Starts	1	10th	Bill Elliott – 12
Laps Led	1,237	3rd	Bill Elliott – 1,920
Races Led	17	5th	Darrell Waltrip – 21
Times Led	63	3rd	Bill Elliott – 80
Miles Led	1,092	4th	Bill Elliott – 3,188
Times Led Most Laps	4	2nd	Bill Elliott – 7
Bonus Points	105	4th	Bill Elliott – 130
Laps Completed	8,231	10th	Darrell Waltrip – 8,932
Miles Completed	9,149	15th	Darrell Waltrip – 10,910
Points per Race	127.2	8th	Darrell Waltrip – 153.2
Fin. on Lead Lap	9	5th	Darrell Waltrip – 17

As Earnhardt's legend grew with his fans, even his crewmen became famous. Long-time Earnhardt crewman Chocolate Myers, whose tough and gruff image reflected his boss' reputation, is the most recognizable nondriver on the Winston Cup circuit. *Bill Burt*

1985 Performance Chart

No. 3 RCR Enterprises Chevrolet

Career Race	Season Race	Date	Race	St.	Fin.	Total Laps	Laps Completed	Laps Led	Condition	Money	Pts.	Bonus Pts.	Point Standing	Behind Leader	Points Leader
189	1	Feb 17	Daytona: Daytona 500	18	32	200	84	0	DNF - Engine	$17,150	67	0	32	-118	Elliott
190	2	Feb 24	Richmond: Miller High Life 400	4	1	400	400	95	Running	33,625	180	5	8	-93	D. Waltrip
191	3	Mar 3	Rockingham: Carolina 500	11	10	492	491	13	Running	16,300	139	5	7	-83	Speed
192	4	Mar 17	Atlanta: Coca-Cola 500	8	9	328	326	0	Running	12,125	138	0	6	-94	G. Bodine
193	5	Apr 6	Bristol: Valleydale 500	12	1	500	500	214	Running	31,525	185	10	3	-29	T. Labonte
194	6	Apr 14	Darlington: TranSouth 500	8	24	367	293	130	DNF - Engine	9,180	96	5	6	-98	T. Labonte
195	7	Apr 21	North Wilkesboro: Northwestern Bank 400	8	8	400	398	1	Running	8,340	147	5	6	-97	T. Labonte
196	8	Apr 28	Martinsville: Sovran Bank 500	4	25	500	345	1	DNF - Engine	8,975	93	5	9	-168	G. Bodine
197	9	May 5	Talladega: Winston 500	13	21	188	155	12	DNF - Engine	11,410	105	5	10	-205	T. Labonte
198	10	May 19	Dover: Budweiser 500	9	25	500	219	0	DNF - Engine	9,050	88	0	11	-259	Elliott
199	11	May 26	Charlotte: Coca-Cola World 600	5	4	400	399	97	Running	49,238	170	10	11	-222	T. Labonte
200	12	June 2	Riverside: Budweiser 400	13	40	95	19	0	DNF - Engine	8,240	43	0	11	-364	T. Labonte
201	13	June 9	Pocono: Van Scoy Diamond Mine 500	4	39	200	3	0	DNF - Engine	8,700	46	0	14	-449	Elliott
202	14	June 16	Michigan: Miller 400	14	5	200	200	19	Running	17,925	160	5	12	-469	Elliott
203	15	July 4	Daytona: Pepsi Firecracker 400	18	9	160	159	0	Running	13,400	138	0	12	-511	Elliott
204	16	July 21	Pocono: Summer 500	11	39	200	11	0	DNF - Engine	8,700	46	0	12	-645	Elliott
205	17	July 28	Talladega: Talladega 500	14	24	188	156	8	Running	11,080	96	5	12	-719	Elliott
206	18	Aug 11	Michigan: Champion Spark Plug 400	12	22	200	191	0	Running	9,525	97	0	12	-802	Elliott
207	19	Aug 24	Bristol: Busch 500	1	1	500	500	343	Running	34,675	185	10	12	-777	Elliott
208	20	Sep 1	Darlington: Southern 500	5	19	367	349	147	DNF - Engine	12,835	116	10	12	-841	Elliott
209	21	Sep 8	Richmond: Wrangler Sanfor-Set 400	9	4	400	400	24	Running	12,050	165	5	11	-803	Elliott
210	22	Sep 15	Dover: Delaware 500	8	7	500	496	0	Running	12,600	146	0	11	-765	Elliott
211	23	Sep 22	Martinsville: Goody's 500	11	1	500	500	58	Running	37,725	180	5	11	-697	Elliott
212	24	Sep 29	North Wilkesboro: Holly Farms 400	7	4	400	400	37	Running	10,960	165	5	10	-635	D. Waltrip
213	25	Oct 6	Charlotte: Miller High Life 500	5	20	334	301	0	Running	12,050	103	0	10	-697	D. Waltrip
214	26	Oct 20	Rockingham: Nationwise 500	15	8	492	489	32	Running	11,800	147	5	10	-730	D. Waltrip
215	27	Nov 3	Atlanta: Atlanta Journal 500	13	4	328	328	0	Running	15,300	160	0	9	-740	D. Waltrip
216	28	Nov 17	Riverside: Winston Western 500	7	5	119	119	6	Running	13,175	160	5	8	-731	D. Waltrip

"When most drivers look into a pack of cars, they see traffic. Dale looks into the thickest pack and sees opportunity."
—Richard Childress

1986: The Second Championship

When Darrell Waltrip and Dale Earnhardt emerged on the Winston Cup scene in the 1970s, race fans assumed the brash Tennessean and the soft-spoken North Carolinian would become rivals for years to come. And while DW and the Intimidator dueled often for the lead on every track on the circuit over the next two decades, rarely did the rivalry manifest over the course of a full season.

Waltrip's best seasons—his title years in 1981, 1982 and 1985—came during Earnhardt's most fallow period. And in Dale's seven title seasons, DW was not typically the man he had to beat. Except in 1986.

For the previous two years, Earnhardt and car owner Richard Childress tried to put together a championship-worthy combination. They found it on the third try. Coupling the staying power he had in 1984 with the horsepower of 1985, the RCR Enterprises Chevrolet was a force all season. Earnhardt seized control of the points lead (from Waltrip) with a runner-up finish at Talladega the first weekend in May and never looked back.

His run to the top started slightly earlier, when he won back-to-back starts at Darlington and North Wilkesboro. A third win at Charlotte in the Coca Cola 600 followed in June. He nailed the Charlotte double in October, then sealed the crown with a victory at Atlanta in the season's penultimate race. Though he remained the closest pursuer almost all season long, Waltrip simply couldn't keep up with Dale's week-in, week-out brilliance.

Earnhardt was a factor in every race. He led all but three events, but placed no worse than seventh in any of the races he didn't lead. And in the four races that he failed to finish, Dale led no fewer than 34 laps in any of them.

Earnhardt in 1986

Category	Earnhardt's Total	Earnhardt's Rank	1986 Leader*
Money	$1,783,880	1st	(Darrell Waltrip – 1,099,735)
Total Points	4,468	1st	(Darrell Waltrip – 4,180)
Avg. Start	6.9	3rd	Geoffrey Bodine – 4.2
Avg. Finish	7.4	1st	(Tim Richmond – 9.9)
Wins	5	2nd	Tim Richmond – 7
Top 5s	16	2nd	Darrell Waltrip – 21
Top 10s	23	1st	(Darrell Waltrip – 22)
DNFs	4	34th	Morgan Shepherd – 15
Poles	1	5th	Geoffrey Bodine – 9
Front Row Starts	4	5th	G. Bodine, Richmond – 15
Laps Led	2,127	1st	(Geoffrey Bodine – 1,676)
Races Led	26	1st	(Geoffrey Bodine – 25)
Times Led	103	1st	(Geoffrey Bodine – 82)
Miles Led	2,439	1st	(Geoffrey Bodine – 2,055)
Times Led Most Laps	7	1st	(Geoffrey Bodine – 6)
Bonus Points	165	1st	(Geoffrey Bodine – 155)
Laps Completed	9,212	1st	(Bill Elliott – 8,549)
Miles Completed	11,164	1st	(Bill Elliott – 10,591)
Points per Race	154.1	1st	(Darrell Waltrip – 144.1)
Fin. on Lead Lap	15	2nd	Darrell Waltrip – 17

*2nd-place driver listed in parentheses if Earnhardt is category leader.

Earnhardt vs. Waltrip

1986 Season Comparison

Driver	Points	Wins	Top 5s	Top 10s	Poles	Laps Led
Dale Earnhardt	4,468	5	16	23	1	2,127
Darrell Waltrip	4,180	3	21	22	1	573

Earnhardt vs. Waltrip

Career Comparison

Driver	W.C. Titles	Wins	Top 5s	Poles	Laps Led	Money
Earnhardt	7	76	281	22	25,713	$41,641,084
Waltrip	3	84	276	59	23,130	22,493,879

The most common view of the No. 3 Chevy for Winston Cup competitors was its back bumper as Earnhardt pulled away. *Bill Burt*

1986 Performance Chart

No. 3 RCR Enterprises Chevrolet

Career Race	Season Race	Date	Race	St.	Fin.	Total Laps	Laps Completed	Laps Led	Condition	Money	Pts.	Bonus Pts.	Point Standing	Behind Leader	Points Leader
217	1	Feb 16	Daytona: Daytona 500	4	14	200	197	34	DNF - Engine	$61,655	126	5	14	-59	G. Bodine
218	2	Feb 23	Richmond: Miller High Life 400	10	3	400	400	299	Running	19,310	175	10	4	-31	G. Bodine
219	3	Mar 2	Rockingham: Goodwrench 500	5	8	492	490	69	Running	19,510	147	5	3	-42	D. Waltrip
220	4	Mar 16	Atlanta: Motorcraft 500	1	2	328	328	168	Running	51,300	180	10	3	-27	D. Waltrip
221	5	Apr 6	Bristol: Valleydale 500	6	10	500	497	106	Running	10,650	139	5	3	-58	D. Waltrip
222	6	Apr 13	Darlington: TranSouth 500	4	1	367	367	335	Running	52,250	185	10	2	-48	D. Waltrip
223	7	Apr 20	North Wilkesboro: First Union 400	5	1	400	400	195	Running	38,550	185	10	2	-23	D. Waltrip
224	8	Apr 27	Martinsville: Sovran Bank 500	3	21	500	347	102	DNF - Engine	9,915	105	5	2	-5	D. Waltrip
225	9	May 4	Talladega: Winston 500	14	2	188	188	18	Running	53,900	175	5	1	+109	(D. Waltrip)
226	10	May 18	Dover: Budweiser 500	2	3	500	499	57	Running	24,900	170	5	1	+124	(D. Waltrip)
227	11	May 25	Charlotte: Coca-Cola 600	3	1	400	400	26	Running	98,150	180	5	1	+144	(D. Waltrip)
228	12	June 1	Riverside: Budweiser 400	10	5	95	95	0	Running	14,125	155	0	1	+119	(D. Waltrip)
229	13	June 8	Pocono: Miller High Life 500	8	2	200	200	8	Running	29,750	175	5	1	+251	(D. Waltrip)
230	14	June 15	Michigan: Miller American 400	11	6	200	200	21	Running	17,650	155	5	1	+251	(D. Waltrip)
231	15	July 4	Daytona: Firecracker 400	5	27	160	151	69	DNF - Crash	14,895	92	10	1	+178	(D. Waltrip)
232	16	July 20	Pocono: Summer 500	10	7	150	150	0	Running	14,655	146	0	1	+159	(D. Waltrip)
233	17	July 27	Talladega: Talladega 500	2	26	188	153	54	DNF - Engine	15,355	95	10	1	+161	(D. Waltrip)
234	18	Aug 10	Watkins Glen: The Bud at the Glen	10	3	90	90	0	Running	25,250	165	0	1	+151	(D. Waltrip)
235	19	Aug 17	Michigan: Champion Spark Plug 400	12	5	200	199	34	Running	18,750	160	5	1	+141	(D. Waltrip)
236	20	Aug 23	Bristol: Busch 500	5	4	500	499	71	Running	12,800	165	5	1	+121	(D. Waltrip)
237	21	Aug 31	Darlington: Southern 500	21	9	367	366	17	Running	15,735	143	5	1	+109	(D. Waltrip)
238	22	Sep 7	Richmond: Wrangler Jeans Indigo 400	5	2	400	400	24	Running	24,525	175	5	1	+118	(Richmond)
239	23	Sep 14	Dover: Delaware 500	3	21	500	432	3	Running	10,750	105	5	1	+138	(Richmond)
240	24	Sep 21	Martinsville: Goody's 500	2	12	500	494	56	Running	11,770	132	5	1	+136	(Richmond)
241	25	Sep 28	North Wilkesboro: Holly Farms 400	14	9	400	398	24	Running	9,500	143	5	1	+122	(D. Waltrip)
242	26	Oct 5	Charlotte: Oakwood Homes 500	3	1	334	334	80	Running	82,050	180	5	1	+159	(D. Waltrip)
243	27	Oct 19	Rockingham: Nationwise 500	10	6	492	491	94	Running	15,750	155	5	1	+144	(D. Waltrip)
244	28	Nov 2	Atlanta: Atlanta Journal 500	4	1	328	328	162	Running	67,950	185	10	1	+278	(D. Waltrip)
245	29	Nov 16	Riverside: Winston Western 500	8	2	119	119	1	Running	26,750	175	5	1	+288	(D. Waltrip)

*2nd-place driver listed in parentheses if Earnhardt is current points leader

"There is a fine line between hard racing and reckless driving, and Earnhardt clearly stepped over that line Sunday. We simply cannot tolerate or condone such actions. We must preserve the integrity of our sport."
—NASCAR official after the sanctioning body fined Earnhardt $5,000 in 1986

1987: The Third Championship, Back-to-Back for the First Time

Dale Earnhardt's championship season in 1986 was a mere glimpse into the excellence on the horizon. His 1987 campaign was simply awe-inspiring. After his annual Daytona disappointment, Earnhardt won six of the next seven races (failing only at Atlanta when he started from the pole) and took the championship by the throat. Back-to-back victories at Rockingham and Richmond, then four straight at Darlington, North Wilkesboro, Bristol and Martinsville, put him 157 points in front of Bill Elliott.

And so it went. Earnhardt rolled through his campaign, building his lead over runner-up Elliott to an astonishing 608 points by early September. In the end, Earnhardt posted 11 victories, including sweeps at Darlington, Bristol and Richmond. He also added dominating triumphs at Michigan and Pocono. The wins hardly told the entire story, however. Dale led all but two races, for an astounding 3,358 laps, the fifth highest single-season total in the modern era. Looked at another way, in the 1987 season, more than a third of all competitive laps found Earnhardt at the front of the field. His only DNF was posted at Dover, when engine trouble knocked him out after 304 laps. Of the circuit's 29 races, Dale finished in the Top 5 21 times.

The 1987 season was the finest of Earnhardt's career, maybe the finest of anyone's, and marked the first time he displayed all of his promise during the course of an entire season. By winning his third championship, equaling the number of titles won by legends David Pearson, Lee Petty, Darrell Waltrip and Cale Yarborough, Earnhardt answered any remaining doubt about his position among NASCAR's all-time greats.

Earnhardt in 1987

Category	Earnhardt's Total	Earnhardt's Rank	1987 Leader*
Money	$2,099,243	1st	(Bill Elliott – 1,599,210)
Total Points	4,696	1st	(Bill Elliott – 4,207)
Avg. Start	7.3	3rd	Bill Elliott – 6.1
Avg. Finish	5.9	1st	(Bill Elliott – 5.9)
Wins	11	1st	(Bill Elliott – 6)
Top 5s	21	1st	(Bill Elliott – 16)
Top 10s	24	1st	(Terry Labonte – 22)
DNFs	2	70th	Harry Gant – 21
Poles	1	6th	Bill Elliott – 8
Front Row Starts	5	3rd	Bill Elliott – 11
Laps Led	3,358	1st	(Bill Elliott – 1,399)
Races Led	27	1st	(Bill Elliott – 22)
Times Led	116	1st	(Bill Elliott – 73)
Miles Led	3,399	1st	(Bill Elliott – 2,040)
Times Led Most Laps	13	1st	(Bill Elliott – 5)
Bonus Points	200	1st	(Bill Elliott – 135)
Laps Completed	9,043	1st	(Darrell Waltrip – 8,996)
Miles Completed	10,898	2nd	Darrell Waltrip – 11,034
Points per Race	161.9	1st	(Bill Elliott – 144.9)
Fin. on Lead Lap	23	1st	(Bill Elliott – 17)

*2nd-place driver listed in parentheses if Earnhardt is category leader.

Most Laps Led, Single Season

Modern Era

Driver	Laps Led	Year
Bobby Allison	4,343	1972
Cale Yarborough	3,791	1976
Cale Yarborough	3,587	1978
Cale Yarborough	3,530	1974
Dale Earnhardt	3,358	1987

Earnhardt's greatest season came in 1987 when he won a career-high 11 races and led 3,358 laps—over one-third of the laps run that season. He took the 1987 championship—his third—by nearly 500 points over second-place Bill Elliott. Because of that kind of performance, Earnhardt's cars often drew crowds, even when parked. *David Stringer*

1987 Performance Chart

No. 3 RCR Enterprises Chevrolet

Career Race	Season Race	Date	Race	St.	Fin.	Total Laps	Laps Completed	Laps Led	Condition	Money	Pts.	Bonus Pts.	Point Standing	Behind Leader	Points Leader
246	1	Feb 15	Daytona: Daytona 500	13	5	200	200	16	Running	$64,925	160	5	5	-25	Elliott
247	2	Mar 1	Rockingham: Goodwrench 500	14	1	492	492	319	Running	53,900	185	10	1 (tie)	—	(Elliott)
248	3	Mar 8	Richmond: Miller High Life 400	3	1	400	400	235	Running	49,150	185	10	1	+20	(Elliott)
249	4	Mar 15	Atlanta: Motorcraft Quality Parts 500	1	16	328	322	196	Running	19,520	125	10	1	+61	(Elliott)
250	5	Mar 29	Darlington: TranSouth 500	2	1	367	367	239	Running	52,985	185	10	1	+71	(Elliott)
251	6	Apr 5	North Wilkesboro: First Union 400	3	1	400	400	319	Running	44,675	185	10	1	+117	(Elliott)
252	7	Apr 12	Bristol: Valleydale Meats 500	3	1	500	500	134	Running	43,850	180	5	1	+127	(Elliott)
253	8	Apr 26	Martinsville: Sovran Bank 500	4	1	500	500	156	Running	50,850	185	10	1	+157	(Elliott)
254	9	May 3	Talladega: Winston 500	5	4	178	178	10	Running	31,350	165	5	1	+220	(Elliott)
255	10	May 24	Charlotte: Coca-Cola 600	3	20	400	305	0	Running	19,600	103	0	1	+219	(Elliott)
256	11	May 31	Dover: Budweiser 500	10	4	500	498	15	Running	20,775	165	5	1	+209	(Elliott)
257	12	June 14	Pocono: Miller High Life 500	7	5	200	200	56	Running	22,400	160	5	1	+194	(Elliott)
258	13	June 21	Riverside: Budweiser 400	8	7	95	95	0	Running	13,500	146	0	1	+185	(Elliott)
259	14	June 28	Michigan: Miller American 400	5	1	200	200	152	Running	60,250	185	10	1	+304	(Elliott)
260	15	July 4	Daytona: Pepsi Firecracker 400	13	6	160	160	22	Running	22,160	155	5	1	+327	(Elliott)
261	16	July 19	Pocono: Summer 500	16	1	200	200	85	Running	55,875	185	10	1	+409	(Bonnett)
262	17	July 26	Talladega: Talladega 500	2	3	188	188	8	Running	35,050	170	5	1	+430	(Elliott)
263	18	Aug 10	Watkins Glen: The Bud at the Glen	11	8	90	90	6	Running	17,005	147	5	1	+483	(T. Labonte)
264	19	Aug 16	Michigan: Champion Spark Plug 400	8	2	200	200	63	Running	34,325	180	10	1	+498	(Elliott)
265	20	Aug 22	Bristol: Busch 500	6	1	500	500	415	Running	47,175	185	10	1	+545	(Elliott)
266	21	Sep 6	Darlington: Southern 500	5	1	202	202	109	Running	64,650	185	10	1	+583	(Elliott)
267	22	Sep 13	Richmond: Wrangler Jeans Indigo 400	8	1	400	400	220	Running	44,950	185	10	1	+608	(Elliott)
268	23	Sep 20	Dover: Delaware 500	22	31	500	304	18	DNF - Engine	12,700	75	5	1	+518	(Elliott)
269	24	Sep 27	Martinsville: Goody's 500	8	2	500	500	170	Running	29,875	180	10	1	+568	(Elliott)
270	25	Oct 4	North Wilkesboro: Holly Farms 400	10	2	400	400	137	Running	26,950	175	5	1	+573	(Elliott)
271	26	Oct 11	Charlotte: Oakwood Homes 500	9	12	334	329	2	Running	16,440	132	5	1	+525	(Elliott)
272	27	Oct 25	Rockingham: AC Delco 500	2	2	492	492	122	Running	38,915	175	5	1	+515	(Elliott)
273	28	Nov 8	Riverside: Winston Western 500	8	30	119	93	1	DNF - Engine	11,975	78	5	1	+499	(Elliott)
274	29	Nov 22	Atlanta: Atlanta Journal 500	2	2	328	328	133	Running	35,350	175	5	1	+489	(Elliott)

*2nd-place driver (or co-leader) listed in parentheses if Earnhardt is current points leader

"With Earnhardt, every lap is a controlled crash."
—*Darrell Waltrip*

1988: The Morning After

A repeat of Earnhardt's phenomenal 1987 season was a little too much to expect as the calendar rolled to 1988. But considering the heights he had ascended, his 1988 effort represented a precipitous drop-off. Though never far removed from the top of the standings, Dale was also not a serious factor in the last third of the season, ultimately won by Bill Elliott. Earnhardt placed third in the final standings, 232 points behind Elliott.

No. 3 held the points lead for seven races, from Darlington to Dover in early spring. He surrendered the advantage despite a respectable fourth-place run at Riverside, but plunged the following race with a DNF at Pocono. A mid-season flurry pulled him within 58 points of then-leader Rusty Wallace, but a poor effort at Michigan (29th) began his slow drop from contender status.

Wins were logged at Atlanta in the Motorcraft Quality Parts 500, at Martinsville in the Pannill Sweatshirts 500 and in the Busch 500 at Bristol. The three races after the Bristol win illustrated how 1988 wasn't going to be Earnhardt's year. Despite a run of one third and two seconds, Dale still lost a point to Elliott in the points battle.

By falling short of winning the championship in 1988, Earnhardt missed a chance to match Cale Yarborough's record three straight titles. Though he would also miss in his next two opportunities to win three straight, no driver has won back-to-back championships more often than Earnhardt.

Earnhardt in 1988

Category	Earnhardt's Total	Earnhardt's Rank	1988 Leader
Money	$1,214,089	3rd	Bill Elliott – 1,554,639
Total Points	4,256	3rd	Bill Elliott – 4,488
Avg. Start	10.2	7th	Geoffrey Bodine – 6.8
Avg. Finish	8.8	3rd	Bill Elliott – 6.6
Wins	3	3rd	B. Elliott, R. Wallace – 6
Top 5s	13	3rd	Rusty Wallace – 19
Top 10s	19	3rd	Rusty Wallace – 23
DNFs	1	52nd	Derrike Cope – 16
Poles	0	—	Bill Elliott – 6
Front Row Starts	5	5th	Bill Elliott – 10
Laps Led	1,808	1st	(Bill Elliott – 1,598)
Races Led	20	T-1st	(Bill Elliott – 20)
Times Led	63	1st	(Darrell Waltrip – 57)
Miles Led	1,792	2nd	Bill Elliott – 1,851
Times Led Most Laps	7	1st	(Bill Elliott – 6)
Bonus Points	135	1st	(Bill Elliott – 130)
Laps Completed	9,561	2nd	Bill Elliott – 9,647
Miles Completed	11,314	2nd	Bill Elliott – 11,521
Points per Race	146.8	3rd	Bill Elliott – 154.8
Fin. on Lead Lap	17	2nd	Rusty Wallace – 21

*2nd-place driver listed in parentheses if Earnhardt is category leader.

NASCAR's Back-to-Back Champions

Driver	Championship Seasons
Cale Yarborough	1976-77-78
Dale Earnhardt	1986-87, 1990-91, 1993-94
Richard Petty	1971-72, 1974-75
Buck Baker	1956-57
Jeff Gordon	1997-98
David Pearson	1968-69
Lee Petty	1958-59
Darrell Waltrip	1981-82
Joe Weatherly	1962-63

In 1988, Richard Childress Racing took on GM Goodwrench as its primary sponsor. With a change in team colors, the No. 3 car's paint scheme changed from a cheery blue and yellow to an ominous black. The stock car racing world would never be the same. *Bill Burt*

1988 Performance Chart

No. 3 RCR Enterprises Chevrolet

Career Race	Season Race	Date	Race	St.	Fin.	Total Laps	Laps Completed	Laps Led	Condition	Money	Pts.	Bonus Pts.	Point Standing	Behind Leader	Points Leader
275	1	Feb 14	Daytona: Daytona 500	6	10	200	200	2	Running	$52,540	139	5	9	-46	B. Allison
276	2	Feb 21	Richmond: Pontiac Excitement 400	2	10	400	399	151	Running	16,245	144	10	7	-62	Bonnett
277	3	Mar 6	Rockingham: Goodwrench 500	22	5	492	492	22	Running	19,865	160	5	3	-87	Bonnett
278	4	Mar 20	Atlanta: Motorcraft Quality Parts 500	2	1	328	328	270	Running	67,950	185	10	2	-4	Bonnett
279	5	Mar 27	Darlington: TranSouth 500	2	11	367	363	0	Running	14,825	130	0	1	+20	(Bonnett)
280	6	Apr 10	Bristol: Valleydale Meats 500	4	14	500	461	95	Running	12,050	126	5	1	+7	(Marlin)
281	7	Apr 17	North Wilkesboro: First Union 400	10	3	400	400	265	Running	22,115	175	10	1	+53	(Wallace)
282	8	Apr 24	Martinsville: Pannill Sweatshirts 500	14	1	500	500	182	Running	53,550	185	10	1	+77	(Marlin)
283	9	May 1	Talladega: Winston 500	16	9	188	188	0	Running	21,500	138	0	1	+60	(Marlin)
284	10	May 29	Charlotte: Coca-Cola 600	7	13	400	394	0	Running	19,205	124	0	1	+71	(Wallace)
285	11	June 5	Dover: Budweiser 500	9	16	500	495	0	Running	13,450	115	0	1	+16	(Wallace)
286	12	June 12	Riverside: Budweiser 400	6	4	95	95	7	Running	18,600	165	5	2	-4	Wallace
287	13	June 19	Pocono: Miller High Life 500	18	33	200	93	0	DNF - Engine	13,045	64	0	2	-110	Wallace
288	14	June 26	Michigan: Miller High Life 400	9	4	200	200	12	Running	26,175	165	5	2	-130	Wallace
289	15	July 2	Daytona: Pepsi Firecracker 400	20	4	160	160	53	Running	22,825	170	10	2	-87	Wallace
290	16	July 24	Pocono: AC Spark Plug 500	9	11	200	200	0	Running	15,025	130	0	3	-48	Wallace
291	17	July 31	Talladega: Talladega DieHard 500	6	3	188	188	37	Running	37,775	170	5	3	-33	Wallace
292	18	Aug 14	Watkins Glen: The Bud at the Glen	19	6	90	90	0	Running	18,530	150	0	3	-58	Wallace
293	19	Aug 21	Michigan: Champion Spark Plug 400	5	29	200	194	39	Running	14,315	81	5	3	-157	Wallace
294	20	Aug 27	Bristol: Busch 500	5	1	500	500	220	Running	48,500	185	10	3	-126	Elliott
295	21	Sep 4	Darlington: Southern 500	2	3	367	367	85	Running	31,375	170	5	3	-141	Elliott
296	22	Sep 11	Richmond: Miller High Life 400	19	2	400	400	78	Running	29,625	175	5	2	-117	Elliott
297	23	Sep 18	Dover: Delaware 500	12	2	500	500	50	Running	37,450	175	5	2	-127	Elliott
298	24	Sep 25	Martinsville: Goody's 500	10	8	500	498	0	Running	13,050	142	0	3	-140	Elliott
299	25	Oct 9	Charlotte: Oakwood Homes 500	11	17	334	328	83	Running	24,300	122	10	3	-183	Elliott
300	26	Oct 16	North Wilkesboro: Holly Farms 400	22	6	400	400	107	Running	15,475	155	5	3	-188	Elliott
301	27	Oct 23	Rockingham: AC Delco 500	13	5	492	491	1	Running	27,965	160	5	3	-198	Elliott
302	28	Nov 6	Phoenix: Checker 500	13	11	312	311	0	Running	15,100	130	0	3	-228	Elliott
303	29	Nov 20	Atlanta: Atlanta Journal 500	2	14	328	326	49	Running	16,750	126	5	3	-232	Elliott

*2nd-place driver listed in parentheses if Earnhardt is current points leader

1989: Carolina Blues, 12 Points Short of The Fourth Championship

As a native of Kannapolis and a product of the state's dirt tracks, Dale Earnhardt certainly qualified as one of North Carolina's favorite sons. But his home state did him no favors during the 1989 Winston Cup season. Heading into Charlotte with five races to go, Earnhardt led Rusty Wallace in the championship battle by 75 points. That margin evaporated just 13 laps into the All Pro Auto Parts 500, when a broken crankshaft ended his day early and relegated him to 42nd place, his career-worst finish. Earnhardt's 75-point lead became a 35-point deficit.

Disappointment turned to anger the following week at North Wilkesboro. Earnhardt thoroughly dominated the Holly Farms 400—leading 343 of 400 laps—but saw a sure win degrade into a 10th place finish when he and Ricky Rudd made contact and spun out on the race's final lap. Had Earnhardt won, he would have overtaken Wallace in the point standings and enjoyed a 12-point advantage with three races to go. Instead, the spin actually dropped Dale two points further behind Wallace.

The series stayed in the Tar Heel state another week for a trip to Rockingham, but Earnhardt's luck didn't get any better. Momentum now squarely behind Wallace, Earnhardt finished in 20th place and fell 109 behind. A sixth-place effort at Phoenix and a win at Atlanta could not help him overcome the deficit. At season's end, all that stood between Earnhardt and Wallace was 12 points—the third tightest points battle in Winston Cup history.

How close was the Earnhardt-Wallace battle? Dale actually led Wallace in average finish (10.28 to 10.34), but lost the title on bonus points; Rusty accumulated 20 more points than Earnhardt by leading one more race than Earnhardt and by leading the most laps three more times. That, along with the North Wilkesboro fiasco, was the difference.

The victory at Atlanta was Earnhardt's fifth of the year, following earlier triumphs at North Wilkesboro, Darlington and a sweep of the two visits to Dover. Earnhardt's performance at Dover was stunning. He led a track record 831 of 1,000 laps run on the track. For the season, he led 2,735 laps, a total he bettered during his career only once (in 1987).

Earnhardt in 1989

Category	Earnhardt's Total	Earnhardt's Rank	1989 Leader*
Money	$1,435,730	2nd	Rusty Wallace – 2,237,950
Total Points	4,164	2nd	Rusty Wallace – 4,176
Avg. Start	8.0	5th	Mark Martin – 5.3
Avg. Finish	10.3	1st	(Rusty Wallace – 10.34)
Wins	5	2nd	R. Wallace, D. Waltrip – 6
Top 5s	14	T-1st	(M. Martin, D. Waltrip – 14)
Top 10s	19	2nd	Rusty Wallace – 20
DNFs	2	48th	J. Means, G. Sacks – 13
Poles	0	—	A. Kulwicki, M. Martin – 6
Front Row Starts	3	8th	Mark Martin – 9
Laps Led	2,735	1st	(Rusty Wallace – 2,021)
Races Led	22	2nd	Rusty Wallace – 23
Times Led	88	1st	(Rusty Wallace – 77)
Miles Led	2,624	1st	(Rusty Wallace – 2,549)
Times Led Most Laps	6	2nd	Rusty Wallace – 9
Bonus Points	140	2nd	Rusty Wallace – 160
Laps Completed	9,112	3rd	Darrell Waltrip – 9,333
Miles Completed	10,796	4th	Ricky Rudd – 11,075
Points per Race	143.6	2nd	Rusty Wallace – 144.0
Fin. on Lead Lap	19	1st	(Mark Martin – 16)

*2nd-place driver listed in parentheses if Earnhardt is category leader.

Closest Championships in Winston Cup History

Year	Point Differential	Result
1992	10	Alan Kulwicki tops Bill Elliott
1979	11	Richard Petty tops Darrell Waltrip
1989	12	Wallace tops Earnhardt
1997	14	Jeff Gordon tops Dale Jarrett
1980	19	Earnhardt top Cale Yarborough

One of the most heartbreaking races in Earnhardt's career came at North Wilkesboro Speedway in the fall of 1989. He led 343 of 400 laps and appeared ready to take over the points lead from Rusty Wallace. On the final lap, Earnhardt's hopes were dashed when he made contact with Ricky Rudd and spun out. Instead of winning and taking the points lead, Earnhardt dropped to 10th and lost ground to Wallace. He ended the 1989 championship chase in second, just 12 points behind Wallace. *Bill Burt*

1989 Performance Chart

No. 3 RCR Enterprises Chevrolet

Career Race	Season Race	Date	Race	St.	Fin.	Total Laps	Laps Completed	Laps Led	Condition	Money	Pts.	Bonus Pts.	Point Standing	Behind Leader	Points Leader
304	1	Feb 19	Daytona: Daytona 500	8	3	200	200	3	Running	$95,550	170	5	3	-10	D. Waltrip
305	2	Mar 5	Rockingham: Goodwrench 500	19	3	492	492	0	Running	24,200	165	0	1	+5	(Bodine)
306	3	Mar 19	Atlanta: Motorcraft Quality Parts 500	5	2	328	328	92	Running	39,675	175	5	1	+69	(Bodine)
307	4	Mar 26	Richmond: Pontiac Excitement 400	6	3	400	400	43	Running	30,900	170	5	1	+64	(Kulwicki)
308	5	Apr 2	Darlington: TranSouth 500	11	33	367	290	35	Running	10,655	69	5	2	-18	Kulwicki
309	6	Apr 9	Bristol: Valleydale Meats 500	5	16	500	492	74	Running	21,280	120	5	4	-31	Bodine
310	7	Apr 16	North Wilkesboro: First Union 400	3	1	400	400	296	Running	51,225	185	10	1	+3	(Bodine)
311	8	Apr 23	Martinsville: Pannill Sweatshirts 500	7	2	500	500	103	Running	34,525	175	5	1	+58	(Bodine)
312	9	May 7	Talladega: Winston 500	17	8	188	188	2	Running	20,450	147	5	1	+77	(D. Waltrip)
313	10	May 28	Charlotte: Coca-Cola 600	14	38	400	223	2	DNF - Engine	10,750	54	5	3	-49	D. Waltrip
314	11	June 4	Dover: Budweiser 500	2	1	500	500	456	Running	59,350	185	10	2	-2	D. Waltrip
315	12	June 11	Sears Point: Banquet Frozen Foods 300	10	4	74	74	0	Running	20,350	160	0	1	+109	(D. Waltrip)
316	13	June 18	Pocono: Miller High Life 500	7	3	200	200	12	Running	29,250	170	5	1	+190	(Wallace)
317	14	June 25	Michigan: Miller High Life 400	6	17	200	198	0	Running	13,775	112	0	1	+122	(Wallace)
318	15	July 1	Daytona: Pepsi 400	13	18	160	158	33	Running	13,180	114	5	1	+124	(Wallace)
319	16	July 23	Pocono: AC Spark Plug 500	3	9	200	200	3	Running	14,275	143	5	1	+87	(Wallace)
320	17	July 30	Talladega: Talladega DieHard 500	9	11	188	188	0	Running	15,020	130	0	1	+90	(D. Waltrip)
321	18	Aug 13	Watkins Glen: The Bud at the Glen	4	3	90	90	21	Running	38,140	170	5	1	+126	(Martin)
322	19	Aug 20	Michigan: Champion Spark Plug 400	15	17	200	198	0	Running	13,450	112	0	1	+82	(Wallace)
323	20	Aug 26	Bristol: Busch 500	7	14	500	490	145	Running	11,650	126	5	1	+53	(Wallace)
324	21	Sep 3	Darlington: Heinz Southern 500	10	1	367	367	153	Running	71,150	185	10	1	+73	(Wallace)
325	22	Sep 10	Richmond: Miller High Life 400	8	2	400	400	135	Running	31,475	175	5	1	+63	(Wallace)
326	23	Sep 17	Dover: Peak Performance 500	15	1	500	500	375	Running	59,950	185	10	1	+102	(Wallace)
327	24	Sep 24	Martinsville: Goody's 500	1	9	500	499	74	Running	15,950	143	5	1	+75	(Wallace)
328	25	Oct 8	Charlotte: All Pro Auto Parts 500	12	42	334	13	0	DNF - Crankshaft	11,250	37	0	2	-35	Wallace
329	26	Oct 15	North Wilkesboro: Holly Farms 400	1	10	400	400	343	Running	15,155	144	10	2	-37	Wallace
330	27	Oct 22	Rockingham: AC Delco 500	5	20	492	484	86	Running	13,775	108	5	2	-109	Wallace
331	28	Nov 5	Phoenix: Autoworks 500	7	6	312	312	0	Running	16,995	150	0	3	-79	Wallace
332	29	Nov 19	Atlanta: Atlanta Journal 500	3	1	328	328	249	Running	81,700	185	10	2	-12	Wallace

*2nd-place driver listed in parentheses if Earnhardt is current points leader

1990: The Fourth Championship

When Mark Martin looks back on the 1990 season, the 46 points NASCAR stripped from him after his victory at Richmond surely loom large, particularly considering the deficit between he and champion Dale Earnhardt at the end of the season was a mere 26 points. But a look at the record book indicates those points lost at the beginning of the season were not nearly as important as the points seized by Earnhardt at the end of the season.

With clutch performances in the final two races of the 1990 season, Earnhardt converted a 45-point deficit into a championship-winning 26-point lead. At Phoenix, the next-to-last race on the circuit, while Martin was tooling around to a 10th-place finish, Earnhardt turned in the most dominating effort in track history. He maximized his opportunity by leading a record 262 laps en route to the victory, capturing all 185 points available to him. The amazing win gave Earnhardt the points lead for the first time in five months by a narrow six-point margin.

Perhaps remembering the sting of defeat from 1989, Earnhardt followed his triumphant Phoenix run with a flawless performance in the season finale at Atlanta. Driving aggressive early to claim valuable bonus points for leading a lap, he kept his car in the Top 5 and Martin in his rear view mirror. Earnhardt finished third, good enough to win his fourth Winston Cup crown, lifting him to second all-time on the Winston Cup leaderboard.

The thrilling finish closed one of the best championship battles in NASCAR history. During the second half of the season, Earnhardt and Martin were never separated by more than 63 points. After Earnhardt's incredible run at Talladega – during which he won the pole, led 134 of 188 laps and won the race—the margin between the two was a single point.

Earnhardt finished 1990 with a series-high nine victories, including back-to-back wins at Atlanta and Darlington in the spring, Michigan and Daytona in the summer and Darlington-Richmond in the fall. A sweep of the Talladega races completed his victory tour. Altogether, Dale had 18 Top 5 finishes and 23 Top 10s, both series-leading.

Earnhardt in 1990

Category	Earnhardt's Total	Earnhardt's Rank	1990 Leader*
Money	$3,083,056	1st	(Mark Martin – 1,302,958)
Total Points	4,430	1st	(Mark Martin – 4,404)
Avg. Start	5.9	2nd	Mark Martin – 5.4
Avg. Finish	8.0	2nd	Mark Martin – 6.6
Wins	9	1st	(M. Martin, G. Bodine – 3)
Top 5s	18	1st	(Mark Martin – 16)
Top 10s	23	T-1st	(Mark Martin – 23)
DNFs	1	61st	R. Moroso, R. Wilson – 15
Poles	4	T-1st	(Mark Martin – 4)
Front Row Starts	7	2nd	Mark Martin – 11
Laps Led	2,438	1st	(Bill Elliott – 1,182)
Races Led	22	1st	(Geoffrey Bodine – 21)
Times Led	84	1st	(Geoffrey Bodine – 60)
Miles Led	3,203	1st	(Bill Elliott – 1,512)
Times Led Most Laps	10	1st	(Rusty Wallace – 5)
Bonus Points	160	1st	(Geoffrey Bodine – 125)
Laps Completed	9,162	3rd	Mark Martin – 9,636
Miles Completed	10,955	3rd	Mark Martin – 11,487
Points per Race	152.8	1st	(Mark Martin – 151.9)
Fin. on Lead Lap	20	2nd	Mark Martin – 22

*2nd-place driver listed in parentheses if Earnhardt is category leader.

Earnhardt and Mark Martin (right) share thoughts before the 2000 spring race at Rockingham. The two drivers staged one of the most memorable championship battles in NASCAR history in 1990. Martin was penalized 46 points early that season by NASCAR in a disputed ruling (NASCAR claimed Martin had used an illegally prepared intake manifold). Earnhardt later caught Martin in the standings and won the championship by 26 points. *Bill Burt*

1990 Performance Chart

No. 3 RCR Enterprises Chevrolet

Career Race	Season Race	Date	Race	St.	Fin.	Total Laps	Laps Completed	Laps Led	Condition	Money	Pts.	Bonus Pts.	Point Standing	Behind Leader	Points Leader
333	1	Feb 18	Daytona: Daytona 500	2	5	200	200	155	Running	$109,325	165	10	4	-15	Cope
334	2	Feb 25	Richmond: Pontiac Excitement 400	4	2	400	400	41	Running	42,600	175	5	1	+5	(Rudd)
335	3	Mar 4	Rockingham: GM Goodwrench 500	4	10	492	489	0	Running	17,150	134	0	1	+8	Wallace)
336	4	Mar 18	Atlanta: Motorcraft Quality Parts 500	1	1	328	328	216	Running	85,000	185	10	1	+59	(Shepherd)
337	5	Apr 1	Darlington: TranSouth 500	15	1	367	367	129	Running	61,985	180	5	1	+78	(Shepherd)
338	6	Apr 8	Bristol: Valleydale Meats 500	9	19	500	451	0	Running	10,990	106	0	1	+42	(Shepherd)
339	7	Apr 22	North Wilkesboro: First Union 400	4	3	400	400	72	Running	21,775	170	5	1	+57	(Shepherd)
340	8	Apr 29	Martinsville: Hanes Activewear 500	2	5	500	499	21	Running	20,800	160	5	1	+52	(Shepherd)
341	9	May 6	Talladega: Winston 500	5	1	188	188	107	Running	98,975	185	10	1	+90	(Shepherd)
342	10	May 27	Charlotte: Coca-Cola 600	12	30	400	262	0	Running	13,950	73	0	1	+21	(Shepherd)
343	11	June 3	Dover: Budweiser 500	4	31	500	159	0	DNF - Engine	12,600	70	0	3	-59	Shepherd
344	12	June 10	Sears Point: Banquet Frozen Foods 300	3	34	74	65	0	Running	12,650	61	0	4	-136	Martin
345	13	June 17	Pocono: Miller Genuine Draft 500	6	13	200	200	3	Running	14,150	129	5	5	-133	Martin
346	14	June 24	Michigan: Miller Genuine Draft 400	5	1	200	200	22	Running	72,950	180	5	5	-118	Martin
347	15	July 7	Daytona: Pepsi 400	3	1	160	160	127	Running	72,850	185	10	2	-63	Martin
348	16	July 22	Pocono: AC Spark Plug 500	11	4	200	200	6	Running	22,800	165	5	2	-48	Martin
349	17	July 29	Talladega: DieHard 500	1	1	188	188	134	Running	152,975	185	10	2	-1	Martin
350	18	Aug 12	Watkins Glen: The Bud at the Glen	1	7	90	90	11	Running	22,380	151	5	2	-10	Martin
351	19	Aug 19	Michigan: Champion Spark Plug 400	7	8	200	200	50	Running	19,400	147	5	2	-48	Martin
352	20	Aug 25	Bristol: Busch 500	1	8	500	499	350	Running	30,125	152	10	2	-61	Martin
353	21	Sep 2	Darlington: Heinz Southern 500	1	1	367	367	99	Running	210,350	185	10	2	-26	Martin
354	22	Sep 9	Richmond: Miller Genuine Draft 400	6	1	400	400	173	Running	59,225	185	10	2	-16	Martin
355	23	Sep 16	Dover: Peak AntiFreeze 500	3	3	500	500	102	Running	29,375	170	5	2	-21	Martin
356	24	Sep 23	Martinsville: Goody's 500	8	2	500	500	25	Running	30,550	175	5	2	-16	Martin
357	25	Sep 30	North Wilkesboro: Tyson/Holly Farms 400	8	2	400	400	291	Running	32,075	180	10	2	-16	Martin
358	26	Oct 7	Charlotte: Mello Yello 500	15	25	334	320	0	Running	12,275	88	0	2	-49	Martin
359	27	Oct 21	Rockingham: AC Delco 500	20	10	492	490	0	Running	19,750	134	0	2	-45	Martin
360	28	Nov 4	Phoenix: Checker 500	3	1	312	312	262	Running	72,100	185	10	1	+6	(Martin)
361	29	Nov 18	Atlanta: Atlanta Journal 500	6	3	328	328	42	Running	26,700	170	5	1	+26	(Martin)

*2nd-place driver listed in parentheses if Earnhardt is current points leader

1991: The Fifth Championship

Before the 1984 season, Dale Earnhardt and Ricky Rudd exchanged rides, with Earnhardt returning to the blossoming Richard Childress Racing team and its Chevrolet and Rudd taking over Bud Moore's Ford. In 1991, those two drivers would again be linked, this time as the principal combatants in the Winston Cup points race. Adding texture to the points battle was their somewhat contentious rivalry, fueled two seasons earlier by an incident in the fall race at North Wilkesboro. Rudd and Earnhardt tangled on the last lap in that race, robbing a sure win from Earnhardt and stunting his drive for the championship (which he lost to Rusty Wallace by a mere 12 points).

In 1991, from the second race until season's end, with the exception of a one-race interlude by Davey Allison, Earnhardt and Rudd occupied the top two spots in the standings. Earnhardt seized the lead with a victory in the second race at Richmond, moving up from his 19th starting position. He gave the points lead to Rudd at Darlington in early April, but reclaimed it with a victory at Martinsville and a third at Talladega in early May.

Throughout their points battle, Earnhardt's largest deficit was 142 points, while the largest his lead got was 195 (the margin at the end of the season). Besides the two early victories, Earnhardt triumphed at Talladega in July at the DieHard 500. When he topped the field at North Wilkesboro late in the season, his lead ballooned from 59 to 112 with four races remaining.

Oddly, the turning point in the season came in a race Earnhardt failed to finish at Charlotte. For just the second time all season, Earnhardt wasn't running at the end of the fall Charlotte race, going out with valve problems after 302 laps. Rudd, however, couldn't capitalize on Earnhardt's misfortune: he had crashed out on lap 232 and fell 26 points further in debt. Sensing another championship, Earnhardt eased into Top 10 finishes at Rockingham, Phoenix and Atlanta in the final three races of the season. The 1991 title sealed, Dale found himself two championships shy of King Richard.

Earnhardt in 1991

Category	Earnhardt's Total	Earnhardt's Rank	1991 Leader*
Money	$2,396,685	1st	(Davey Allison – 1,712,924)
Total Points	4,287	1st	(Ricky Rudd – 4,092)
Avg. Start	11.1	10th	Alan Kulwicki – 6.8
Avg. Finish	8.6	1st	(Ricky Rudd – 9.5)
Wins	4	3rd	D. Allison, H. Gant – 5
Top 5s	14	2nd	Harry Gant – 15
Top 10s	21	1st	Ernie Irvan – 19
DNFs	2	40th	D. Cope, J. Spencer – 14
Poles	0	—	Mark Martin – 5
Front Row Starts	1	15th	A. Kulwicki, M. Martin – 8
Laps Led	1,125	3rd	Harry Gant – 1,684
Races Led	20	2nd	Davey Allison – 23
Times Led	63	2nd	Davey Allison – 72
Miles Led	1,525	2nd	Davey Allison – 1,879
Times Led Most Laps	4	3rd	D. Allison, H. Gant – 5
Bonus Points	120	2nd	Davey Allison – 140
Laps Completed	9,541	2nd	Ricky Rudd – 9,561
Miles Completed	11,435	1st	(Ricky Rudd – 11,427)
Points per Race	147.8	1st	(Ricky Rudd – 141.1)
Fin. on Lead Lap	17	1st	(Allison, Irvan, Martin – 16)

*2nd-place driver listed in parentheses if Earnhardt is category leader.

Earnhardt vs. Rudd

Career Comparison, After Swapping Rides in 1984

Driver	Races	W.C. Titles	Wins	Top 5s	Poles	Money
Earnhardt	518	6	67	225	17	39,592,832
Rudd	518	0	18	133	17	19,051,770

In spite of his image, Earnhardt was accommodating with fellow drivers and was rarely alone at the race track. Other drivers eagerly sought his advice, or were the butt of his practical jokes. *Bill Burt*

1991 Performance Chart

No. 3 RCR Enterprises Chevrolet

Career Race	Season Race	Date	Race	St.	Fin.	Total Laps	Laps Completed	Laps Led	Condition	Money	Pts.	Bonus Pts.	Point Standing	Behind Leader	Points Leader
362	1	Feb 17	Daytona: Daytona 500 by STP	4	5	200	200	46	Running	$113,850	160	5	5	-20	Irvan
363	2	Feb 24	Richmond: Pontiac Excitement 400	19	1	400	400	150	Running	67,950	180	5	1	+22	(Rudd)
364	3	Mar 3	Rockingham: GM Goodwrench 500	13	8	492	489	0	Running	18,850	142	0	1	+4	(Rudd)
365	4	Mar 18	Atlanta: Motorcraft Quality Parts 500	21	3	328	328	21	Running	37,000	170	5	1	+24	(Rudd)
366	5	Apr 7	Darlington: TranSouth 500	7	29	367	332	0	DNF - Cylinder	14,310	76	0	2	-80	Rudd
367	6	Apr 14	Bristol: Valleydale Meats 500	2	20	500	484	0	Running	15,525	103	0	3	-142	Rudd
368	7	Apr 21	North Wilkesboro: First Union 400	17	2	400	400	19	Running	35,225	175	5	2	-97	Rudd
369	8	Apr 28	Martinsville: Hanes 500	10	1	500	500	251	Running	63,600	185	10	2	-42	Rudd
370	9	May 6	Talladega: Winston 500	8	3	188	188	112	Running	56,100	175	10	1	+4	(Rudd)
371	10	May 26	Charlotte: Coca-Cola 600	14	3	400	400	26	Running	53,650	170	5	1	+36	(Rudd)
372	11	June 2	Dover: Budweiser 500	10	2	500	500	187	Running	44,275	180	10	1	+82	(Rudd)
373	12	June 9	Sears Point: Banquet Frozen Foods 300	3	7	74	74	0	Running	14,400	146	0	1	+53	(Rudd)
374	13	June 16	Pocono: Champion Spark Plug 500	21	2	200	200	28	Running	43,775	175	5	1	+120	(Rudd)
375	14	June 23	Michigan: Miller Genuine Draft 400	6	4	200	200	14	Running	30,950	165	5	1	+138	(Rudd)
376	15	July 6	Daytona: Pepsi 400	12	7	160	160	8	Running	23,200	151	5	1	+146	(Rudd)
377	16	July 21	Pocono: Miller Genuine Draft 500	16	22	179	175	0	Running	15,350	97	0	1	+140	(Rudd)
378	17	July 28	Talladega: DieHard 500	4	1	188	188	101	Running	88,670	185	10	1	+160	(Rudd)
379	18	Aug 11	Watkins Glen: The Bud at the Glen	8	15	90	90	1	Running	16,180	123	5	1	+108	(Rudd)
380	19	Aug 18	Michigan: Champion Spark Plug 400	26	24	200	194	0	Running	16,425	91	0	1	+69	(Rudd)
381	20	Aug 24	Bristol: Bud 500	13	7	500	498	0	Running	16,025	146	0	1	+60	(Rudd)
382	21	Sep 1	Darlington: Heinz Southern 500	3	8	367	365	22	Running	20,470	147	5	1	+89	(Rudd)
383	22	Sep 7	Richmond: Miller Genuine Draft 400	16	11	400	398	5	Running	13,750	135	5	1	+64	(Rudd)
384	23	Sep 15	Dover: Peak AntiFreeze 500	12	15	500	447	21	Running	16,700	123	5	1	+36	(Rudd)
385	24	Sep 22	Martinsville: Goody's 500	5	3	500	500	9	Running	30,350	170	5	1	+59	(Rudd)
386	25	Sep 29	North Wilkesboro: Tyson/Holly Farms 400	16	1	400	400	9	Running	69,350	180	5	1	+112	(Rudd)
387	26	Oct 6	Charlotte: Mello Yello 500	15	25	334	302	56	DNF - Valve	22,460	93	5	1	+138	(Rudd)
388	27	Oct 20	Rockingham: AC Delco 500	4	7	492	490	0	Running	19,250	146	0	1	+157	(Rudd)
389	28	Nov 3	Phoenix: Pyroil 500	12	9	312	311	0	Running	18,200	138	0	1	+156	(D. Allison)
390	29	Nov 17	Atlanta: Hardee's 500	5	5	328	328	39	Running	27,825	160	5	1	+195	(Rudd)

*2nd-place driver listed in parentheses if Earnhardt is current points leader

1992: Falling Down

After winning four Winston Cup championships in six seasons—and missing a fifth by 12 points in 1989 – Earnhardt might have been due for a down campaign. The 1992 season fit the bill. A wild chase to the 1992 title, eventually won by the late Alan Kulwicki, did not involve Earnhardt. In fact, Earnhardt finished 1992 in 12th place, matching the worst points finish of his career.

A major reason for Earnhardt's quiet season was the sheer dominance of the Ford Thunderbird. Fords won the first nine races of 1992 and finished with 16 victories in the season's 29 races, easily beating out Chevy (eight wins), Pontiac (three) and Oldsmobile (two). That performance translated to points supremacy, with Ford drivers taking the top three spots in the championship standings and four of the top six. Ricky Rudd, who ended the season in seventh while piloting the No. 17 car for Rick Hendrick, was the top-finishing Chevy in the points battle.

Simply no match for Fords driven by Davey Allison, Alan Kulwicki, Bill Elliott and Mark Martin, Earnhardt nevertheless contributed one win to the Chevy effort by taking the Coca Cola 600 in May at Charlotte. With just the one victory, the 1992 season was undeniably atypical for Earnhardt. He netted just six Top 5 finishes and 15 Top 10s.

Six of those Top 10s came in a row, with the last of those six—a sixth-place showing at Sears Point—actually moving Earnhardt into second place in the point standings, 28 points behind Davey Allison. From that point forward, however, Earnhardt slid steadily down the points scale. He failed to finish three of the next five races, registering two 40th-place efforts that sent him spiraling down the standings. Earnhardt never recovered and finished 504 points behind Kulwicki, who rallied past Allison in the season's final event at Atlanta to win the championship.

Earnhardt's stat sheet for 1992 reflects his sub-par season. His highest finish in any category was a tie for seventh in poles, accomplished with his single start from there at Watkins Glen. He led just nine races all season for 483 laps. Not once did he pick up the five extra bonus points for leading the most laps. It was not a Dale Earnhardt season. The next one would be.

Earnhardt in 1992

Category	Earnhardt's Total	Earnhardt's Rank	1992 Leader
Money	915,463	8th	Alan Kulwicki – 2,322,561
Total Points	3,574	12th	Alan Kulwicki – 4,078
Avg. Start	14.7	14th	Ernie Irvan – 7.1
Avg. Finish	14.9	12th	Alan Kulwicki – 10.6
Wins	1	10th	D. Allison, B. Elliott: 5
Top 5s	6	11th	Davey Allison – 15
Top 10s	15	8th	Ricky Rudd – 18
DNFs	4	27th	D. Marcis, J. Means – 14
Poles	1	7th	Alan Kulwicki – 6
Front Row Starts	2	10th	Kulwicki, Marlin, Martin, Rudd – 6
Laps Led	483	8th	Davey Allison – 1,377
Races Led	9	10th	Alan Kulwicki – 20
Times Led	19	10th	Alan Kulwicki – 51
Miles Led	466	9th	Davey Allison – 2,315
Times Led Most Laps	0	—	Davey Allison – 6
Bonus Points	45	12th	Alan Kulwicki – 125
Laps Completed	8,694	14th	Ted Musgrave – 9,253
Miles Completed	10,198	17th	Harry Gant – 11,220
Points per Race	123.2	12th	Alan Kulwicki – 140.6
Fin. on Lead Lap	9	14th	Alan Kulwicki – 17

Earnhardt's Worst Seasons

Year	Point Standing	Wins	Top 5s	Avg. Fin.	Laps Led	DNFs
1982	12th	1	7	18.8	1,062	18
1992	12th	1	6	14.9	483	4
1998	8th	1	5	16.2	273	3

"I was with my dad and we were outside cutting down a big tree. He was using a chain saw when something happened and he wound up cutting the back of his hand all the way to the bone. It was bad. But what does my dad do? He doesn't even look at his hand. He just keeps cutting down the tree. Man, now that was determination."
—Dale Earnhardt, Jr.

1992 Performance Chart

No. 3 RCR Enterprises Chevrolet

Career Race	Season Race	Date	Race	St.	Fin.	Total Laps	Laps Completed	Laps Led	Condition	Money	Pts.	Bonus Pts.	Point Standing	Behind Leader	Points Leader
391	1	Feb 16	Daytona: Daytona 500 by STP	3	9	200	199	0	Running	$87,000	138	0	9	-47	D. Allison
392	2	Mar 1	Rockingham: GM Goodwrench 500	8	24	492	469	0	Running	16,850	91	0	13	-131	D. Allison
393	3	Mar 8	Richmond: Pontiac Excitement 400	29	11	400	399	0	Running	16,600	130	0	11	-166	D. Allison
394	4	Mar 15	Atlanta: Motorcraft Quality Parts 500	7	3	328	328	0	Running	36,850	165	0	8	-171	D. Allison
395	5	Mar 29	Darlington: TranSouth 500	8	10	367	365	0	Running	20,570	134	0	8	-207	D. Allison
396	6	Apr 5	Bristol: Food City 500	18	18	500	471	28	Running	18,130	114	5	8	-177	D. Allison
397	7	Apr 12	North Wilkesboro: First Union 400	9	6	400	400	36	Running	32,540	155	5	8	-202	D. Allison
398	8	Apr 26	Martinsville: Hanes 500	2	9	500	497	167	Running	22,550	143	5	7	-144	D. Allison
399	9	May 3	Talladega: Winston 500	10	3	188	188	10	Running	46,970	170	5	6	-159	D. Allison
400	10	May 24	Charlotte: Coca-Cola 600	13	1	400	400	54	Running	125,100	180	5	5	-144	D. Allison
401	11	May 31	Dover: Budweiser 500	24	2	500	500	52	Running	43,720	175	5	3	-99	D. Allison
402	12	June 7	Sears Point: Save Mart 300K	12	6	74	74	0	Running	21,910	150	0	2	-28	D. Allison
403	13	June 14	Pocono: Champion Spark Plug 500	17	28	200	148	0	DNF - Engine	16,600	79	0	5	-109	D. Allison
404	14	June 21	Michigan: Miller Genuine Draft 400	22	9	200	199	0	Running	23,110	138	0	5	-156	D. Allison
405	15	July 4	Daytona: Pepsi 400	22	40	160	7	0	DNF - Engine	16,355	43	0	5	-252	D. Allison
406	16	July 19	Pocono: Miller Genuine Draft 500	29	23	200	199	0	Running	16,540	94	0	6	-241	Elliott
407	17	July 26	Talladega: DieHard 500	30	40	188	52	0	DNF - Engine	18,140	43	0	8	-359	Elliott
408	18	Aug 9	Watkins Glen: The Bud at the Glen	1	9	51	51	10	Running	22,430	143	5	8	-336	Elliott
409	19	Aug 16	Michigan: Champion Spark Plug 400	41	16	200	199	0	Running	19,665	115	0	10	-396	Elliott
410	20	Aug 29	Bristol: Bud 500	23	2	500	500	0	Running	39,325	170	0	7	-376	Elliott
411	21	Sep 6	Darlington: Mountain Dew Southern 500	13	29	298	241	0	Running	16,555	76	0	9	-470	Elliott
412	22	Sep 12	Richmond: Miller Genuine Draft 400	11	4	400	400	0	Running	29,655	160	0	9	-431	Elliott
413	23	Sep 20	Dover: Peak AntiFreeze 500	5	21	500	470	82	Running	17,880	105	5	9	-506	Elliott
414	24	Sep 28	Martinsville: Goody's 500	11	31	500	111	0	DNF - Engine	14,550	70	0	12	-509	Elliott
415	25	Oct 5	North Wilkesboro: Tyson/Holly Farms 400	13	19	400	395	0	Running	15,350	106	0	14	-488	Elliott
416	26	Oct 11	Charlotte: Mello Yello 500	11	14	334	332	0	Running	19,050	121	0	13	-445	Elliott
417	27	Oct 25	Rockingham: AC Delco 500	12	8	492	490	0	Running	22,350	142	0	12	-468	Elliott
418	28	Nov 1	Phoenix: Pyroil 500	19	10	312	311	0	Running	21,370	134	0	11	-444	D. Allison
419	29	Nov 15	Atlanta: Hooters 500	3	26	328	299	44	Running	20,670	90	5	12	-504	Kulwicki

1993: The Sixth Championship

Earnhardt took the checkered flag six times in 1993, though that wasn't the determining factor in his sixth Winston Cup championship. If wins and laps led were the only benchmark, Rusty Wallace's name would have been inscribed on the championship trophy.

Rusty won 10 races and led 2,860 laps, the most laps led by a driver since Earnhardt led 3,358 during his amazing 1987 season. Wallace's laps led total almost doubled Earnhardt's total of 1,475. Despite this disparity, Earnhardt actually led more miles, 2,485 vs. 2,333, illustrating Wallace's short-track acumen and Earnhardt's superspeedway muscle.

Of course, championships are determined by how you finish, not how dominant a car you bring to the track. Here, Earnhardt enjoyed the advantage, posting 21 Top 10 finishes. More importantly, he suffered only two DNFs, neither of which dropped him out of the Top 30 in either race. While Rusty was frequently up front during each race, Earnhardt had a stranglehold on the championship points race.

Dale took the top points spot from Rusty with a sixth-place showing at Sears Point in the season's 10th race, and never relinquished his advantage. Once in command, Earnhardt tightened his grip with five wins in the next eight starts. Consecutive triumphs at Charlotte and Dover, another at Daytona three races later and two more in a row at Pocono and Talladega boosted his lead to 234 points. Trailing by 309 points with nine races left, Wallace made a late surge, eventually whittling the deficit to 80 points.

With his 12-point loss to Wallace in 1989 still in mind, Earnhardt did his part to lock Wallace out of the title chase by finishing in the Top 10 in seven of those final nine events. His 10th-place showing at Atlanta cemented his sixth title, leaving him just one championship shy of Richard Petty.

Earnhardt in 1993

Category	Earnhardt's Total	Earnhardt's Rank	1993 Leader*
Money	$3,353,789	1st	(Rusty Wallace – 1,702,154)
Total Points	4,526	1st	(Rusty Wallace – 4,446)
Avg. Start	9.7	4th	Ernie Irvan – 7.7
Avg. Finish	8.2	1st	(Rusty Wallace – 9.4)
Wins	6	2nd	Rusty Wallace – 10
Top 5s	17	2nd	Rusty Wallace – 19
Top 10s	21	T-1st	(Rusty Wallace – 21)
DNFs	2	41st	Jeff Gordon – 11
Poles	2	5th	Ken Schrader – 6
Front Row Starts	4	5th	Ernie Irvan – 9
Laps Led	1,475	2nd	Rusty Wallace – 2,860
Races Led	21	1st	(M. Martin, R. Wallace – 20)
Times Led	81	1st	(Mark Martin – 68)
Miles Led	2,485	1st	(Rusty Wallace – 2,333)
Times Led Most Laps	9	T-1st	(Rusty Wallace – 9)
Bonus Points	150	1st	(Rusty Wallace – 145)
Laps Completed	9,787	1st	(Rusty Wallace – 9,641)
Miles Completed	11,808	1st	(M. Shepherd – 11,406)
Points per Race	150.9	1st	(Rusty Wallace – 148.2)
Fin. on Lead Lap	21	2nd	Rusty Wallace – 23

*2nd-place driver listed in parentheses if Earnhardt is category leader.

Earnhardt vs. Wallace

1993 Statistical Comparison

Driver	Points	Avg. Start	Avg. Finish	Wins	Top 10s	Outside Top 30	DNFs
Earnhardt	4,526	9.7	8.2	6	21	0	2
Wallace	4,446	11.9	9.4	10	21	3	5

The tragic mishaps visited upon the No. 28 Robert Yates team robbed NASCAR fans of possible championship challengers to Earnhardt during the 1993 and 1994 seasons. In 1993, Earnhardt and Davey Allison stood first and fifth in the points standings when Allison died in a July helicopter crash at Talladega. A year later, Ernie Irvan and Earnhardt appeared headed for a tight struggle when Irvan was nearly killed in a wreck at Michigan. *Bill Burt*

1993 Performance Chart

No. 3 RCR Enterprises Chevrolet

Career Race	Season Race	Date	Race	St.	Fin.	Total Laps	Laps Completed	Laps Led	Condition	Money	Pts.	Bonus Pts.	Point Standing	Behind Leader	Points Leader
420	1	Feb 14	Daytona: Daytona 500 by STP	4	2	200	200	107	Running	$181,825	180	10	2	0	Jarrett[1]
421	2	Feb 28	Rockingham: GM Goodwrench 500	7	2	492	492	133	Running	47,585	175	5	1	+25	(Jarrett)
422	3	Mar 7	Richmond: Pontiac Excitement 400	11	10	400	399	0	Running	17,000	134	0	2	-1	Jarrett
423	4	Mar 20	Atlanta: Motorcraft Quality Parts 500	2	11	328	325	0	Running	15,595	130	0	1	+19	(Bodine)
424	5	Mar 28	Darlington: TranSouth 500	1	1	367	367	212	Running	64,815	185	10	1	+57	(Wallace)
425	6	Apr 4	Bristol: Food City 500	6	2	500	500	15	Running	47,760	175	5	1	+47	(Wallace)
426	7	Apr 18	North Wilkesboro: First Union 400	21	16	400	396	0	Running	13,130	115	0	2	-18	Wallace
427	8	Apr 25	Martinsville: Hanes 500	21	22	500	453	1	DNF - Engine	10,625	102	5	2	-101	Wallace
428	9	May 2	Talladega: Winston 500	1	4	188	188	102	Running	39,870	170	10	2	-86	Wallace
429	10	May 16	Sears Point: Save Mart Supermarket 300K	1	6	74	74	33	Running	27,790	160	10	1	+20	(Wallace)
430	11	May 30	Charlotte: Coca-Cola 600	14	1	400	400	152	Running	156,650	185	10	1	+129	(Wallace)
431	12	June 6	Dover: Budweiser 500	8	1	500	500	226	Running	68,030	185	10	1	+209	(Wallace)
432	13	June 13	Pocono: Champion Spark Plug 500	5	11	200	200	20	Running	14,815	135	5	1	+225	(D. Allison)
433	14	June 20	Michigan: Miller Genuine Draft 400	6	14	200	199	27	Running	16,385	126	5	1	+213	(Jarrett)
434	15	July 3	Daytona: Pepsi 400	5	1	160	160	110	Running	75,940	185	10	1	+251	(Jarrett)
435	16	July 11	New Hampshire: Slick 50 300	24	26	300	296	0	Running	15,300	85	0	1	+171	(Jarrett)
436	17	July 18	Pocono: Miller Genuine Draft 500	11	1	200	200	71	Running	66,795	185	10	1	+209	(Jarrett)
437	18	July 25	Talladega: DieHard 500	11	1	188	188	59	Running	87,315	185	10	1	+234	(Jarrett)
438	19	Aug 8	Watkins Glen: The Bud at the Glen	5	18	90	90	26	Running	13,510	114	5	1	+281	(Jarrett)
439	20	Aug 15	Michigan: Champion Spark Plug 400	7	9	200	200	0	Running	19,215	138	0	1	+259	(Jarrett)
440	21	Aug 28	Bristol: Bud 500	19	3	500	500	0	Running	32,325	165	0	1	+309	(Wallace)
441	22	Sep 5	Darlington: Mountain Dew Southern 500	6	4	351	351	101	Running	31,090	165	5	1	+304	(Wallace)
442	23	Sep 11	Richmond: Miller Genuine Draft 400	8	3	400	400	0	Running	35,780	165	0	1	+284	(Wallace)
443	24	Sep 19	Dover: SplitFire Spark Plug 500	9	27	500	404	0	Running	14,555	82	0	1	+181	(Wallace)
444	25	Sep 26	Martinsville: Goody's 500	7	29	500	440	0	DNF - Axle	10,525	76	0	1	+82	(Wallace)
445	26	Oct 3	North Wilkesboro: Tyson/Holly Farms 400	10	2	400	400	59	Running	46,285	175	5	1	+72	(Wallace)
446	27	Oct 10	Charlotte: Mello Yello 500	9	3	334	334	3	Running	56,900	170	5	1	+82	(Wallace)
447	28	Oct 24	Rockingham: AC Delco 500	22	2	492	492	14	Running	49,550	175	5	1	+72	(Wallace)
448	29	Oct 31	Phoenix: Slick 50 500	11	4	312	312	2	Running	29,980	165	5	1	+126	(Wallace)
449	30	Nov 14	Atlanta: Hooters 500	19	10	328	327	2	Running	19,300	139	5	1	+80	(Wallace)

*2nd-place driver listed in parentheses if Earnhardt is current points leader
[1]As race winner, Jarrett designated points leader

1994: The Seventh Championship

So much for unbreakable records. In 1994 Dale Earnhardt accomplished what many observers never thought possible, especially after the modern era's shorter, more stable schedule and increased number of deep-pocketed sponsors widened the distribution of capable teams within NASCAR. Earnhardt did the unthinkable when he matched Richard Petty's all-time series record of seven career Winston Cup championships.

For all of its historic import, however, the seventh championship can only be described as bittersweet. From the early stages of the 1994 campaign, the battle at the top of the point standings pitted Earnhardt against his latest rival, Ernie Irvan. The matchup had all the makings of a classic duel. Earnhardt overtook Irvan with a late-March victory at Darlington, but gave the points lead back two races later at Martinsville. The lead would swing three more times, the last time back to Earnhardt when Dale finished fifth in the first Brickyard 400.

All signs pointed to a memorable finish. It never happened. The title chase, which saw Earnhardt clinging to a 27-point lead, became secondary when the series made its second visit to Michigan Speedway in August. During practice for the GM Goodwrench Dealer 400, Irvan slammed into the turn 4 wall, suffering head injuries that not only ended his season, but put his life in jeopardy. The tragedy likely hit home for Earnhardt when he considered Irvan's career. Mirroring the development of Earnhardt, Irvan went from being reviled for his hard-charging style (with Earnhardt among those questioning Irvan's tactics) to gaining respect as he matured.

With his closest competitor violently removed from the equation, Dale had little trouble securing the seventh title, winning by 444 points over Mark Martin. The margin of victory was the fourth-largest in the modern era.

Earnhardt in 1994

Category	Earnhardt's Total	Earnhardt's Rank	1994 Leader*
Money	$3,300,733	1st	(R. Wallace – 1,959,072)
Total Points	4,694	1st	(Mark Martin – 4,250)
Avg. Start	15.3	10th	Ernie Irvan – 6.6
Avg. Finish	8.0	1st	(Ernie Irvan – 9.0)
Wins	4	2nd	Rusty Wallace – 8
Top 5s	20	1st	(Rusty Wallace – 17)
Top 10s	25	1st	(R. Wallace, Martin – 20)
DNFs	3	35th	Geoffrey Bodine – 15
Poles	2	5th	G. Bodine, E. Irvan – 5
Front Row Starts	4	4th	Geoffrey Bodine – 10
Laps Led	1,014	4th	Rusty Wallace – 2,142
Races Led	23	1st	(Geoffrey Bodine – 20)
Times Led	76	2nd	Ernie Irvan – 79
Miles Led	1,322	4th	Ernie Irvan – 2,419
Times Led Most Laps	3	4th	Ernie Irvan – 10
Bonus Points	130	2nd	Ernie Irvan – 135
Laps Completed	9,546	5th	Darrell Waltrip – 9,905
Miles Completed	11,409	7th	Ricky Rudd – 12,046
Points per Race	151.4	1st	(Ernie Irvan – 151.3)
Fin. on Lead Lap	22	1st	(Martin, Shepherd, Wallace – 17)

*2nd-place driver listed in parentheses if Earnhardt is category leader.

Earnhardt's Championship Seasons

Year	Avg. Start	Avg. Fin	Wins	Top 5s	Points	Point Differential
1980	9.1	8.2	5	19	4,661	19 over C. Yarborough
1986	6.9	7.4	5	16	4,468	288 over D. Waltrip
1987	7.3	5.9	11	21	4,696	489 over B. Elliott
1990	5.9	8.0	9	18	4,430	26 over M. Martin
1991	11.1	8.6	4	14	4,287	195 over R. Rudd
1993	9.7	8.2	6	17	4,526	80 over R. Wallace
1994	15.3	8.0	4	20	4,694	444 over M. Martin

The top three starters of the inaugural Brickyard 400 gathered to meet Mary Fendrich Hulman, chair of the Indianapolis Motor Speedway, during prerace festivities. Earnhardt, center, earned a front-row starting spot for NASCAR's first Indy race next to pole-winner Rick Mast, right. Jeff Gordon, left, qualified third and went on to win the race. Earnhardt won the Brickyard in 1995. *David Stringer*

1994 Performance Chart

No. 3 RCR Enterprises

Career Race	Season Race	Date	Race	St.	Total Fin.	Total Laps	Laps Completed	Led	Condition	Money	Bonus Pts.	Point Pts.	Behind Standing	Points Leader	Leader
450	1	Feb 20	Daytona: Daytona 500	2	7	200	200	45	Running	$110,340	151	5	6	-29	Marlin
451	2	Feb 27	Rockingham: Goodwrench 500	19	7	492	491	17	Running	25,785	151	5	3	-53	Marlin
452	3	Mar 6	Richmond: Pontiac Excitement 400	9	4	400	400	10	Running	29,550	165	5	2	-53	Irvan
453	4	Mar 13	Atlanta: Purolator 500	16	12	328	325	0	Running	24,550	127	0	3	-111	Irvan
454	5	Mar 27	Darlington: TranSouth Financial 400	9	1	293	293	166	Running	70,190	185	10	2	-81	Irvan
455	6	Apr 10	Bristol: Food City 500	24	1	500	500	183	Running	72,570	185	10	1	+40	(Irvan)
456	7	Apr 17	North Wilkesboro: First Union 400	19	5	400	400	0	Running	26,740	155	0	1	+20	(Irvan)
457	8	Apr 24	Martinsville: Hanes 500	8	11	500	499	0	Running	21,060	130	0	2	-25	Irvan
458	9	May 1	Talladega: Winston Select 500	4	1	188	188	64	Running	94,865	180	5	2	-25	Irvan
459	10	May 15	Sears Point: Save Mart Supermarkets 300	4	3	74	74	3	Running	37,825	170	5	2	-40	Irvan
460	11	May 29	Charlotte: Coca-Cola 600	24	9	400	397	0	Running	37,950	138	0	2	-62	Irvan
461	12	June 5	Dover: Budweiser 500	14	28	500	425	0	Running	22,065	79	0	2	-163	Irvan
462	13	June 12	Pocono: UAW-GM Teamwork 500	19	2	200	200	6	Running	46,425	175	5	2	-139	Irvan
463	14	June 19	Michigan: Miller Genuine Draft 400	24	2	200	200	18	Running	55,905	175	5	2	-78	Irvan
464	15	July 2	Daytona: Pepsi 400	1	3	160	160	31	Running	50,050	170	5	2	-88	Irvan
465	16	July 10	New Hampshire: Slick 50 300	28	2	300	300	29	Running	68,000	175	5	1	+4	(Irvan)
466	17	July 17	Pocono: Miller Genuine Draft 500	20	7	200	200	0	Running	26,210	146	0	1	+83	(Irvan)
467	18	July 24	Talladega: DieHard 500	1	34	188	80	41	DNF - Engine	30,725	66	5	2	-16	Irvan
468	19	Aug 6	Indianapolis: Brickyard 400	2	5	160	160	2	Running	121,625	160	5	1	+27	(Irvan)
469	20	Aug 14	Watkins Glen: The Bud at the Glen	6	3	90	90	5	Running	39,605	170	5	1	+27	(Irvan)
470	21	Aug 21	Michigan: GM Goodwrench Dealer 400	11	37	200	54	0	DNF - Crash	22,915	52	0	1	+79	(Irvan)
471	22	Aug 27	Bristol: Goody's 500	14	3	500	500	25	Running	33,265	170	5	1	+201	(Martin)
472	23	Sep 4	Darlington: Mountain Dew Southern 500	27	2	367	367	87	Running	45,030	175	5	1	+227	(Wallace)
473	24	Sep 10	Richmond: Miller Genuine Draft 400	12	3	400	400	41	Running	38,830	170	5	1	+232	(Wallace)
474	25	Sep 18	Dover: SplitFire Spark Plug 500	37	2	500	500	62	Running	47,980	175	5	1	+227	(Wallace)
475	26	Sep 25	Martinsville: Goody's 500	20	2	500	500	10	Running	42,400	175	5	1	+217	(Wallace)
476	27	Oct 2	North Wilkesboro: Tyson Holly Farms 400	3	7	400	398	38	Running	21,315	151	5	1	+208	(Wallace)
477	28	Oct 9	Charlotte: Mello Yello 500	38	3	334	334	6	Running	66,000	170	5	1	+321	(Wallace)
478	29	Oct 23	Rockingham: AC Delco 500	20	1	492	492	108	Running	60,600	185	10	1	+448	(Wallace)
479	30	Oct 30	Phoenix: Slick 50 500	8	40	312	91	0	DNF - Engine	19,575	43	0	1	+379	(Wallace)
480	31	Nov 13	Atlanta: Hooters 500	30	2	328	328	17	Running	55,950	175	5	1	+444	(Martin)

*2nd-place driver listed in parentheses if Earnhardt is current points leader

1995: No. 8 Eludes Earnhardt

One more race. That's all Dale Earnhardt may have needed in 1995 to earn his King-usurping eighth Winston Cup championship. With four races left in the season, he trailed young gun Jeff Gordon by a seemingly insurmountable 302 points. Too much to make up, right? Well, Earnhardt gave it his best shot and nearly pulled it off.

Earnhardt started his final-four run with a second-place finish at Charlotte that trimmed Gordon's lead by almost 100 points, followed by a seventh-place showing at Rockingham that sliced the difference to just 162 points. The Intimidator continued to do his part at Phoenix, running a solid third, but Gordon's fifth-place finish allowed Earnhardt to narrow the gap by just 15 points. At the season-ending race at Atlanta, Dale did everything he could, winning the race and leading the most laps. Gordon, however, needed only to start the race—and finish 42nd or better. Gordon essentially did just enough when he finished 32nd, 17 laps off of Earnhardt's pace. Gordon won his first Cup title by 34 points, the eighth closest race in Winston Cup history. For Earnhardt his role in the chase was reminiscent of Cale Yarborough hunting a young Earnhardt in 1980. Like Earnhardt staring down the wily Yarborough, Gordon gained instant credibility by surviving the feverish charge from Earnhardt, the most talented and toughest veteran in the series.

Those last four races were just an extension of a season-ending run that saw Dale stake a claim to the Top 10 in '95's final 10 races. Besides Atlanta, his other win in that span came at Martinsville, where he led 253 of the 500 trips around the track. Those victories were two of five on the season, including one at North Wilkesboro, which was in its final season on the Winston Cup schedule. His two biggest victories, however, were logged at Indianapolis, where Dale claimed the second Brickyard 400 at historic Indianapolis Motor Speedway, and at Sears Point.

Though the Save Mart 300 does not quite have the same ring as 'Daytona 500' or 'Brickyard 400,' winning it was a significant accomplishment in Earnhardt's career. The triumph was the first and only time Dale earned the checkered flag on one of NASCAR's road courses, a prize he long coveted. The road-course win left Dale with just one hole left on his impressive resume, a victory in the Daytona 500. That void required three more years to fill.

Earnhardt in 1995

Category	Earnhardt's Total	Earnhardt's Rank	1995 Leader*
Money	$3,154,241	2nd	Jeff Gordon – 4,347,343
Total Points	4,580	2nd	Jeff Gordon – 4,614
Avg. Start	13.8	5th	Jeff Gordon – 5.0
Avg. Finish	9.2	1st	(Jeff Gordon – 9.5)
Wins	5	2nd	Jeff Gordon – 7
Top 5s	19	1st	(Jeff Gordon – 17)
Top 10s	23	T-1st	(Jeff Gordon – 23)
DNFs	2	40th	G. Sacks, D. Waltrip – 11
Poles	3	3rd	Jeff Gordon – 8
Front Row Starts	6	4th	Jeff Gordon – 12
Laps Led	1,583	2nd	Jeff Gordon – 2,600
Races Led	24	2nd	Jeff Gordon – 29
Times Led	71	2nd	Jeff Gordon – 94
Miles Led	1,739	2nd	Jeff Gordon – 3,458
Times Led Most Laps	2	2nd	Jeff Gordon – 11
Bonus Points	140	2nd	Jeff Gordon – 200
Laps Completed	9,625	2nd	Sterling Marlin – 9,728
Miles Completed	11,714	3rd	Sterling Marlin – 11,936
Points per Race	147.7	2nd	Jeff Gordon – 148.8
Fin. on Lead Lap	22	2nd	Jeff Gordon – 23

*2nd-place driver listed in parentheses if Earnhardt is category leader.

Making a Charge

Earnhardt vs. Gordon in the final 10 races of 1995

Driver	Points	Wins	Top 5s	Top 10s	Laps Led
Earnhardt	1,689	2	8	10	1,010
Gordon	1,409	2	4	7	689

Earnhardt's magical early-1990s run—which saw him win championships in 1990, 1991, 1993, and 1994—came to an end in 1995 with the ascension of Hendrick Motorsports' three-car team. Ken Schrader (25) and Jeff Gordon (24) spearheaded the reintroduction of the Chevy Monte Carlo in 1995. Thanks to Gordon and teammate Terry Labonte, Hendrick Motorsports won four straight Winston Cup titles between 1995 and 1998. *Bill Burt*

1995 Performance Chart

No. 3 RCR Enterprises Chevrolet

Career Race	Season Race	Date	Race	St.	Fin.	Total Laps	Laps Completed	Laps Led	Condition	Money	Pts.	Bonus Pts.	Point Standing	Behind Leader	Points Leader
481	1	Feb 19	Daytona: Daytona 500	2	2	200	200	23	Running	$269,750	175	5	2	-10	Marlin
482	2	Feb 26	Rockingham: Goodwrench 500	23	3	492	492	72	Running	40,740	170	5	1	+29	(Martin)
483	3	Mar 5	Richmond: Pontiac Excitement 400	26	2	400	400	11	Running	57,200	175	5	1	+53	(Marlin)
484	4	Mar 12	Atlanta: Purolator 500	1	4	328	328	62	Running	52,950	165	5	1	+72	(Marlin)
485	5	Mar 26	Darlington: TranSouth Financial 400	23	2	293	293	37	Running	54,355	175	5	1	+67	(Marlin)
486	6	Apr 2	Bristol: Food City 500	25	25	500	479	0	Running	36,360	88	0	1	+17	(Marlin)
487	7	Apr 9	North Wilkesboro: First Union 400	5	1	400	400	227	Running	77,400	185	10	1	+56	(Marlin)
488	8	Apr 23	Martinsville: Hanes 500	20	29	356	331	0	Running	27,515	76	0	1	+8	(Marlin)
489	9	Apr 30	Talladega: Winston Select 500	16	21	188	188	6	Running	34,735	105	5	2	0	Gordon[1]
490	10	May 7	Sears Point: Save Mart Supermarkets 300	4	1	74	74	2	Running	74,860	180	5	1	+9	Earnhardt
491	11	May 28	Charlotte: Coca-Cola 600	34	6	400	399	38	Running	52,500	155	5	1	+80	Earnhardt
492	12	June 4	Dover: Miller Genuine Draft 500	23	5	500	500	10	Running	45,545	160	5	1	+100	Earnhardt
493	13	June 11	Pocono: UAW-GM Teamwork 500	24	8	200	200	0	Running	32,455	142	0	1	+77	Earnhardt
494	14	June 18	Michigan: Miller Genuine Draft 400	7	35	200	127	2	DNF - Crash	29,945	63	5	2	-6	Marlin
495	15	July 1	Daytona: Pepsi 400	1	3	160	160	11	Running	66,200	170	5	3	-16	Marlin
496	16	July 9	New Hampshire: Slick 50 300	18	22	300	298	24	Running	43,350	102	5	3	-92	Gordon
497	17	July 16	Pocono: Miller Genuine Draft 500	5	20	200	199	0	Running	31,555	103	0	4	-164	Gordon
498	18	July 23	Talladega: DieHard 500	5	3	188	188	20	Running	57,105	170	5	3	-146	Gordon
499	19	Aug 5	Indianapolis: Brickyard 400	13	1	160	160	28	Running	565,600	180	5	3	-121	Gordon
500	20	Aug 13	Watkins Glen: The Bud at the Glen	15	23	90	89	0	Running	30,890	94	0	4	-197	Gordon
501	21	Aug 20	Michigan: GM Goodwrench Dealer 400	8	35	200	87	0	DNF - Timing Belt	29,965	58	0	4	-314	Gordon
502	22	Aug 26	Bristol: Goody's 500	7	2	500	500	91	Running	66,890	175	5	4	-294	Gordon
503	23	Sep 3	Darlington: Mountain Dew Southern 500	3	2	367	367	208	Running	62,155	180	10	3	-294	Gordon
504	24	Sep 9	Richmond: Miller Genuine Draft 400	1	3	400	400	73	Running	54,005	170	5	2	-279	Gordon
505	25	Sep 17	Dover: MBNA 500	28	5	500	500	0	Running	40,970	155	0	2	-309	Gordon
506	26	Sep 24	Martinsville: Goody's 500	2	1	500	500	253	Running	78,150	185	10	2	-275	Gordon
507	27	Oct 1	North Wilkesboro: Tyson/Holly Farms 400	13	9	400	399	5	Running	27,850	143	5	2	-302	Gordon
508	28	Oct 8	Charlotte: UAW-GM Quality 500	43	2	334	334	2	Running	86,800	175	5	2	-205	Gordon
509	29	Oct 22	Rockingham: AC Delco 400	20	7	393	393	39	Running	34,050	151	5	2	-162	Gordon
510	30	Oct 29	Phoenix: Dura-Lube 500	2	3	312	312	71	Running	49,105	170	5	2	-147	Gordon
511	31	Nov 12	Atlanta: NAPA 500	11	1	328	328	268	Running	141,850	185	10	2	-34	Gordon

*2nd-place driver or co-leader listed in parentheses if Earnhardt is current points leader
[1]Despite points tie, Gordon assumed points lead due to greater number of wins (3-1)

1996: Talladega Crash Derails Title Hopes

For Earnhardt, the middle of the 1996 season was the summer of his discontent. During the first 15 events of the year, Earnhardt was at his front-running best. A runner-up finish at Daytona, followed by a victory at Rockingham, put Earnhardt at the top of the points chase early. After a hiccup at Richmond, Dale went on to post ten Top 10 finishes in the next dozen races. When he finished fourth at Daytona on the sixth of July, Earnhardt had a narrow lead over Terry Labonte. From there, he slid backwards.

Starting with the Jiffy Lube 300 at New Hampshire July 14 and ending with the Hanes 500 at Martinsville Sept. 29, a span of 11 races, Earnhardt notched only one Top 10, a sixth-place at the Bud at the Glen. The stretch, which included one DNF, dropped him to fourth place, 351 points behind points leader Jeff Gordon.

That one DNF was a painful one. At Talladega, Earnhardt got caught in the "big one"—the field-thinning wreck that seems to occur during Talladega races. Contact between Ernie Irvan and Sterling Marlin sent Earnhardt hurtling into the outside retaining wall along the track's front stretch. Flipped on its side, Earnhardt's car was plowed into by three cars, including one shot to the roof of the No. 3 Chevy. Earnhardt, deservedly viewed as one of the toughest drivers on the track, emerged from the wreckage gingerly, but with a wave to the crowd. The veteran driver was rushed to a local hospital and diagnosed with a broken sternum and collarbone.

At that point in his career, the Talladega wreck was Earnhardt's most serious since his violent 1979 crash at Pocono (which forced him out of action for four races). As he had in 1979, Earnhardt demonstrated his toughness immediately. Less than a week after the Talladega incident, Earnhardt qualified 12th and started the Brickyard 400 before getting relief help from future teammate Mike Skinner. The next week, Earnhardt won the pole at Watkins Glen, led a race-high 54 laps and stayed in the car for the entire race in an amazing effort.

The Watkins Glen pole had significance for another reason, though no one knew it at the time: It was the 22nd and final time Earnhardt won a pole. A strong finish to the season, with four Top 10s in the final five races, including a second place in the final race at North Wilkesboro, was not enough to counteract the painful summer. Labonte earned his second crown, while Dale was fourth, 330 points back.

Earnhardt in 1996

Category	Earnhardt's Total	Earnhardt's Rank	1996 Leader*
Money	$2,285,926	4th	Terry Labonte – 4,030,648
Total Points	4,327	4th	Terry Labonte – 4,657
Avg. Start	14.6	6th	Jeff Gordon – 6.3
Avg. Finish	10.7	4th	Terry Labonte – 8.2
Wins	2	4th	Jeff Gordon – 10
Top 5s	13	5th	J. Gordon, T. Labonte – 21
Top 10s	17	6th	J. Gordon, T. Labonte – 24
DNFs	2	39th	Andretti, Cope, D. Waltrip – 11
Poles	2	5th	Jeff Gordon – 5
Front Row Starts	2	8th	Jeff Gordon – 15
Laps Led	614	7th	Jeff Gordon – 2,314
Races Led	18	4th	Jeff Gordon – 25
Times Led	54	3rd	Jeff Gordon – 97
Miles Led	929	5th	Jeff Gordon – 2,386
Times Led Most Laps	3	3rd	Jeff Gordon – 10
Bonus Points	105	4th	Jeff Gordon – 175
Laps Completed	9,530	1st	(Terry Labonte – 9,443)
Miles Completed	11,523	1st	(Terry Labonte – 11,522)
Points per Race	139.6	4th	Terry Labonte – 150.2
Fin. on Lead Lap	21	5th	J. Gordon, T. Labonte – 24

*2nd-place driver listed in parentheses if Earnhardt is category leader.

"There'll come a Sunday when there won't be enough wreckers to pick up the pieces of his car."
—*Richard Petty*

1996 Performance Chart

No. 3 RCR Enterprises Chevrolet Monte Carlo

Career Race	Season Race	Date	Race	St.	Fin.	Total Laps	Laps Completed	Laps Led	Condition	Money	Pts.	Bonus Pts.	Point Standing	Behind Leader	Points Leader
512	1	Feb 18	Daytona: Daytona 500	1	2	200	200	32	Running	$215,065	175	5	2	-5	Jarrett
513	2	Feb 25	Rockingham: Goodwrench Service 400	18	1	393	393	95	Running	83,840	180	5	1 (tie)	—	(Jarrett)
514	3	Mar 3	Richmond: Pontiac Excitement 400	9	31	400	393	0	Running	27,265	70	0	4	-105	Jarrett
515	4	Mar 10	Atlanta: Purolator 500	18	1	328	328	136	Running	91,050	185	10	2	-50	Jarrett
516	5	Mar 24	Darlington: TranSouth Financial 400	27	14	293	292	1	Running	28,080	126	5	2	-47	Jarrett
517	6	Mar 31	Bristol: Food City 500	19	4	342	342	0	Running	35,351	160	0	2	-37	Jarrett
518	7	Apr 14	North Wilkesboro: First Union 400	26	3	400	400	0	Running	38,525	165	0	2	-2	Jarrett
519	8	Apr 21	Martinsville: Goody's Headache Powder 500	8	5	500	500	12	Running	35,195	160	5	1	+76	(Gordon)
520	9	Apr 28	Talladega: Winston Select 500	16	3	188	188	26	Running	64,620	170	5	1	+77	(Jarrett)
521	10	May 5	Sears Point: Save Mart Supermarkets 300	5	4	74	74	6	Running	39,160	165	5	1	+115	(Jarrett)
522	11	May 26	Charlotte: Coca-Cola 600	20	2	400	400	7	Running	97,000	175	5	1	+105	(Jarrett)
523	12	June 2	Dover: Miller 500	14	3	500	500	89	Running	60,080	170	5	1	+136	(T. Labonte)
524	13	June 16	Pocono: UAW-GM Teamwork 500	10	32	200	135	0	DNF - Engine	26,035	67	0	1	+52	(T. Labonte)
525	14	June 23	Michigan: Miller 400	11	9	200	200	0	Running	33,350	138	0	1	+15	(T. Labonte)
526	15	July 6	Daytona: Pepsi 400	7	4	117	117	0	Running	97,960	160	0	1	+5	(T. Labonte)
527	16	July 14	New Hampshire: Jiffy Lube 300	5	12	300	300	12	Running	32,225	132	5	2	-18	T. Labonte
528	17	July 21	Pocono: Miller 500	8	14	200	199	0	Running	27,925	121	0	2	-12	T. Labonte
529	18	July 28	Talladega: DieHard 500	4	28	129	117	40	DNF - Crash	31,020	89	10	3	-23	Gordon
530	19	Aug 3	Indianapolis: Brickyard 400[1]	12	15	160	160	1	Running	84,460	123	5	2	-61	T. Labonte
531	20	Aug 11	Watkins Glen: The Bud at the Glen	1	6	90	90	54	Running	52,960	160	10	2	-76	T. Labonte
532	21	Aug 18	Michigan: GM Goodwrench Dealer 400	16	17	200	200	0	Running	32,865	112	0	3	-134	T. Labonte
533	22	Aug 24	Bristol: Goody's Headache Powder 500	23	24	500	476	0	Running	32,310	91	0	4	-198	T. Labonte
534	23	Sep 1	Darlington: Mountain Dew Southern 500	12	12	367	365	0	Running	30,545	127	0	4	-161	T. Labonte
535	24	Sep 7	Richmond: Miller 400	23	20	400	398	0	Running	30,100	103	0	4	-218	T. Labonte
536	25	Sep 15	Dover: MBNA 500	20	16	500	498	11	Running	31,515	120	5	4	-279	Gordon
537	26	Sep 22	Martinsville: Hanes 500	19	15	500	498	0	Running	29,100	118	0	4	-341	Gordon
538	27	Sep 29	North Wilkesboro: Tyson Holly Farms 400	11	2	400	400	35	Running	51,940	175	5	4	-351	Gordon
539	28	Oct 6	Charlotte: UAW-GM Quality 500	34	6	334	334	15	Running	44,700	155	5	4	-271	Gordon
540	29	Oct 20	Rockingham: AC Delco 400	15	9	393	393	37	Running	30,700	143	5	4	-292	T. Labonte
541	30	Oct 27	Phoenix: Dura-Lube 500	24	12	312	312	0	Running	29,055	127	0	4	-335	T. Labonte
542	31	Nov 10	Atlanta: NAPA 500	17	4	328	328	4	Running	47,400	165	5	4	-330	T. Labonte

*2nd-place driver or co-leader listed in parentheses if Earnhardt is current points leader

[1]Relieved by Mike Skinner

73

1997: A Winless Season

For 15 consecutive years, when the Winston Cup season came to a close and Dale Earnhardt took stock of his campaign, he always had a victory to point to. A checkered flag at Charlotte here, a romp at Richmond there. Of course, there's always Talladega. But when the 1997 campaign wrapped up, Earnhardt had no such triumph to reflect upon. Earnhardt's streak of 15 seasons with at least one victory, and usually far more, came to an end in 1997. Four runner-up finishes, including the Winston 500 when he led 76 of 188 laps, was the best he could do. As a result, Earnhardt's career-worst winless streak grew to 59 races.

Despite his failure to find victory lane, Dale was consistently good enough to finish fifth in the final points standings, a result of his impressive, if slightly misleading, run of 33 races without a DNF. The No. 3 car was running at the end of every race, even if Dale was only in it on 32 of those occasions.

In the August 31 Southern 500 at Darlington, Earnhardt's afternoon came to a quick and mystifying early end. On the opening lap, Earnhardt apparently blacked out and crashed into the Turn 3 wall. Though able to return to the pits, Earnhardt was removed from the car and immediately hospitalized for observation. Tests throughout the week turned up nothing unusual, and Earnhardt was back behind the wheel for the next race seven days later at Richmond. The cause of the blackout is still unknown. The cause of the winless season also remains a mystery.

Earnhardt's Longest Winless Streaks

No. of Races	Season(s)	Streak Breaker
59	Race 5, 1996 – Race 32, 1997	1998 Daytona 500
40	Race 2, 1998 – Race 8, 1999	Talladega – 1999 DieHard 500
40	Race 7, 1982 – Race 16, 1983	Nashville – 1983 Busch Nashville 420
39	Race 29, 1980 – Race 5, 1982	Darlington – 1982 CRC Chemicals Rebel 500
29	Race 20, 1983 – Race 18, 1984	Talladega – 1984 Talladega 500

Earnhardt in 1997

Category	Earnhardt's Total	Earnhardt's Rank	1997 Leader
Money	$2,151,909	7th	Jeff Gordon – 6,375,658
Total Points	4,216	5th	Jeff Gordon – 4,710
Avg. Start	19.9	13th	Dale Jarrett – 7.2
Avg. Finish	12.1	4th	Mark Martin – 8.9
Wins	0	—	Jeff Gordon – 10
Top 5s	7	8th	Jeff Gordon – 22
Top 10s	16	7th	Mark Martin – 24
DNFs	0	—	Dallenbach, K & R Wallace: 10
Poles	0	—	B. Labonte, Jarrett, Martin: 3
Front Row Starts	1	17th	Gordon, Jarrett, Martin – 6
Laps Led	220	12th	Dale Jarrett – 2,083
Races Led	10	11th	Jeff Gordon – 24
Times Led	28	6th	Dale Jarrett – 71
Miles Led	503	9th	Dale Jarrett – 2,541
Times Led Most Laps	1	8th	Dale Jarrett – 8
Bonus Points	55	11th	Dale Jarrett – 150
Laps Completed	9,693	2nd	Dale Jarrett – 9,769
Miles Completed	12,509	3rd	Dale Jarrett – 12,652
Points per Race	131.8	5th	Jeff Gordon – 147.2
Fin. on Lead Lap	21	5th	Jeff Burton – 24

Winston Cup crew chief and later Fox Sports color commentator Larry McReynolds arrived with great fanfare when he accepted the top job with the No. 3 Goodwrench team in 1997. In their two-plus years together, however, McReynolds and Earnhardt never prospered as expected. Earnhardt went winless in 1997 but did win the 1998 Daytona 500 with McReynolds' help. *David Stringer*

1997 Performance Chart

No. 3 Richard Childress Racing Chevrolet Monte Carlo

Career Race	Season Race	Date	Race	St.	Fin.	Total Laps	Laps Completed	Laps Led	Condition	Money	Pts.	Bonus Pts.	Point Standing	Behind Leader	Points Leader
543	1	Feb 16	Daytona: Daytona 500	4	31	200	195	48	Running	$72,545	75	5	30	-105	Gordon
544	2	Feb 23	Rockingham: Goodwrench Service 400	27	11	393	393	0	Running	32,000	130	0	19	-155	Gordon
545	3	Mar 2	Richmond: Pontiac Excitement 400	4	25	400	397	0	Running	27,940	88	0	24	-232	Gordon
546	4	Mar 9	Atlanta: Primestar 500	26	8	328	328	0	Running	40,975	142	0	16	-199	Jarrett
547	5	Mar 23	Darlington: TranSouth Financial 400	43	15	293	292	0	Running	28,625	118	0	15	-266	Jarrett
548	6	Apr 6	Texas: Interstate Batteries 500	15	6	334	334	0	Running	111,700	150	0	10	-291	Jarrett
549	7	Apr 13	Bristol: Food City 500	29	6	500	500	0	Running	32,970	150	0	8	-301	Jarrett
550	8	Apr 20	Martinsville: Goody's Headache Powder 500	25	12	500	500	0	Running	28,400	127	0	8	-289	Jarrett
551	9	May 4	Sears Point: SaveMart Supermarkets 300	32	12	74	74	0	Running	39,580	127	0	7	-327	Jarrett
552	10	May 10	Talladega: Winston 500	3	2	188	188	76	Running	85,445	180	10	6	-257	T. Labonte
553	11	May 25	Charlotte: Coca-Cola 600	33	7	333	333	2	Running	54,400	151	5	6	-253	T. Labonte
554	12	June 1	Dover: Miller 500	43	16	500	497	0	Running	33,265	115	0	6	-259	T. Labonte
555	13	June 8	Pocono: Pocono 500	12	10	200	200	0	Running	34,025	134	0	6	-268	Gordon
556	14	June 15	Michigan: Miller 400	22	7	200	200	0	Running	41,375	146	0	6	-277	Gordon
557	15	June 22	California: California 500	14	16	250	249	0	Running	41,975	115	0	6	-347	Gordon
558	16	July 5	Daytona: Pepsi 400	2	4	160	160	7	Running	52,475	165	5	6	-287	Gordon
559	17	July 13	New Hampshire: Jiffy Lube 300	26	2	300	300	0	Running	82,950	170	0	6	-214	T. Labonte
560	18	July 20	Pocono: Pennsylvania 500	5	12	200	200	2	Running	29,490	132	5	6	-254	Gordon
561	19	Aug 2	Indianapolis: Brickyard 400	5	29	160	158	0	Running	76,310	76	0	6	-343	Gordon
562	20	Aug 10	Watkins Glen: The Bud at the Glen	3	16	90	90	0	Running	29,575	115	0	6	-413	Gordon
563	21	Aug 17	Michigan: DeVilbiss 400	28	9	200	200	0	Running	37,940	138	0	6	-450	Gordon
564	22	Aug 23	Bristol: Goody's Headache Powder 500	34	14	500	497	0	Running	32,515	121	0	6	-405	Gordon
565	23	Aug 31	Darlington: Mountain Dew Southern 500[1]	36	30	367	282	0	Running	30,925	73	0	6	-499	Gordon
566	24	Sep 6	Richmond: Exide 400	22	15	400	398	0	Running	33,775	118	0	6	-546	Gordon
567	25	Sep 14	New Hampshire: CMT 300	30	8	300	300	0	Running	49,025	142	0	6	-589	Gordon
568	26	Sep 21	Dover: MBNA 400	33	2	400	400	4	Running	63,105	175	5	6	-565	Gordon
569	27	Sep 29	Martinsville: Hanes 500	13	2	500	500	0	Running	65,800	170	0	5	-560	Gordon
570	28	Oct 5	Charlotte: UAW-GM Quality 500	19	3	334	334	31	Running	85,650	170	5	5	-545	Gordon
571	29	Oct 12	Talladega: DieHard 500	12	29	188	167	25	Running	48,500	81	5	6	-527	Gordon
572	30	Oct 27	Rockingham: AC Delco 400	26	8	393	393	0	Running	32,800	142	0	6	-550	Gordon
573	31	Nov 2	Phoenix: Dura-Lube 500	7	5	312	312	1	Running	39,300	160	5	6	-502	Gordon
574	32	Nov 16	Atlanta: NAPA 500	6	16	325	322	24	Running	43,075	120	5	5	-494	Gordon

[1] Relieved by Mike Dillon

1998: Victory in the Daytona 500 (Finally)

In the first race of the 1998 season, Earnhardt finally slayed his biggest and last remaining demon: the Daytona 500. Around the front of the field all day, leading 107 of 200 laps, Earnhardt held the advantage during a restart with 23 laps remaining. He held off challenges from Jeff Gordon, Rusty Wallace, Jeremy Mayfield and Bobby Labonte, then watched as a Lap 199 accident brought out the white and yellow flags simultaneously. The yellow prevented a last-lap duel with runner-up and pole winner, Bobby Labonte.

Following his Daytona 500 victory, Earnhardt enjoyed some of the most touching and memorable moments of his career. In a genuine, impromptu reaction that reflected the admiration and respect Earnhardt commanded among his peers, members of every NASCAR team lined pit road to salute his long-overdue victory.

Though certainly well-deserved, Earnhardt's win at Daytona couldn't have been more improbable. Earnhardt hadn't won a race in 59 starts, the longest drought of his career. He entered the Daytona 500 with lower expectations, at least in the eyes of others, than at any time since the early 1980s. Perhaps this made the triumph more likely, and what followed more foreseeable. In his previous 19 seasons, Earnhardt seemed to use his annual Daytona disappointment to fuel his effort during the rest of the season. In 1998, when he finally had a Daytona 500 to his name, the opposite happened. The '98 season soon became one of the worst in his career.

Over the next 32 races, Earnhardt was rarely a factor, compiling just 13 Top 10 finishes and a career-low five Top 5s. Moreover, by season's end, Earnhardt was 1,400 points in arrears of champion Jeff Gordon, the biggest difference between the series winner and Earnhardt in his storied career. Of course, in light of Gordon's historic campaign in '98, the same fate befell many drivers that season. Earnhardt still earned a place in New York at NASCAR's annual year-end banquet at the Waldorf-Astoria with an eighth-place finish in the season standings. Largest Point Difference Between Earnhardt and the Winston Cup Champion.

Year	Point Standing	No. of Points Behind (Champion)
1998	8th	1,400 (Jeff Gordon)
1982	12th	1,087 (Darrell Waltrip)
1979	7th	1,081 (Richard Petty)
1983	8th	935 (Bobby Allison)
1981	7th	905 (Darrell Waltrip)

Earnhardt in 1998

Category	Earnhardt's Total	Earnhardt's Rank	1998 Leader
Money	$2,990,749	4th	Jeff Gordon – 9,306,584
Total Points	3,928	8th	Jeff Gordon – 5,328
Avg. Start	26.5	40th	Jeff Gordon – 6.9
Avg. Finish	16.2	8th	Jeff Gordon – 5.7
Wins	1	6th	Jeff Gordon – 13
Top 5s	5	8th	Jeff Gordon – 26
Top 10s	13	9th	Jeff Gordon – 28
DNFs	3	32nd	Kenny Wallace – 13
Poles	0	—	Jeff Gordon – 7
Front Row Starts	1	12th	Jeff Gordon – 11
Laps Led	273	10th	Mark Martin – 1,730
Races Led	14	5th	Jeff Gordon – 26
Times Led	25	6th	Jeff Gordon – 76
Miles Led	536	7th	Jeff Gordon – 2,765
Times Led Most Laps	1	7th	J. Gordon, M. Martin – 8
Bonus Points	75	6th	Jeff Gordon – 170
Laps Completed	9,459	11th	Bobby Hamilton – 9,840
Miles Completed	12,278	12th	Jeff Gordon – 12,785
Points per Race	119.0	8th	Jeff Gordon – 161.5
Fin. on Lead Lap	16	10th	Jeff Gordon – 28

"I always used to tell him, 'I won seven championships.' He'd say, 'Yeah, but I won Daytona.' He can't say that no more."
—*Dale Earnhardt talking about Darrell Waltrip, after winning the Daytona 500 in 1998*

1998 Performance Chart

No. 3 RCR Enterprisces Chevrolet

Career Race	Season Race	Date	Race	St.	Fin.	Total Laps	Laps Completed	Laps Led	Condition	Money	Pts.	Bonus Pts.	Point Standing	Behind Leader	Points Leader
575	1	Feb 15	Daytona: Daytona 500	4	1	200	200	107	Running	$1,080,233	185	10	1	+10	(Mayfield)
576	2	Feb 22	Rockingham: GM Goodwrench Service Plus 400	37	17	393	392	1	Running	32,100	117	5	2	-33	Wallace
577	3	Mar 1	Las Vegas: Las Vegas 400	26	8	267	267	1	Running	84,500	147	5	2	-56	Wallace
578	4	Mar 9	Atlanta: Primestar 500	30	13	325	324	2	Running	39,055	129	5	3	-87	Wallace
579	5	Mar 22	Darlington: TranSouth Financial 400	27	12	293	292	0	Running	37,595	127	0	3	-130	Wallace
580	6	Mar 29	Bristol: Food City 500	37	22	500	496	0	Running	33,715	97	0	5	-106	Wallace
581	7	Apr 5	Texas: Texas 500	34	35	334	205	0	Running	58,200	58	0	9	-176	Wallace
582	8	Apr 20	Martinsville: Goody's Headache Powder 500	31	4	500	500	33	Running	49,475	165	5	8	-166	Wallace
583	9	Apr 26	Talladega: Diehard 500	2	36	188	144	10	DNF - Crash	38,250	60	5	9	-233	Wallace
584	10	May 3	California: California 500	43	9	250	250	0	Running	53,800	138	0	7	-234	Mayfield
585	11	May 24	Charlotte: Coca-Cola 600	28	39	400	336	0	DNF - Crash	39,580	46	0	10	-321	Gordon
586	12	May 31	Dover: MBNA Platinum 400	34	25	400	395	0	Running	33,205	88	0	12	-408	Gordon
587	13	June 6	Richmond: Pontiac Excitement 400	38	21	400	398	0	Running	34,250	100	0	12	-411	Mayfield
588	14	June 14	Michigan: Miller Lite 400	25	15	200	199	0	Running	38,650	118	0	12	-448	Mayfield
589	15	June 21	Pocono: Pocono 500	11	8	200	200	1	Running	34,625	147	5	10	-486	Mayfield
590	16	June 28	Sears Point: Save Mart/Kragen 350	17	11	112	112	0	Running	44,950	130	0	10	-505	Gordon
591	17	July 12	New Hampshire: Jiffy Lube 300	20	18	300	299	0	Running	47,150	109	0	10	-566	Gordon
592	18	July 26	Pocono: Pennsylvania 500	9	7	200	200	14	Running	49,890	151	5	9	-600	Gordon
593	19	Aug 1	Indianapolis: Brickyard 400	28	5	160	160	6	Running	169,275	160	5	9	-625	Gordon
594	20	Aug 9	Watkins Glen: The Bud at the Glen	22	11	90	90	0	Running	36,355	130	0	9	-680	Gordon
595	21	Aug 16	Michigan: Pepsi 400	37	18	200	198	3	Running	34,840	114	5	8	-746	Gordon
596	22	Aug 22	Bristol: Goody's Headache Powder 500	30	6	500	500	34	Running	42,540	155	5	8	-746	Gordon
597	23	Aug 30	New Hampshire: Farm Aid on CMT 300	18	9	300	300	0	Running	50,550	138	0	8	-788	Gordon
598	24	Sep 6	Darlington: Mountain Dew Southern 500	18	4	367	367	0	Running	64,465	160	0	8	-808	Gordon
599	25	Sep 12	Richmond: Exide Batteries 400	34	38	400	260	0	Running	34,495	49	0	8	-934	Gordon
600	26	Sep 20	Dover: MBNA Gold 400	43	23	400	396	0	Running	32,140	94	0	8	-1,015	Gordon
601	27	Sep 27	Martinsville: NAPA Autocare 500	33	22	500	495	0	Running	32,950	97	0	8	-1,088	Gordon
602	28	Oct 4	Charlotte: UAW-GM Quality 500	33	29	334	278	0	Running	31,300	76	0	8	-1,172	Gordon
603	29	Oct 11	Talladega: Winston 500	14	32	188	175	12	DNF - Rear End	40,920	72	5	8	-1,275	Gordon
604	30	Oct 17	Daytona: Pepsi 400	5	10	160	160	41	Running	57,375	139	5	8	-1,321	Gordon
605	31	Oct 25	Phoenix: Dura Lube/KMart 500	39	3	257	257	0	Running	57,175	165	0	8	-1,307	Gordon
606	32	Nov 1	Rockingham: AC Delco 400	29	9	393	393	8	Running	34,400	143	5	8	-1,339	Gordon
607	33	Nov 8	Atlanta: NAPA 500	37	13	221	221	0	Running	46,025	124	0	8	-1,400	Gordon

*2nd-place driver listed in parentheses if Earnhardt is current points leader

"We won it! We won it! We won it! The Daytona 500 is ours!"
—Dale Earnhardt, emerging from his car in Victory Lane

1999: Talladega Sweep, Bristol Controversy

Dale Earnhardt long championed the end of restrictor plate racing—that NASCAR creation that keeps drivers bunched together on the circuit's two fastest tracks, Daytona and Talladega. Despite his public statements, Earnhardt seemed to gravitate to the three-wide challenge they presented. Especially in 1999, Earnhardt thoroughly dominated the series' restrictor-plate events.

His Daytona scorecard for the 1999 season featured two runner-up finishes, plus his annual romp in his half of the Twin 125s. But it was at Talladega where Dale did his best work, claiming both the spring and fall races. He led 70 of 188 laps in his DieHard 500 win, coming to the front from the 17th starting spot. He charged even harder in the October race, moving up from 27th to the top spot.

Bristol, however, provided the most memorable moment of the 1999 season. The Earnhardt of old was on full display in the track's much-anticipated night race. Passed by Terry Labonte on the next-to-last lap, Earnhardt reclaimed the lead with a "rattle his cage a little" tap on the final lap. The jostle sent Labonte into a race-conceding spin and allowed Earnhardt to sneak to his ninth Bristol win. As Earnhardt emerged from his car in victory lane, he heard something normally reserved for Jeff Gordon: thunderous boos cascaded from the crowd.

Three wins and 21 Top 10s would normally boost Earnhardt into the heat of a points race. That wasn't a realistic expectation in 1999, thanks to Dale Jarrett, who crafted one of the most consistent seasons in NASCAR history. DJ won just one more time than Earnhardt, but his 29 Top 10s, the most in the modern era, erased all doubts about the identity of the 1999 champion.

Earnhardt's Performance in NASCAR's 53 Restrictor Plate Races

Category	Earnhardt's Total	Earnhardt's Rank	Category Leader*
Avg. Start	8.6	2nd	Davey Allison – 5.7
Avg. Finish	9.4	1st	(Jeff Gordon – 14.2)
Poles	6	T-1st	(E. Irvan, S. Marlin – 6)
Wins	11	1st	(Jeff Gordon – 6)
Top 5s	32	1st	(Sterling Marlin – 18)
Top 10s	40	1st	(Marlin, Schrader – 28)
Laps Led	2,134	1st	(Sterling Marlin – 833)
DNFs	7	31st	Derrike Cope – 20

*2nd-place driver or co-leader listed in parentheses if Earnhardt is the category leader

Earnhardt in 1999

Category	Earnhardt's Total	Earnhardt's Rank	1999 Leader
Money	$3,048,236	7th	Dale Jarrett – 6,649,596
Total Points	4,492	7th	Dale Jarrett – 5,262
Avg. Start	24.8	27th	Jeff Gordon – 7.4
Avg. Finish	12.0	6th	Dale Jarrett – 6.8
Wins	3	5th	Jeff Gordon – 7
Top 5s	7	7th	Dale Jarrett – 24
Top 10s	21	5th	Dale Jarrett – 29
DNFs	3	23rd	Andretti, Craven, M. Waltrip – 10
Poles	0	—	Jeff Gordon – 7
Front Row Starts	0	—	Jeff Gordon – 9
Laps Led	230	12th	Jeff Gordon – 1,319
Races Led	8	14th	Bobby Labonte – 30
Times Led	25	9th	Jeff Gordon – 86
Miles Led	395	9th	Jeff Gordon – 1,923
Times Led Most Laps	1	8th	J. Burton, J. Gordon – 6
Bonus Points	45	13th	Bobby Labonte – 165
Laps Completed	9,751	11th	Bobby Labonte – 10,013
Miles Completed	12,762	10th	Bobby Labonte – 13,135
Points per Race	132.1	7th	Dale Jarrett – 154.8
Fin. on Lead Lap	22	6th	D. Jarrett, B. Labonte – 28

One of the best stories in NASCAR in 1999 and 2000 was the rise of Dale Earnhardt Jr. to the Winston Cup series. Here, Dale Jr. closes in on his dad's bumper during the 1999 NAPA 500 at Atlanta, one of five races the younger Earnhardt competed in that season. *David Stringer*

1999 Performance Chart

No. 3 RCR Enterprises Chevrolet

Career Race	Season Race	Date	Race	St.	Fin.	Total Laps	Laps Completed	Laps Led	Condition	Money	Pts.	Bonus Pts.	Point Standing	Behind Leader	Points Leader
608	1	Feb 14	Daytona: Daytona 500	4	2	200	200	0	Running	$613,659	170	0	2	-10	Gordon
609	2	Feb 21	Rockingham: Dura-Lube/Big Kmart 400	18	41	393	275	0	DNF - Crash	36,725	40	0	17	-105	Skinner
610	3	Mar 7	Las Vegas: Las Vegas 400	38	7	267	267	0	Running	91,350	146	0	12	-119	Skinner
611	4	Mar 14	Atlanta: Cracker Barrel Old Country Store 500	33	40	325	151	0	DNF - Handling	41,625	43	0	18	-231	Skinner
612	5	Mar 21	Darlington: TranSouth Financial 400	30	25	164	163	0	Running	37,020	88	0	20	-276	J. Burton
613	6	Mar 28	Texas: Primestar 500	38	8	334	334	0	Running	97,775	142	0	16	-280	J. Burton
614	7	Apr 11	Bristol: Food City 500	34	10	500	500	0	Running	48,630	134	0	14	-301	J. Burton
615	8	Apr 18	Martinsville: Goody's Body Pain 500	39	19	500	498	0	Running	39,150	106	0	15	-370	J. Burton
616	9	Apr 25	Talladega: Diehard 500	17	1	188	188	70	Running	147,795	185	10	9	-315	J. Burton
617	10	May 2	California: California 500	9	12	250	249	2	Running	55,425	132	5	11	-358	J. Burton
618	11	May 15	Richmond: Pontiac Excitement 400	37	8	400	400	0	Running	48,540	142	0	9	-341	Jarrett
619	12	May 30	Charlotte: Coca-Cola 600	15	6	400	400	0	Running	70,225	150	0	7	-346	Jarrett
620	13	June 6	Dover: MBNA Platinum 400	34	11	400	398	0	Running	49,510	130	0	7	-376	Jarrett
621	14	June 13	Michigan: Kmart 400	15	16	200	198	0	Running	39,825	115	0	8	-446	Jarrett
622	15	June 20	Pocono: Pocono 500	25	7	200	200	0	Running	57,190	146	0	7	-475	Jarrett
623	16	June 27	Sears Point: Save Mart/Kragen 350k	23	9	112	112	0	Running	46,165	138	0	7	-487	Jarrett
624	17	July 3	Daytona: Pepsi 400	10	2	160	160	18	Running	92,175	175	5	7	-492	Jarrett
625	18	July 11	New Hampshire: Jiffy Lube 300	14	8	300	300	0	Running	56,675	142	0	7	-515	Jarrett
626	19	July 25	Pocono: Pennsylvania 500	11	9	200	200	4	Running	48,765	143	5	7	-547	Jarrett
627	20	Aug 7	Indianapolis: Brickyard 400	18	10	160	160	0	Running	135,525	134	0	7	-598	Jarrett
628	21	Aug 15	Watkins Glen: Frontier @ the Glen	14	20	90	90	0	Running	41,525	103	0	7	-655	Jarrett
629	22	Aug 22	Michigan: Pepsi 400	38	5	200	200	27	Running	51,005	160	5	7	-660	Jarrett
630	23	Aug 28	Bristol: Goody's Headache Powder 500	26	1	500	500	46	Running	89,880	180	5	7	-529	Jarrett
631	24	Sep 5	Darlington: Pepsi Southern 500	25	22	270	268	0	Running	42,470	97	0	7	-552	Jarrett
632	25	Sep 11	Richmond: Exide Batteries 400	33	6	400	400	0	Running	47,055	150	0	7	-567	Jarrett
633	26	Sep 19	New Hampshire: Dura-Lube/Kmart 300	16	13	300	300	0	Running	55,125	124	0	7	-557	Jarrett
634	27	Sep 26	Dover: MBNA Gold 400	37	8	400	399	0	Running	52,065	142	0	7	-585	Jarrett
635	28	Oct 3	Martinsville: NAPA AutoCare 500	38	2	500	500	45	Running	70,225	175	5	7	-544	Jarrett
636	29	Oct 10	Charlotte: UAW-GM Quality 500	17	12	334	332	0	Running	44,450	127	0	7	-568	Jarrett
637	30	Oct 17	Talladega: Winston 500	27	1	188	188	18	Running	120,290	180	5	7	-563	Jarrett
638	31	Oct 24	Rockingham: Pop Secret Popcorn 400	37	40	393	318	0	DNF - Crash	36,900	43	0	7	-690	Jarrett
639	32	Nov 7	Phoenix: Checker Auto Parts/Dura-Lube 500K	14	11	312	312	0	Running	57,225	130	0	7	-715	Jarrett
640	33	Nov 14	Homestead: Pennzoil 400	23	8	267	266	0	Running	65,575	142	0	7	-733	Jarrett
641	34	Nov 21	Atlanta: NAPA 500	36	9	325	325	0	Running	54,550	138	0	7	-770	Jarrett

2000: Making a Run at No. 8

For much of the first half of the 2000 Winston Cup season, when the name Dale Earnhardt came up, it wasn't the Intimidator on people's minds. Dale Earnhardt Jr. exploded on the Winston Cup scene in 2000, becoming the series' first two-time winner and claiming the Winston all-star race, all in the season's first three months.

But Little E, who obviously has the best of both worlds in the ongoing nature vs. nurture debate, quickly faded from the scene, showing he still has a thing or two to learn from the old man. While the elder Earnhardt came up short in his final bid to become the series' first eight-time champion, he provided an enduring lesson to Junior in what it takes to reach the ultimate goal of a NASCAR driver. Earnhardt won the Cracker Barrel Old Country Store 500 in the season's fourth race, but it was a stretch later in the spring that vaulted him into the heat of the points standings. From the May 6 Pontiac Excitement 400 at Richmond to the New England 300 at New Hampshire in July, Earnhardt posted eight straight Top 10s. That run moved him into second place, just 45 points behind Bobby Labonte. Unfortunately for Earnhardt, he never got any closer as Labonte maintained his steadiness all season.

Earnhardt created one of his most thrilling moments in 2000 when he roared from 22nd to first in just a handful of laps to win yet another restrictor-plate race at Talladega in October. A runner-up finish in the season's final race at Atlanta allowed Earnhardt to overtake Jeff Burton and reclaim the runner-up spot in the season standings. And his season-long presence running at the front left no doubt that a record eighth championship could have been in the cards in 2001.

Perhaps indicating what the future had in store for the NASCAR legend, in simple victory terms, Earnhardt actually had a better season as a car owner (of the No. 8 and No. 1 cars) than as a driver in 2000. Besides his son's two victories, Earnhardt the owner also witnessed Steve Park's first career victory at Watkins Glen.

Earnhardt in 2000

Category	Earnhardt's Total	Earnhardt's Rank	2000 Leader*
Money	$4,918,886	4th	Bobby Labonte – 7,361,386
Total Points	4,865	2nd	Bobby Labonte – 5,130
Avg. Start	21.1	18th	Rusty Wallace – 10.0
Avg. Finish	9.4	2nd	Bobby Labonte – 7.4
Wins	2	6th	Tony Stewart – 6
Top 5s	13	4th	Bobby Labonte – 19
Top 10s	24	T-1st	(D. Jarrett, B. Labonte – 24)
DNFs	0	—	J. Mayfield, S. Pruett – 11
Poles	0	—	Rusty Wallace – 9
Front Row Starts	0	—	Rusty Wallace – 11
Laps Led	353	12th	Rusty Wallace – 1,731
Races Led	17	5th	J. Burton, B. Labonte – 23
Times Led	38	7th	Rusty Wallace – 61
Miles Led	508.3	13th	Rusty Wallace – 1,868.8
Times Led Most Laps	0	—	Rusty Wallace – 6
Bonus Points	85	8th	Jeff Burton – 140
Laps Completed	10,005	3rd	Bobby Labonte – 10,158
Miles Completed	13,183.7	2nd	Bobby Labonte – 13,268.0
Points per Race	143.1	2nd	Bobby Labonte – 150.9
Fin. on Lead Lap	28	T-1st	(Bobby Labonte – 28)

*2nd-place driver listed in parentheses if Earnhardt is category leader.

2000 Season Comparison

Driver	Avg. Start	Avg. Fin.	Wins	Top 5s	Top 10s	Laps Led	DNFs
B. Labonte	11.6	7.4	4	19	24	465	0
D. Earnhardt	21.1	9.4	2	13	24	353	0

In his last run for an eighth Winston Cup championship, Earnhardt chased Bobby Labonte for much of the 2000 season before settling for second place. Labonte held off Earnhardt by 265 points. Here, Earnhardt and Labonte race side-by-side at Michigan during the 1996 Miller 400. *Don Hamilton*

2000 Performance Chart

No. 3 Richard Childress Racing Chevrolet

Career Race	Season Race	Date	Race	St.	Fin.	Total Laps	Laps Completed	Laps Led	Condition	Money	Pts.	Bonus Pts.	Point Standing	Behind Leader	Points Leader
642	1	Feb 20	Daytona: Daytona 500	21	21	200	200	0	Running	$116,075	100	0	21	-85	Jarrett
643	2	Feb 27	Rockingham: Dura Lube/Kmart 400	4	2	393	393	1	Running	78,610	175	5	7	-65	Jarrett
644	3	Mar 5	Las Vegas: Carsdirect.com 400	33	8	148	148	0	Running	94,900	142	0	7	-73	B.Labonte
645	4	Mar 12	Atlanta: Cracker Barrel Old Country Store 500	35	1	325	325	34	Running	123,100	180	5	3	-68	B.Labonte
646	5	Mar 19	Darlington: Mall.com 400	4	3	293	293	0	Running	68,590	165	0	3	-32	B.Labonte
647	6	Mar 26	Bristol: Food City 500	11	39	500	346	2	Running	45,215	51	5	5	-131	B.Labonte
648	7	Apr 2	Texas: DirecTV 500	17	7	334	334	0	Running	108,750	146	0	4	-155	B.Labonte
649	8	Apr 9	Martinsville: Goody's Body Pain 500	17	9	500	500	42	Running	48,550	143	5	5	-144	B.Labonte
650	9	Apr 16	Talladega: DieHard 500	4	3	188	188	5	Running	92,630	170	5	4	-98	Martin
651	10	Apr 30	California: NAPA Auto Parts 500	35	17	250	250	0	Running	59,075	112	0	5	-132	B.Labonte
652	11	May 6	Richmond: Pontiac Excitement 400	31	10	400	400	19	Running	52,800	139	5	5	-78	B.Labonte
653	12	May 28	Charlotte: Coca-Cola 600	15	3	400	400	23	Running	103,250	170	5	4	-83	B.Labonte
654	13	June 4	Dover: MBNA Platinum 400	30	6	400	399	49	Running	75,455	155	5	3	-98	B.Labonte
655	14	June 11	Michigan: Kmart 400	9	2	194	194	0	Running	80,575	170	0	2	-98	B.Labonte
656	15	June 18	Pocono: Pocono 500	16	4	200	200	17	Running	87,495	165	5	2	-57	B.Labonte
657	16	June 25	Sears Point: Save Mart/Kragen 300	29	6	112	112	0	Running	65,165	150	0	2	-67	B.Labonte
658	17	July 1	Daytona: Pepsi 400	18	8	160	160	0	Running	64,375	142	0	2	-52	B.Labonte
659	18	July 9	New Hampshire: Thatlook.com 300	24	6	273	273	0	Running	69,425	150	0	2	-45	B.Labonte
660	19	July 23	Pocono: Pennsylvania 500	25	25	200	199	6	Running	48,915	93	5	3	-107	B.Labonte
661	20	Aug 5	Indianapolis: Brickyard 400	8	8	160	160	0	Running	143,510	142	0	3	-145	B.Labonte
662	21	Aug 13	Watkins Glen: Global Crossing @ The Glen	3	25	90	90	0	Running	45,180	88	0	3	-217	B.Labonte
663	22	Aug 20	Michigan: Pepsi 400	37	6	200	200	0	Running	51,190	150	0	3	-237	B.Labonte
664	23	Aug 26	Bristol: Goracing.com 500	17	4	500	500	2	Running	62,980	165	5	3	-195	B.Labonte
665	24	Sep 3	Darlington: Southern 500	6	3	328	328	47	Running	82,745	170	5	3	-205	B.Labonte
666	25	Sep 9	Richmond: Chevrolet Monte Carlo 400	22	2	400	400	0	Running	81,190	170	0	2	-158	B.Labonte
667	26	Sep 17	New Hampshire – Dura Lube 300	37	12	300	299	0	Running	62,550	127	0	4	-201	B.Labonte
668	27	Sep 24	Dover: MBNA.com 400	37	17	400	398	0	Running	63,390	112	0	2	-249	B.Labonte
669	28	Oct 1	Martinsville: NAPA AutoCare 500	12	2	500	500	0	Running	77,925	170	0	2	-213	B.Labonte
670	29	Oct 8	Charlotte: UAW-GM Quality 500	37	11	334	334	58	Running	58,750	135	5	3	-258	B.Labonte
671	30	Oct 15	Talladega: Winston 500	20	1	188	188	34	Running	1,135,900	180	5	2	-210	B.Labonte
672	31	Oct 22	Rockingham: Pop Secret 400	27	17	393	393	1	Running	46,625	117	5	2	-201	B.Labonte
673	32	Nov 5	Phoenix: Checker Auto Parts/DuraLube 500K	31	9	312	312	1	Running	69,300	143	5	2	-218	B.Labonte
674	33	Nov 12	Homestead: Pennzoil 400	37	20	267	264	0	Running	60,700	103	0	3	-280	B.Labonte
675	34	Nov 21	Atlanta: NAPA 500	8	2	325	325	12	Running	99,750	175	5	2	-265	B.Labonte

2001: NASCAR Loses Its Greatest Driver

Dale Earnhardt's quest for that eighth Winston Cup championship had a chance in 2001. The series has never been more competitive—as many as 10, perhaps 15, drivers could legitimately claim a solid chance at winning the '01 title – but signs pointed to another strong Earnhardt run. The most obvious sign was his performance during the 2000 season, in which he finished second only to the dominating Pontiac of Bobby Labonte.

Another, perhaps more important, fact: Earnhardt and his teams at Dale Earnhardt, Inc. and Richard Childress Racing were the lead developers of the 2000 Monte Carlo—a solid car that seemed to be getting better. The last time a new Chevy had been introduced—in 1995—the lead development team (Hendrick Motorsports) went on a Winston Cup championship binge and catapulted Jeff Gordon to stardom.

This time, Earnhardt was the lead driver of the lead development team. Though the 2000 Monte Carlo was not nearly as successful as the 1995 version, the Chevy teams were able to use the 2000 car to stem the onslaught of the Fords and Pontiacs. In 2000, Chevy teams held their own on the circuit's down-force tracks, rather that automatically concede them as they had in 1999.

In other words, Earnhardt had the car and he had momentum. Sure, Speed Weeks seemed inauspicious. For the first time in 14 years, Earnhardt didn't win the Budweiser Shootout or a Twin 125 or the IROC race. But Daytona disappointment was never an indicator of future Earnhardt success. Perhaps the better indication of what awaited was Earnhardt's demeanor. He was more relaxed than ever. When Eddie Cheever ran him off the road in the IROC race—precipitating a spectacular save by Earnhardt—the "Intimidator" gave him a harmless shove on the cool-down lap, then laughed it off by giving a nervous Cheever a pat on the back after the race. Before the Daytona 500, a TV reporter preparing to interview Earnhardt nearly had to wake him up first, so completely was Earnhardt at ease with his situation. In those now-famous last scenes on pit road with his son, Dale Jr., and wife, Teresa, Earnhardt seemed content and ultra confident in his team's potential. He even predicted a win for Waltrip's No. 15 car. Then came the wreck. As usual, Earnhardt left NASCAR fans guessing and wishing they had more.

2001 Performance Chart

No. 3 Richard Childress Racing Chevrolet

Career Race	Season Race	Date	Race	St.	Fin.	Total Laps	Laps Completed	Laps Led	Condition	Money	Pts.	Bonus Pts.	Point Standing	Behind Leader	Points Leader
676	1	Feb 18	Daytona: Daytona 500	7	12	200	199	16	DNF - Crash	$194,111	132	5	11	-48	M. Waltrip

"Dale Earnhardt is the only driver I've ever seen who I feel was born to be a race car driver."
—*Ned Jarrett*

A week after the 2001 Daytona 500, Dale Earnhardt Jr. suffered a first-lap, race-ending crash at Rockingham. The wreck was eerily similar to Dale Sr.'s, as Junior's car fishtailed after contact from another, then shot up the banking and into the wall between Turns 3 and 4. He walked away from the crash with a limp but was not seriously hurt. Earnhardt Jr. is pictured here during driver introductions before the 2000 spring race at Rockingham. *Bill Burt*

As the most well-known driver in a booming sport, Earnhardt usually found himself surrounded by fans and well-wishers whenever he was not strapped into his car. *David Stringer*

"Earnhardt is the resurrected Confederate soldier."
—*Humpy Wheeler, President, Charlotte Motor Speedway*

The Tracks

Chapter 4

Dale Earnhardt's Career on Current and Former Winston Cup Tracks

The Winston Cup schedule includes a variety of tracks, from short tracks (less than one mile, such as Bristol), to one-mile ovals (Dover) to speedways (less than two miles, such as Darlington) to superspeedways (two miles or greater, such as Talladega) to road courses (Watkins Glen). Each track demands a different touch, a different set of skills. Over the course of a driver's career, patterns emerge that provide a glimpse into the style and skill of a driver. This section lays out in detail Earnhardt's career on each Winston Cup track.

For each track on which Earnhardt competed there is a statistical comparison to determine his place in the track's history. This comparison extends to 22 different statistical categories. Earnhardt's total for each category is listed, along with his rank and that category's leader. If Earnhardt is the leader in a category, the second-place driver is listed in parentheses with his total. For the older tracks—that is, tracks that have been part of the Winston Cup circuit for more than 30 years—the comparison is limited to the modern era (1972 to the present).

Accompanying the statistical comparison is a track summary that puts Earnhardt's career at the track in context or details memorable moments. Perhaps most useful to understanding Earnhardt's development at each track is the inclusion of a "performance chart" that lists in detail every race he started at the track. Listed for each race are the year, date, and race name, along with Earnhardt's start, finish, total laps, laps completed, laps led, race-ending condition, money, points earned and bonus points.

Track	Page
Atlanta Motor Speedway	86
Bristol Motor Speedway	88
California Speedway	90
\Darlington Raceway	92
Daytona International Speedway	94
Dover Downs International Speedway	96
Homestead-Miami Speedway	98
Indianapolis Motor Speedway	100
Las Vegas Motor Speedway	102
Lowe's Motor Speedway	104
Martinsville Speedway	106
Michigan International Speedway	108
Nashville Speedway	110
New Hampshire International Speedway	112
North Carolina Speedway	114
North Wilkesboro Speedway	116
Ontario Motor Speedway	118
Phoenix International Raceway	119
Pocono Raceway	120
Richmond International Raceway	122
Riverside International Raceway	124
Sears Point Raceway	126
Talladega SuperSpeedway	128
Texas Motor Speedway	130
Texas World Speedway	131
Watkins Glen International	132

Earnhardt and a crew member take in the scene at Rockingham. The North Carolina track has proven to be one of Earnhardt's least favorite venues. In 44 starts, he has just three wins and 12 Top 5 finishes, well off his performance at other Winston Cup tracks. *Bill Burt*

Whether a rookie or a seven-time Winston Cup champion, every driver must submit his car to NASCAR officials for pre-race inspection. Of course, anti-Earnhardt fans claimed NASCAR casted a forgiving eye on Earnhardt – during inspection and during the race. *Bill Burt*

Earnhardt avoided trouble and the spinning Morgan Shepherd (No. 46) on the backstretch at Bristol during the 1998 Food City 500. Though he later experienced handling problems and dropped to 22nd in the finishing order, Earnhardt ended the race on the track. In 43 races at the half-mile oval, he has failed to finish just twice. He is currently on a DNF-less string of 38 races at Bristol. *Bill Burt*

Earnhardt at Atlanta Motor Speedway

Dale Earnhardt's by-a-nose victory over Bobby Labonte in the 2000 Atlanta spring race was a fine encapsulation of the 1.5-mile track's history. Labonte has emerged as the new dominant driver at Atlanta, claiming four wins and eight Top 5s in nine Atlanta races between 1996 and 2000. For all of his success, however, Labonte has a long way to go to match Earnhardt's Atlanta achievements.

Earnhardt is the Hampton, Georgia track's all-time greatest performer—holding track records in wins, Top 5s, Top 10s, prize winnings and laps led. In other words, his career at Atlanta is unparalleled. Over a nine-year, 17-race stretch between 1984 and 1992, Earnhardt logged 14 Top 5 finishes and five victories. He followed up with five straight Top 4 finishes and two wins between 1994 and 1996. Those amazing runs pushed Earnhardt past legends Cale Yarborough and Buddy Baker as Atlanta's most prolific winner.

Earnhardt fell on uncharacteristic hard times after the 1996 season. Poor qualifying—Earnhardt's average starting spot at Atlanta was 28th during the 1997-1999 seasons—and inconsistent finishes marked the Goodwrench team's effort. Earnhardt's failure to finish the spring race in 1999 was his first DNF at Atlanta since 1983. In 2000, Earnhardt regained his old Atlanta form. Besides the thrilling win over Labonte in the spring, Earnhardt finished second after a wild late-race shootout in the fall event.

Memorable Atlanta Moments

1986 Atlanta Journal 500. Earnhardt led all but three of the final 138 to claim his third Atlanta victory and clinch his second Winston Cup championship. The championship was the first for the Earnhardt-Richard Childress team, which formed in 1984. They went on to win five more titles together.

1988 Motorcraft Quality Parts 500. Earnhardt set the modern era record for laps led in an Atlanta race by pacing the field for 270 laps, bettering the record held by Cale Yarborough

Most Laps Led at Atlanta
Single Race (Modern Era)

Driver	No. Laps Led	Race
Dale Earnhardt	270	1988 Motorcraft Quality Parts 500
Cale Yarborough	269	1980 Atlanta Journal 500
Dale Earnhardt	268	1995 NAPA 500
Bobby Allison	261	1978 Atlanta 500
Dale Jarrett	253	1997 Primestar 500
Jeff Gordon	250	1995 Purolator 500

Atlanta Record Book – Modern Era
(min. 5 starts)

Category	Earnhardt's Total	Earnhardt's Rank	Modern Era Track Leader*
Money Won	$1,796,825	1st	(Bobby Labonte – 1,223,855)
Career Starts	46	4th	Darrell Waltrip – 56
Total Points	6,715	1st	(Darrell Waltrip – 6,531.25)
Avg. Start	12.1	11th	David Pearson – 4.7
Avg. Finish	9.5	1st	(Cale Yarborough – 10.8)
Wins	9	1st	(Bill Elliott – 5)
Winning Pct.	19.6	2nd	Bobby Labonte – 25.0
Top 5s	26	1st	(D. Waltrip, C. Yarborough – 18)
Top 10s	30	1st	(Darrell Waltrip – 28)
DNFs	7	34th	Dave Marcis – 19
Poles	4	2nd	Buddy Baker – 5
Front Row Starts	10	1st	(Geoffrey Bodine – 7)
Laps Led	2,647	1st	(Cale Yarborough – 2,205)
Pct. Led	17.7	3rd	Cale Yarborough – 21.2
Races Led	32	1st	(Darrell Waltrip – 27)
Times Led	125	1st	(Cale Yarborough – 108)
Times Led Most Laps	9	1st	(B. Allison, B. Elliott, D. Pearson, C. Yarborough – 5)
Bonus Points	205	1st	(Cale Yarborough – 150)
Laps Completed	13,834	2nd	Darrell Waltrip – 14,818
Pct. of Laps Completed	92.7	22nd	Steve Park – 99.2
Points per Race	146.0	1st	(Bobby Labonte – 140.4)
Lead Lap Finishes	26	1st	(Bill Elliott – 13)

* 2nd-place driver or co-leader listed in parentheses if Earnhardt is track leader.

Atlanta was one of Earnhardt's best tracks. He had more wins there than any other driver. Over a nine-year, 17-race stretch between 1984 and 1992, Earnhardt logged 14 Top 5 finishes and 5 victories. *Bill Burt*

Track Performance Chart
Atlanta Motor Speedway

Hampton, Georgia, 1.5 miles, 24° banking

Year	Date	Race	St.	Fin.	Total Laps	Laps Completed	Laps Led	Condition	Money	Pts.	Bonus Pts.
1976	Nov 7	Dixie 500	16	19	328	260	0	DNF - Crash	$1,360	106	0
1978	Nov 5	Dixie 500	10	4	328	327	0	Running	7,500	160	0
1979	Mar 18	Atlanta 500	17	12	328	321	0	Running	4,835	127	0
	Nov 4	Dixie 500	7	2	328	328	69	Running	16,700	175	5
1980	Mar 16	Atlanta 500	31	1	328	328	50	Running	36,200	180	5
	Nov 2	Atlanta Journal 500	13	3	328	327	1	Running	14,700	170	5
1981	Mar 15	Coca-Cola 500	5	3	328	327	0	Running	19,400	165	0
	Nov 8	Atlanta Journal 500	9	25	328	222	0	DNF - Engine	4,290	88	0
1982	Mar 21	Coca-Cola 500	1	28	287	211	155	DNF - Engine	21,375	89	10
	Nov 7	Atlanta Journal 500	8	34	328	85	3	DNF - Crash	8,385	66	5
1983	Mar 27	Coca-Cola 500	8	33	328	246	34	DNF - Engine	8,075	69	5
	Nov 6	Atlanta Journal 500	2	33	328	49	19	DNF - Clutch	7,995	69	5
1984	Mar 18	Coca-Cola 500	9	2	328	328	26	Running	26,935	175	5
	Nov 11	Atlanta Journal 500	10	1	328	328	48	Running	40,610	180	5
1985	Mar 17	Coca-Cola 500	8	9	328	326	0	Running	12,125	138	0
	Nov 3	Atlanta Journal 500	13	4	328	328	0	Running	15,300	160	0
1986	Mar 16	Motorcraft 500	1	2	328	328	168	Running	51,300	180	10
	Nov 2	Atlanta Journal 500	4	1	328	328	162	Running	67,950	185	10
1987	Mar 15	Motorcraft Quality Parts 500	1	16	328	322	196	Running	19,520	125	10
	Nov 22	Atlanta Journal 500	2	2	328	328	133	Running	35,350	175	5
1988	Mar 20	Motorcraft Quality Parts 500	2	1	328	328	270	Running	67,950	185	10
	Nov 20	Atlanta Journal 500	2	14	328	326	49	Running	16,750	126	5
1989	Mar 19	Motorcraft Quality Parts 500	5	2	328	328	92	Running	39,675	175	5
	Nov 19	Atlanta Journal 500	3	1	328	328	249	Running	81,700	185	10
1990	Mar 18	Motorcraft Quality Parts 500	1	1	328	328	216	Running	85,000	185	10
	Nov 18	Atlanta Journal 500	6	3	328	328	42	Running	26,700	170	5
1991	Mar 18	Motorcraft Quality Parts 500	21	3	328	328	21	Running	37,000	170	5
	Nov 17	Hardee's 500	5	5	328	328	39	Running	27,825	160	5
1992	Mar 15	Motorcraft Quality Parts 500	7	3	328	328	0	Running	36,850	165	0
	Nov 15	Hooters 500	3	26	328	299	44	Running	20,670	90	5
1993	Mar 20	Motorcraft Quality Parts 500	2	11	328	325	0	Running	15,595	130	0
	Nov 14	Hooters 500	19	10	328	327	2	Running	19,300	139	5
1994	Mar 13	Purolator 500	16	12	328	325	0	Running	24,550	127	0
	Nov 13	Hooters 500	30	2	328	328	17	Running	55,950	175	5
1995	Mar 12	Purolator 500	1	4	328	328	62	Running	52,950	165	5
	Nov 12	NAPA 500	11	1	328	328	268	Running	141,850	185	10
1996	Mar 10	Purolator 500	18	1	328	328	136	Running	91,050	185	10
	Nov 10	NAPA 500	17	4	328	328	4	Running	47,400	165	5
1997	Mar 9	Primestar 500	26	8	328	328	0	Running	40,975	142	0
	Nov 16	NAPA 500	6	16	325	322	24	Running	43,075	120	5
1998	Mar 8	Primestar 500	30	13	325	324	2	Running	39,055	129	5
	Nov 8	NAPA 500	37	13	221	221	0	Running	46,025	124	0
1999	Mar 14	Cracker Barrel 500	33	40	325	151	0	DNF - Handling	41,625	43	0
	Nov 21	NAPA 500	36	9	325	325	0	Running	54,550	138	0
2000	Mar 12	Cracker Barrel 500	35	1	325	325	34	Running	123,100	180	5
	Nov 21	NAPA 500	8	2	325	325	12	Running	99,750	175	5

Earnhardt at Bristol Motor Speedway

Dale Earnhardt entered big-league stock car racing with a reputation for short-track virtuosity. Nowhere was his innate ability for claustrophobic racing better showcased than at Bristol Motor Speedway. Earnhardt took to the high-banked, .533-mile track immediately, winning his first start there. Two decades later, in his ninth Bristol win, he flashed his inner bull-ring bully once again with a last-lap tap on Terry Labonte.

Of course, short-track success requires more than a well-used bumper. Earnhardt revealed an unusually high level of skill on the Tennessee track. On no track did he lead more laps and no other short track yielded more wins in his career (see charts). Only Bristol legend Darrell Waltrip (12) claimed more wins at the track than Earnhardt's nine.

Memorable Bristol Moments

1979 Southeastern 500. Earnhardt served notice early that he would be a force on the Winston Cup circuit by winning the seventh race of his first full season and the 16th start of his career. In 1987 at Talladega, Davey Allison won his sixth start in his official rookie season, making him the only modern era driver to better Earnhardt's quick success. Earnhardt's son, Dale Jr., matched his dad's quick start in the seventh race of his rookie season (at Texas). The elder Earnhardt's first win was impressive. He led the most laps (164) and outran some of the greatest short-track racers of all time – Bobby Allison, Darrell Waltrip and Richard Petty.

1999 Goody's 500. Earnhardt stunned, then angered, a capacity crowd of 150,000 by bumping and spinning race leader Terry Labonte on the final lap of a wild Bristol night race. The incident cleared the way for Earnhardt's ninth win at Bristol and unleashed loud boos from the huge crowd. After being spun out by Darrell Waltrip with 10 laps to go, Labonte charged through the field after the restart. Labonte overtook Earnhardt on lap 499 and seemed poised to complete his amazing recovery. But Earnhardt stayed close to Labonte and, between turns 1 and 2 on the final lap, tapped Labonte's rear bumper. Quoted famously later as trying only to "rattle his cage a little," the bump turned Labonte around. Earnhardt cruised unhindered the rest of the way for the victory. Well-known for aggressive, sometimes questionable, driving, Earnhardt was neither penalized nor fined for his actions, despite the fact that a similar incident earlier in the race garnered Jerry Nadeau a black flag.

Earnhardt's crew pushes the damaged Goodwrench Chevy down pit road during the 1995 Food City 500 at Bristol. Earnhardt slammed the wall in Turn 4 after being bumped by Jeff Burton on Lap 117. Earnhardt's car was taken behind the wall for repairs. He re-entered the race 21 laps down and finished in 25th, his fourth-worst finish ever at Bristol. *Jennifer Regruth*

Most Laps Led by Dale Earnhardt
By Track

Track	Laps Led
Bristol	3,758
N. Wilkesboro	2,680
Darlington	2,648
Atlanta	2,635
Dover	2,150

Earnhardt's Short Track Victories
By Track

Track	Victories
Bristol	9
Martinsville	6
N. Wilkesboro	5
Richmond	5
Nashville	2

Bristol Record Book – The Modern Era
(min. 5 starts)

Category	Earnhardt's Total	Earnhardt's Rank	Modern Era Track Leader*
Money Won	$1,278,381	1st	(Rusty Wallace – 1,227,235)
Starts	43	5th	Darrell Waltrip – 52
Total Points	6,303	2nd	Darrell Waltrip – 7,259.75
Avg. Start	13.2	24th	Cale Yarborough – 2.5
Avg. Finish	9.3	6th	Cale Yarborough – 6.6
Wins	9	2nd	Darrell Waltrip – 12
Winning Pct.	20.9	5th	Cale Yarborough – 56.3
Top 5s	20	2nd	Darrell Waltrip – 26
Top 10s	30	3rd	Darrell Waltrip – 32
DNFs	2	78th	J.D. McDuffie – 15
Poles	2	9th	R. Wallace, Yarborough – 7
Front Row Starts	4	11th	Rusty Wallace – 12
Laps Led	3,758	2nd	Cale Yarborough – 3,872
Pct. Led	17.7	3rd	Cale Yarborough – 50.3
Races Led	30	T-1st	(Darrell Waltrip – 30)
Times Led	87	2nd	Darrell Waltrip – 94
Times Led Most Laps	9	2nd	Darrell Waltrip – 10
Bonus Points	195	2nd	Darrell Waltrip – 200
Laps Completed	20,038	3rd	Darrell Waltrip – 22,964
Pct. of Laps Completed	94.2	10th	Kevin Lepage – 98.9
Points per Race	146.6	4th	Rusty Wallace – 148.7
Fin. on Lead Lap	22	2nd	Darrell Waltrip – 24

*2nd-place driver(s) or co-leader(s) listed if Earnhardt is track leader.

Track Performance Chart

Bristol Motor Speedway

Bristol, Tennessee, .533 miles, 36° banking

Year	Date	Race	St.	Fin.	Total Laps	Laps Completed	Laps Led	Condition	Money	Pts.	Bonus Pts.
1979	Apr 1	Southeastern 500	9	1	500	500	163	Running	$19,800	185	10
	Aug 25	Volunteer 500	Did Not Start due to Injury								
1980	Mar 30	Valleydale Southeastern 500	4	1	500	500	208	Running	20,625	185	10
	Aug 23	Busch Volunteer 500	7	2	500	500	24	Running	11,450	175	5
1981	Mar 29	Valleydale 500	2	28	500	140	65	DNF – Crash	7,270	84	5
	Aug 22	Busch 500	14	27	500	31	0	DNF – Crash	2,620	82	0
1982	Mar 14	Valleydale 500	9	2	500	500	255	Running	18,480	180	10
	Aug 28	Busch 500	12	6	500	499	74	Running	9,600	155	5
1983	Mar 21	Valleydale 500	5	9	500	495	116	Running	7,930	143	5
	Aug 27	Busch 500	6	2	419	419	194	Running	15,725	175	5
1984	Apr 1	Valleydale 500	17	7	500	498	2	Running	7,530	151	5
	Aug 25	Busch 500	9	10	500	478	64	Running	7,800	139	5
1985	Apr 6	Valleydale 500	12	1	500	500	214	Running	31,525	185	10
	Aug 24	Busch 500	1	1	500	500	343	Running	34,675	185	10
1986	Apr 6	Valleydale 500	6	10	500	497	106	Running	10,650	139	5
	Aug 23	Busch 500	5	4	500	499	71	Running	12,800	165	5
1987	Apr 12	Valleydale Meats 500	3	1	500	500	134	Running	43,850	180	5
	Aug 22	Busch 500	6	1	500	500	415	Running	47,175	185	10
1988	Apr 10	Valleydale Meats 500	4	14	500	461	95	Running	12,050	126	5
	Aug 27	Busch 500	5	1	500	500	220	Running	48,500	185	10
1989	Apr 9	Valleydale Meats 500	5	16	500	492	74	Running	21,280	120	5
	Aug 26	Busch 500	7	14	500	490	145	Running	11,650	126	5
1990	Apr 8	Valleydale Meats 500	9	19	500	451	0	Running	10,990	106	0
	Aug 25	Busch 500	1	8	500	499	350	Running	30,125	152	10
1991	Apr 17	Valleydale Meats 500	2	20	500	484	0	Running	15,525	103	0
	Aug 24	Bud 500	13	7	500	498	0	Running	16,025	146	0
1992	Apr 5	Food City 500	18	18	500	471	28	Running	18,130	114	5
	Aug 29	Bud 500	23	2	500	500	0	Running	39,325	170	0
1993	Apr 4	Food City 500	6	2	500	500	15	Running	47,760	175	5
	Aug 28	Bud 500	19	3	500	500	0	Running	32,325	165	0
1994	Apr 10	Food City 500	24	1	500	500	183	Running	72,570	185	10
	Aug 27	Goody's 500	14	3	500	500	25	Running	33,265	170	5
1995	Apr 2	Food City 500	25	25	500	479	0	Running	36,360	88	0
	Aug 26	Goody's 500	7	2	500	500	91	Running	66,890	175	5
1996	Mar 31	Food City 500	19	4	342	342	0	Running	35,351	160	0
	Aug 24	Goody's 500	23	24	500	476	0	Running	32,310	91	0
1997	Apr 13	Food City 500	29	6	500	500	0	Running	32,970	150	0
	Aug 23	Goody's 500	34	14	500	497	0	Running	32,515	121	0
1998	Mar 29	Food City 500	37	22	500	496	0	Running	33,715	97	0
	Aug 22	Goody's 500	30	6	500	500	34	Running	42,540	155	5
1999	Apr 11	Food City 500	34	10	500	500	0	Running	48,630	134	0
	Aug 28	Goody's 500	26	1	500	500	46	Running	89,880	180	5
2000	Mar 26	Food City 500	11	39	500	346	2	Running	45,215	51	5
	Aug 26	Goracing.com 500	17	4	500	500	2	Running	62,980	165	5

Earnhardt at California Speedway

'Non-threatening' best described Dale Earnhardt's short-lived career at the California Speedway. In four Winston Cup races at the track, Earnhardt never made a mark in qualifying or at the finish line. In 1998, the Intimidator started 43rd, using a past-champion's provisional. He fought to a respectable ninth-place finish that year (his best finish at California), but on two other occasions, failed to finish on the lead lap—a difficult feat on a two-mile track.

In true Earnhardt fashion, however, not all was lost. Even when his car was a non-factor, Earnhardt found a way to get more from the situation than most. For instance, despite his woeful average starting position (25.3), he was eighth in the track's history in average finish. In his four California races, he finished more laps (998) than all other drivers besides Jeff Gordon and Jeremy Mayfield.

Earnhardt's difficulty at California Speedway was foretold at its sister track, Michigan Speedway. Also a flat, two-mile track, Michigan was one of Earnhardt's least successful tracks. In 43 Michigan starts, Earnhardt had just two wins, no poles and a relatively modest 12 Top 5s. Considering the similarities between the two tracks, Earnhardt's less-than-intimidating performance at California becomes less mysterious.

Nascar fans know what and who they like. Beause of Earnhardt's aggressive, driving style and many victories, almost every fan has some feelings about him, whether good or bad. Some, like this Bill Elliott fan, derisively labeled Earnhardt the 'Instigator.' *David Stringer*

California Record Book – All-Time
(min. 2 starts)

Category	Earnhardt's Total	Earnhardt's Rank	All-Time Track Leader*
Money Won	$210,275	10th	Jeff Gordon – 463,765
Starts	4	T-1st	26 others with 4 starts
Total Points	497	9th	Jeff Gordon – 665
Avg. Start	25.3	29th	Mark Martin – 5.8
Avg. Finish	13.5	8th	Jeff Gordon – 4.3
Wins	0	—	Jeff Gordon – 2
Winning Pct.	0.0	—	Jeff Gordon – 50.0
Top 5s	0	—	Jeff Gordon – 3
Top 10s	1	12th	6 tied with 3 Top 10s
DNFs	0	—	G. Bodine, Martin, Spencer – 2
Poles	0	—	4 tied with 1 pole
Front Row Starts	0	—	8 tied with 1 F.R. Start
Laps Led	2	23rd	Jeff Gordon – 287
Pct. Led	0.2	23rd	Jeff Gordon – 28.7
Races Led	1	13th	Mark Martin – 4
Times Led	1	19th	Jeff Gordon – 18
Times Led Most Laps	0	—	Jeff Gordon – 2
Bonus Points	5	14th	Gordon, Martin – 25
Laps Completed	998	3rd	Jeff Gordon – 1,000
Pct. of Laps Completed	99.8	4th	Gordon, Stewart – 100.0
Points per Race	124.3	10th	Jeff Gordon – 166.3
Fin. on Lead Lap	2	9th	Jeff Gordon – 4

*2nd-place driver listed in parentheses if Earnhardt is track leader.

Track Performance Chart
California Speedway
Fontana, California, 2.0 miles, 14° banking

Year	Date	Race	St.	Fin.	Total Laps	Laps Completed	Laps Led	Condition	Money	Pts.	Bonus Pts.
1997	Jun 22	California 500	14	16	250	249	0	Running	$41,975	115	0
1998	May 3	California 500	43	9	250	250	0	Running	53,800	138	0
1999	May 2	California 500	9	12	250	249	2	Running	55,425	132	5
2000	Apr 30	NAPA Auto Parts 500	35	17	250	250	0	Running	59,075	112	0

In under 17 seconds, the GM Goodwrench crew could change four tires, adds 22 gallons of gasoline and makes precise chassis adjustments to Earnhardt's No. 3 Chevy, *Bill Burt*

Earnhardt at Darlington Raceway

A major contributor to Dale Earnhardt's legend within NASCAR circles was his performance on the Winston Cup series' oldest—and toughest—tracks. Darlington Raceway was a prime example of his ability to conquer the traditional tracks in ways few other drivers can match.

Beginning with his win in the 1982 spring race, Earnhardt amassed nine wins on the oddly configured 1.336-mile track. Only David Pearson had a greater number of Darlington wins (one of which came while driving for the injured Earnhardt in 1979). Earnhardt's ability to lead races at Darlington was also unparalleled. In the modern era, he led nearly 1,000 more laps than the next best driver.

The height of Earnhardt's mastery at Darlington occurred during a 10-race stretch between 1986 and 1990. During those years, no other driver or team could match Earnhardt and his No. 3 crew. He won six races, including three Southern 500s and led 1,201 laps (Geoffrey Bodine was next best with 474 laps led).

Memorable Darlington Moments

1986 TranSouth 500. Earnhardt drove away from the field and led 335 of 367 laps, easily shattering Darlington's modern era record for most laps led in a single race. Earnhardt bettered the previous mark by 58 laps. Earnhardt started fourth, assumed the lead on the sixth lap and never looked back.

Earnhardt Victories on NASCAR's Oldest Tracks

Track	Wins	All-Time Track Rank
Talladega	10	1st
Atlanta	9	1st
Darlington	9	2nd
Bristol	9	2nd
Martinsville	6	3rd
North Wilkesboro	5	3rd
Charlotte	5	3rd
Richmond	5	6th
Rockingham	3	8th
Daytona	3	10th
Michigan	2	11th

Most Laps Led at Darlington Single Race (Modern Era)

Driver	Laps Led	Race
Dale Earnhardt	335 of 367	1986 TranSouth 500
Harry Gant	277 of 367	1984 Southern 500
Cale Yarborough	277 of 367	1973 Southern 500
Jeff Burton	273 of 367	1998 Southern 500
Darrell Waltrip	251 of 367	1984 TranSouth 500

Darlington Record Book – The Modern Era

(min. 5 starts)

Category	Earnhardt's Total	Earnhardt's Rank	Modern Era Track Leader*
Money Won	$1,597,990	1st	(Bill Elliott – 1,076,840)
Starts	44	6th	Darrell Waltrip – 55
Total Points	6,109	3rd	Bill Elliott – 6,532
Avg. Start	12.4	18th	David Pearson – 4.8
Avg. Finish	11.4	4th	Bill Elliott – 8.9
Wins	9	1st	(David Pearson – 8)
Winning Pct.	20.5	3rd	Jeff Gordon – 31.3
Top 5s	19	T-1st	(Bill Elliott – 19)
Top 10s	24	2nd	Bill Elliott – 30
DNFs	6	45th	B. Baker, R. Petty – 19
Poles	1	17th	David Pearson – 10
Front Row Starts	5	6th	David Pearson – 14
Laps Led	2,648	1st	(Darrell Waltrip – 1,723)
Pct. Led	17.7	1st	(David Pearson – 17.5)
Races Led	27	2nd	Darrell Waltrip – 32
Times Led	116	1st	(Darrell Waltrip – 114)
Times Led Most Laps	10	1st	(David Pearson – 7)
Bonus Points	185	2nd	Darrell Waltrip – 190
Laps Completed	14,011	5th	Darrell Waltrip – 16,395
Pct. of Laps Completed	93.8	11th	Jeff Burton – 98.1
Points per Race	138.8	6th	Jeff Burton – 147.5
Fin. on Lead Lap	18	2nd	Bill Elliott – 19

*2nd-place driver or co-leader listed in parentheses if Earnhardt is track leader.

Track Performance Chart

Darlington Raceway

Darlington, South, Carolina, 1.336 miles, 23-25° banking

Year	Date	Race	St.	Fin.	Total Laps	Laps Completed	Laps Led	Condition	Money	Pts.	Bonus Pts.
1978	Sep 4	Southern 500	14	16	367	313	0	Running	$3,100	115	0
1979	Apr 8	CRC Chemicals Rebel 500	13	23	367	300	4	Running	5,600	99	5
	Sep 3	Southern 500	Did Not Start due to Injury								
1980	Apr 13	CRC Chemicals Rebel 500	5	29	189	104	15	DNF - Engine	6,640	81	5
	Sep 1	Southern 500	8	7	367	366	27	Running	11,125	151	5
1981	Apr 12	CRC Chemicals Rebel 500	5	17	367	346	0	Running	9,150	112	0
	Sep 7	Southern 500	10	6	367	366	0	Running	10,695	150	0
1982	Apr 4	CRC Chemicals Rebel 500	5	1	367	367	181	Running	31,450	185	10
	Sep 6	Southern 500	5	3	367	367	36	Running	21,225	170	5
1983	Apr 10	TranSouth 500	17	13	367	348	2	DNF - Engine	7,890	129	5
	Sep 5	Southern 500	17	11	367	363	0	Running	11,855	130	0
1984	Apr 15	TranSouth 500	14	5	367	366	24	Running	12,825	160	5
	Sep 2	Southern 500	20	38	367	57	0	DNF - Engine	7,860	49	0
1985	Apr 14	TranSouth 500	8	24	367	293	130	DNF - Engine	9,180	96	5
	Sep 1	Southern 500	5	19	367	349	147	DNF - Engine	12,835	116	10
1986	Apr 13	TranSouth 500	4	1	367	367	335	Running	52,250	185	10
	Aug 31	Southern 500	21	9	367	366	17	Running	15,735	143	5
1987	Mar 29	TranSouth 500	2	1	367	367	239	Running	52,985	185	10
	Sep 6	Southern 500	5	1	202	202	109	Running	64,650	185	10
1988	May 27	TranSouth 500	2	11	367	363	0	Running	14,825	130	0
	Sep 4	Southern 500	2	3	367	367	85	Running	31,375	170	5
1989	Apr 2	TranSouth 500	11	33	367	290	35	Running	10,655	69	5
	Sep 3	Heinz Southern 500	10	1	367	367	153	Running	71,150	185	10
1990	Apr 1	TranSouth 500	15	1	367	367	129	Running	61,985	180	5
	Sep 2	Heinz Southern 500	1	1	367	367	99	Running	210,350	185	10
1991	Apr 7	TranSouth 500	7	29	367	332	0	DNF - Cylinder	14,310	76	0
	Sep 1	Heinz Southern 500	3	8	367	365	22	Running	20,470	147	5
1992	Mar 29	TranSouth 500	8	10	367	365	0	Running	20,570	134	0
	Sep 6	Mountain Dew Southern 500	13	29	298	241	0	Running	16,555	76	0
1993	Mar 28	TranSouth 500	1	1	367	367	212	Running	64,815	185	10
	Sep 5	Mountain Dew Southern 500	6	4	351	351	101	Running	31,090	165	5
1994	Mar 27	TranSouth 500	9	1	293	293	166	Running	70,190	185	10
	Sep 4	Southern 500	27	2	367	367	87	Running	45,030	175	5
1995	Mar 26	TranSouth 500	23	2	293	293	37	Running	54,355	175	5
	Sep 3	Southern 500	3	2	367	367	208	Running	62,155	180	10
1996	Mar 24	TranSouth 500	27	14	293	292	1	Running	28,080	126	5
	Sep 1	Southern 500	12	12	367	365	0	Running	30,545	127	0
1997	Mar 23	TranSouth Financial 400	43	15	293	292	0	Running	28,625	118	0
	Aug 31	Mountain Dew Southern 500	36	30	367	282	0	Running	30,925	73	0
1998	Mar 22	TranSouth Financial 400	27	12	293	292	0	Running	37,595	127	0
	Sep 6	Southern 500	18	4	367	367	0	Running	64,465	160	0
1999	Mar 21	TranSouth Financial 400	30	25	164	163	0	Running	37,020	88	0
	Sep 5	Pepsi Southern 500	25	22	270	268	0	Running	42,470	97	0
2000	Mar 19	Mall.com 400	4	3	293	293	0	Running	68,590	165	0
	Sep 3	Southern 500	6	3	328	328	47	Running	82,745	170	5

Earnhardt at Daytona International Speedway

Dale Earnhardt's "difficulties" at Daytona were always too delicious to ignore. The inability of the greatest driver in NASCAR history to win a points race on NASCAR's greatest track invited the sort of fascination, debate and psychoanalysis once reserved for picking a college football champion. That he lost his life at Daytona will forever fuel his legend and the track's mystique.

Earnhardt needed 25 tries to get his first Daytona win (in the 1990 Pepsi 400), the most races he ever needed before claiming a Winston Cup points victory on any track. Considering he won his first attempt at Bristol, a track thought to be too tough for rookies, Earnhardt's struggle to win at Daytona was all the more amazing.

In truth, however, Earnhardt never had trouble winning at Daytona. His career at the 2.5-mile track is unmatched. Counting non-points races and his competition in other series, he had a bewildering 34 Daytona wins. Within the Winston Cup series, since its schedule stabilized in 1972, no driver was ever better at Daytona than Earnhardt. Whether the conversation turns to top finishes, laps led, money won, points earned, number of times he led the most laps in a race, lead-lap finishes and so on, the seven-time champ's name can be found at the top of the list.

Still, Earnhardt was more relieved than anyone by his 1998 Daytona 500 win. The second-most famous scene from that triumph (bettered only by the stirring scene on pit road when every other team formed a line to congratulate Earnhardt) was Earnhardt playing up the hype and removing a stuffed monkey from his back. Earnhardt indicated with his act that the pressure was not just a media concoction, but was also self-inflicted. He needed a Daytona 500 win to answer his own questions, not just those from reporters and commentators.

In NASCAR's restrictor plate races, Earnhardt revealed an innate ability to use the draft. In 53 "plate races," he won 11 times and led 2,134 laps, nearly three times the total of the next best driver (Sterling Marlin). *David Stringer*

Daytona Record Book – The Modern Era
(min. 5 starts)

Category	Earnhardt's Total	Earnhardt's Rank	Modern Era Track Leader*
Money Won	$4,498,565	1st	(Dale Jarrett – 4,215,895)
Starts	46	5th	Marcis, D. Waltrip – 55
Total Points	6,507	1st	(Darrell Waltrip – 6,145.75)
Avg. Start	9.4	6th	Bobby Isaac – 4.2
Avg. Finish	10.7	1st	(Jody Ridley – 13.2)
Wins	3	8th	Richard Petty – 7
Winning Pct.	6.5	14th	Jeff Gordon – 23.5
Top 5s	22	1st	(Richard Petty – 16)
Top 10s	34	1st	(B. Elliott, T. Labonte – 24)
DNFs	9	24th	A.J. Foyt – 23
Poles	3	4th	Cale Yarborough – 8
Front Row Starts	8	3rd	Cale Yarborough – 13
Laps Led	1,285	1st	(Buddy Baker – 862)
Pct. Led	15.6	1st	(Bobby Allison – 13.5)
Races Led	36	1st	(Richard Petty – 26)
Times Led	172	1st	(Bobby Allison – 150)
Times Led Most Laps	7	1st	(Bobby Allison – 6)
Bonus Points	215	1st	(B. Allison, Yarborough – 150)
Laps Completed	7,485	5th	Darrell Waltrip – 8,482
Pct. of Laps Completed	90.9	21st	Johnny Benson – 99.4
Points per Race	141.4	1st	(Jeff Gordon – 133.5)
Fin. on Lead Lap	28	1st	(B. Elliott, K. Schrader – 24)

* 2nd-place driver or co-leader listed in parentheses if Earnhardt is track leader.

Most Races Before First Victory

Track	No. Races
Daytona	25
Dover	21
Riverside*	20
Rockingham	17
Michigan	16
North Wilkesboro	15
Pocono	15
Watkins Glen*	15

* Never won at Riverside before track was closed; Never won at Watkins Glen

Earnhardt's Daytona Victories

Event/Series	No. of Wins
Daytona 500	1
Pepsi 400	2
Twin 125s	12
Bud Shootout	6
IROC	6
Busch Series	7
Total Wins	**34**

Track Performance Chart

Daytona International Speedway

Daytona Beach, Florida, 2.5 miles, 31° banking

Year	Date	Race	St.	Fin.	Total Laps	Laps Completed	Laps Led	Condition	Money	Pts.	Bonus Pts.
1978	Jul 4	Firecracker 400	28	7	160	157	0	Running	$3,990	146	0
1979	Feb 18	Daytona 500	10	8	200	199	10	Running	22,845	147	5
	Jul 4	Firecracker 400	21	3	160	160	1	Running	14,980	170	5
1980	Feb 17	Daytona 500	32	4	200	199	10	Running	36,350	165	5
	Jul 4	Firecracker 400	7	3	160	160	44	Running	16,580	170	5
1981	Feb 15	Daytona 500	7	5	200	200	4	Running	37,365	160	5
	Jul 4	Firecracker 400	3	35	160	71	1	DNF - Vibration	8,360	63	5
1982	Feb 14	Daytona 500	10	36	200	44	6	DNF - Engine	14,700	60	5
	Jul 4	Firecracker 400	13	29	160	89	0	DNF - Engine	9,265	76	5
1983	Feb 20	Daytona 500	3	35	200	63	2	DNF - Engine	37,011	63	5
	Jul 4	Firecracker 400	7	9	160	158	19	Running	11,900	143	5
1984	Feb 19	Daytona 500	29	2	200	200	19	Running	81,825	175	5
	Jul 4	Pepsi Firecracker 400	2	8	160	159	5	Running	13,600	147	5
1985	Feb 17	Daytona 500	18	32	200	84	0	DNF - Engine	17,150	67	0
	Jul 4	Pepsi Firecracker 400	18	9	160	159	0	Running	13,400	138	0
1986	Feb 16	Daytona 500	4	14	200	197	34	DNF - Engine	61,655	126	5
	Jul 4	Firecracker 400	5	27	160	151	69	DNF - Crash	14,895	92	10
1987	Feb 15	Daytona 500	13	5	200	200	16	Running	64,925	160	5
	Jul 4	Pepsi Firecracker 400	13	6	160	160	22	Running	22,160	155	5
1988	Feb 14	Daytona 500	6	10	200	200	2	Running	52,540	139	5
	Jul 2	Pepsi Firecracker 400	20	4	160	160	53	Running	22,825	170	10
1989	Feb 19	Daytona 500	8	3	200	200	3	Running	95,550	170	5
	Jul 1	Pepsi 400	13	18	160	158	33	Running	13,180	114	5
1990	Feb 18	Daytona 500	2	5	200	200	155	Running	109,325	165	10
	Jul 7	Pepsi 400	3	1	160	160	127	Running	72,850	185	10
1991	Feb 17	Daytona 500 by STP	4	5	200	200	46	Running	113,850	160	5
	Jul 6	Pepsi 400	12	7	160	160	8	Running	23,200	151	5
1992	Feb 16	Daytona 500 by STP	3	9	200	199	0	Running	87,000	138	0
	Jul 4	Pepsi 400	22	40	160	7	0	DNF - Engine	16,355	43	0
1993	Feb 14	Daytona 500 by STP	4	2	200	200	107	Running	181,825	180	10
	Jul 3	Pepsi 400	5	1	160	160	110	Running	75,940	185	10
1994	Feb 20	Daytona 500	2	7	200	200	45	Running	110,340	151	5
	Jul 2	Pepsi 400	1	3	160	160	31	Running	50,050	170	5
1995	Feb 19	Daytona 500	2	2	200	200	23	Running	269,750	175	5
	Jul 1	Pepsi 400	1	3	160	160	11	Running	66,200	170	5
1996	Feb 18	Daytona 500	1	2	200	200	32	Running	215,065	175	5
	Jul 6	Pepsi 400	7	4	117	117	0	Running	97,960	160	0
1997	Feb 16	Daytona 500	4	31	200	195	48	Running	72,545	75	5
	Jul 5	Pepsi 400	2	4	160	160	7	Running	52,475	165	5
1998	Feb 15	Daytona 500	4	1	200	200	107	Running	1,059,105	185	10
	Oct 17	Pepsi 400	5	10	160	160	41	Running	57,375	139	5
1999	Feb 14	Daytona 500	4	2	200	200	0	Running	613,659	170	0
	Jul 3	Pepsi 400	10	2	160	160	18	Running	92,175	175	5
2000	Feb 20	Daytona 500	21	21	200	200	0	Running	116,075	100	0
	Jul 1	Pepsi 400	18	8	160	160	0	Running	64,375	142	0
2001	Feb 18	Daytona 500	7	12	200	199	16	DNF - Crash	194,111	132	5

Earnhardt at Dover Downs International Speedway

Dale Earnhardt had a checkered past at Dover Downs International Speedway—though not as checkered as he would have liked it. In 44 starts, he took the checkered flag three times and had 19 Top 5 finishes. On the downside, he finished outside of the Top 10 19 times.

For one season, however, Earnhardt truly conquered Dover. In 1989, while winning both races at the 1-mile track, he led an incredible 831 of 1,000 laps, a shattering performance unequalled before or since (see chart). In fact, Earnhardt record is literally unbreakable: today's Dover races have been shortened to 400 laps each (from their former 500). The maximum number of laps a driver can now lead in a season at the track is 800.

To reach 831 laps led, Earnhardt set the track record for laps led in a single race (456) while winning the Budweiser 500. Three months later, he led another 375 laps en route to victory in the Peak Performance 500. The totality of Earnhardt's 1989 performance at Dover is historic: His effort is the third best single-season performance at a single track in the modern era.

Most Laps Led at Dover in a Season

Driver	Laps Led	Year
Dale Earnhardt	831	1989
Richard Petty	701	1974
David Pearson	661	1973
Bill Elliott	595	1988
Neil Bonnett	589	1981

Most Laps Led at a Track in a Season Modern Era

Driver	Laps Led	Track	Year
Bobby Allison	903	Bristol	1972
David Pearson	887	Rockingham	1973
Dale Earnhardt	831	Dover	1989
Cale Yarborough	831	Nashville	1978
Darrell Waltrip	819	Nashville	1982

Dover Record Book – The Modern Era
(min. 5 starts)

Category	Earnhardt's Total	Earnhardt's Rank	Modern Era Track Leader*
Money Won	$1,273,660	1st	(Mark Martin – 1,195,835)
Starts	44	4th	Marcis, D. Waltrip – 53
Total Points	5,953	2nd	Darrell Waltrip – 6,349
Avg. Start	16.4	38th	David Pearson – 2.6
Avg. Finish	12.1	8th	David Pearson – 7.2
Wins	3	7th	Bobby Allison – 6
Winning Pct.	6.8	15th	David Pearson – 35.7
Top 5s	19	1st	(Bobby Allison – 15)
Top 10s	25	1st	(Ricky Rudd – 24)
DNFs	7	30th	J.D. McDuffie – 25
Poles	1	16th	David Pearson – 5
Front Row Starts	4	10th	M. Martin, D. Pearson – 8
Laps Led	2,150	2nd	Bobby Allison – 2,162
Pct. Led	10.1	8th	David Pearson – 28.8
Races Led	26	1st	(B. Allison, M. Martin – 20)
Times Led	81	1st	(Bobby Allison – 74)
Times Led Most Laps	4	6th	Cale Yarborough – 6
Bonus Points	150	1st	(Bobby Allison – 125)
Laps Completed	19,211	4th	Darrell Waltrip – 22,539
Pct. of Laps Completed	90.2	13th	Steve Park – 99.5
Points per Race	135.3	8th	Bobby Allison – 157.0
Fin. on Lead Lap	12	2nd	Mark Martin – 13

*2nd-place driver or co-leader listed in parentheses if Earnhardt is track leader.

Track Performance Chart

Dover Downs International Speedway

Dover, Delaware, 1.0 miles, 24° banking

Year	Date	Race	St.	Fin.	Total Laps	Laps Completed	Laps Led	Condition	Money	Pts.	Bonus Pts.
1979	May 20	Mason-Dixon 500	6	5	500	497	0	Running	$7,750	155	0
	Sep 16	CRC Chemicals 500	1	9	500	495	46	Running	7,000	143	5
1980	May 18	Mason-Dixon 500	16	10	500	475	0	DNF - Engine	7,675	134	0
	Sep 14	CRC Chemicals 500	9	34	500	151	1	DNF - Engine	6,210	66	5
1981	May 17	Mason-Dixon 500	14	3	500	499	0	Running	15,125	165	0
	Sep 20	CRC Chemicals 500	22	15	500	490	0	Running	5,275	118	0
1982	May 16	Mason-Dixon 500	10	3	500	497	11	Running	15,700	170	5
	Sep 19	CRC Chemicals 500	16	20	500	402	101	DNF - Battery	8,825	108	5
1983	May 15	Mason-Dixon 500	17	8	500	491	28	Running	10,500	147	5
	Sep 18	Budweiser 500	3	35	500	90	59	DNF - Gasket	7,890	63	5
1984	May 20	Budweiser 500	11	5	500	499	0	Running	11,600	155	0
	Sep 16	Delaware 500	2	5	500	497	35	Running	11,710	160	5
1985	May 19	Budweiser 500	9	25	500	219	0	DNF - Engine	9,050	88	0
	Sep 15	Delaware 500	8	7	500	496	0	Running	12,600	146	0
1986	May 18	Budweiser 500	2	3	500	499	57	Running	24,900	170	5
	Sep 14	Delaware 500	3	21	500	432	3	Running	10,750	105	5
1987	May 31	Budweiser 500	10	4	500	498	15	Running	20,775	165	5
	Sep 20	Delaware 500	22	31	500	304	18	DNF - Engine	12,700	75	5
1988	Jun 5	Budweiser 500	9	16	500	495	0	Running	13,450	115	0
	Sep 18	Delaware 500	12	2	500	500	50	Running	37,450	175	5
1989	Jun 4	Budweiser 500	2	1	500	500	456	Running	59,350	185	10
	Sep 17	Peak Performance 500	15	1	500	500	375	Running	59,950	185	10
1990	Jun 3	Budweiser 500	4	31	500	159	0	DNF - Engine	12,600	70	0
	Sep 16	Peak Antifreeze 500	3	3	500	500	102	Running	29,375	170	5
1991	Jun 2	Budweiser 500	10	2	500	500	187	Running	44,275	180	10
	Sep 15	Peak Antifreeze 500	12	15	500	447	21	Running	16,700	123	5
1992	May 31	Budweiser 500	24	2	500	500	52	Running	43,720	175	5
	Sep 20	Peak Antifreeze 500	5	21	500	470	82	Running	17,880	105	5
1993	Jun 6	Budweiser 500	8	1	500	500	226	Running	68,030	185	10
	Sep 19	SplitFire Spark Plug 500	9	27	500	404	0	Running	14,555	82	0
1994	Jun 5	Bud 500	14	28	500	425	0	Running	22,065	79	0
	Sep 18	SplitFire 500	37	2	500	500	62	Running	47,980	175	5
1995	Jun 4	Miller 500	23	5	500	500	10	Running	45,545	160	5
	Sep 17	MBNA 500	28	5	500	500	0	Running	40,970	155	0
1996	Jun 2	Miller 500	14	3	500	500	89	Running	60,080	170	5
	Sep 16	MBNA 500	20	16	500	498	11	Running	31,515	120	5
1997	Jun 1	Miller 500	43	16	500	497	0	Running	33,265	115	0
	Sep 21	MBNA 400	33	2	400	400	4	Running	63,105	175	5
1998	May 31	MBNA Platinum 400	34	25	400	395	0	Running	33,205	88	0
	Sep 20	MBNA Gold 400	43	23	400	396	0	Running	32,140	94	0
1999	Jun 6	MBNA Platinum 400	34	11	400	398	0	Running	49,510	130	0
	Sep 26	MBNA Gold 400	37	8	400	399	0	Running	52,065	142	0
2000	Jun 4	MBNA Platinum 400	30	6	400	399	49	Running	75,455	155	5
	Sep 24	MBNA.com 400	37	17	400	398	0	Running	63,390	112	0

Earnhardt at Homestead-Miami Speedway

As a father, Dale Earnhardt likely grew quite fond of the Homestead-Miami Speedway; as a driver, the memories were not quite as pleasant. In 2000, first-time Winston Cup champion Bobby Labonte extinguished any lingering hopes Earnhardt entertained of winning a record eighth championship. Earnhardt fought valiantly in 2000, a season marked by a Chevy slump. He held a Top 5 spot in the championship points standings nearly all season and was second behind Labonte for much of it. Realistically, he lost the championship at Rockingham two week before the Homestead race when a suddenly ill-handling car prevented him from taking advantage of Labonte's misfortune (Labonte was pinned a lap down by an ill-timed yellow flag late in the race).

Labonte didn't formally clinch the title until Homestead however, pulling ahead by an insurmountable 280 points following a solid fourth-place finish. Earnhardt, strong early after starting 37th, eventually faded to 20th place.

Earnhardt's early strength was a reminder of his solid, if non-contending, run in the inaugural Homestead race in 1999 when he had the second-best Chevy in a decidedly Ford-Pontiac show and finished in eighth place.

While those personal recollections never inspired warm thoughts while he was hunting on chilly fall mornings, Earnhardt could turn to the happy Homestead memories of celebrating his son's two Busch series titles at the Florida track in 1998 and 1999.

"It's like the Celtics and the Lakers with no referees . . . He has one of the best cars, the best crew and tremendous natural ability. If I had all that going for me, I'd be showing everybody how good I was, not how bad."
—**Darrell Waltrip, three-time Winston Cup champion**

Homestead Record Book – All-Time

Category	Earnhardt's Total	Earnhardt's Rank	All-Time Track Leader*
Money Won	$126,275	11th	Tony Stewart – 569,590
Career Starts	2	T-1st	34 others with 2 Starts
Total Points	245	11th	Tony Stewart – 365
Avg. Start	30.0	28th	Bobby Labonte – 3.0
Avg. Finish	14.0	11th	Tony Stewart – 1.0
Wins	0	—	Tony Stewart – 2
Winning Pct.	0.0	—	Tony Stewart – 100.0
Top 5s	0	—	B. Labonte, M. Martin, T. Stewart – 2
Top 10s	1	5th	J. Gordon, B. Labonte, M. Martin, T. Stewart – 2
DNFs	0	—	Darrell Waltrip – 2
Poles	0	—	D. Green, S. Park – 1
Front Row Starts	0	—	J. Andretti, D. Green, S. Park, R. Rudd – 1
Laps Led	0	—	Tony Stewart – 210
Pct. Led	0.0	—	Tony Stewart – 39.3
Races Led	0	—	B. Labonte, T. Stewart – 2
Times Led	0	—	Tony Stewart – 8
Times Led Most Laps	0	—	B. Labonte, T. Stewart – 1
Bonus Points	0	—	B. Labonte, T. Stewart – 15
Laps Completed	530	12th	B. Labonte, M. Martin, T. Stewart – 534
Pct. of Laps Completed	99.3	12th	B. Labonte, M. Martin, K. Petty, T. Stewart – 100.0
Points per Race	122.5	11th	Tony Stewart – 182.5
Lead Lap Finishes	0	—	B. Labonte, M. Martin, T. Stewart – 2

*2nd-place driver or co-leader listed in parentheses if Earnhardt is track leader.

Track Performance Chart

Homestead Motorsports Complex

Homestead, Florida, 1.5 miles, 8° banking

Year	Date	Race	St.	Fin.	Total Laps	Laps Completed	Laps Led	Condition	Money	Pts.	Bonus Pts.
1999	Nov 14	Jiffy Lube Miami 400	23	8	267	266	0	Running	$65,575	142	0
2000	Nov 12	Pennzoil 400	37	20	267	264	0	Running	60,700	103	0

Overshadowed by the talent of their driver and questioned often about their generally poor qualifying efforts, the behind-the-scenes GM Goodwrench crew was a frequently forgotten, but essential, part of Earnhardt's tremendous success. *Bill Burt*

Earnhardt at Indianapolis Motor Speedway

Perhaps the only story that could have been more moving than Jeff Gordon's victory in the inaugural Brickyard 400 at historic Indianapolis Motor Speedway would have been a win by Dale Earnhardt. The story line—NASCAR's greatest driver wins the first stock car race at the world's most famous race track—would have fit the event's magnitude. It didn't happen, thanks to a first-lap brush with the turn-4 wall. Forced to pit early, Earnhardt played catch-up all day before settling for fifth place in the inaugural Indy race.

Instead, Earnhardt waited a year to claim a victory at the hallowed 2.5-mile track. If Gordon's victory instantly certified the Brickyard 400 as a race worthy of the NASCAR world's attention, Earnhardt's win cemented Indianapolis as a NASCAR track.

While Earnhardt was rarely a threat to win at Indy, he was one of the track's most consistent drivers, scoring five Top 10s in seven starts (second only to Rusty Wallace during the same stretch). Earnhardt also revealed that he valued his time at Indianapolis, completing all but two of the 1,120 competitive laps staged at the track during his seven starts.

Indianapolis Record Book – All-Time
(min. 3 starts)

Category	Earnhardt's Total	Earnhardt's Rank	All-Time Track Leader*
Money Won	$1,296,305	4th	Jeff Gordon – 2,276,076
Starts	7	T-1st	20 others with 7 starts
Total Points	975	6th	Bobby Labonte – 1,039
Avg. Start	12.3	7th	Jeff Gordon – 8.9
Avg. Finish	10.4	7th	Bobby Labonte – 8.1
Wins	1	3rd	J. Gordon, D. Jarrett – 2
Winning Pct.	14.3	3rd	J. Gordon, D. Jarrett – 28.6
Top 5s	3	5th	4 tied with 4 Top 5s
Top 10s	5	2nd	Rusty Wallace – 6
DNFs	0	—	C. Little, D. Marcis – 6
Poles	0	—	Jeff Gordon – 3
Front Row Starts	1	4th	Jeff Gordon – 3
Laps Led	37	7th	Jeff Gordon – 277
Pct. Led	3.3	7th	Jeff Gordon – 24.7
Races Led	4	2nd	Jeff Gordon – 6
Times Led	4	9th	Jeff Gordon – 21
Times Led Most Laps	0	—	Jeff Gordon – 2
Bonus Points	20	4th	Jeff Gordon – 40
Laps Completed	1,118	2nd	Elliott, B.Labonte, Schrader – 1,119
Pct. of Laps Completed	99.8	6th	M.Shepherd, Skinner – 100.0
Points per Race	139.3	7th	Bobby Labonte – 148.4
Fin. on Lead Lap	6	T-1st	5 others with 6 Lead Lap Fin.

*2nd-place driver or co-leader listed in parentheses if Earnhardt is track leader.

Indianapolis Motor Speedway

Indianapolis, Indiana, 2.5 miles, 9-12° banking

Year	Date	Race	St.	Fin.	Total Laps	Laps Completed	Laps Led	Condition	Money	Pts.	Bonus Pts.
1994	Aug 6	Brickyard 400	2	5	160	160	2	Running	$121,625	160	5
1995	Aug 5	Brickyard 400	13	1	160	160	28	Running	565,600	180	5
1996	Aug 3	Brickyard 400	12	15	160	160	1	Running	84,460	123	5
1997	Aug 3	Brickyard 400	5	29	160	158	0	Running	76,310	76	0
1998	Aug 1	Brickyard 400	28	5	160	160	6	Running	169,275	160	5
1999	Aug 7	Brickyard 400	18	10	160	160	0	Running	135,525	134	0
2000	Aug 5	Brickyard 400	8	8	160	160	0	Running	143,510	142	0

Earnhardt rolls down pit road following his qualifying run for the 1994 Brickyard 400. He ran a lap of 171.726 mph and held the pole for approximately two minutes before Rick Mast, the next qualifier, ran his pole-winning lap of 172.414 mph. Earnhardt started the race in the second position. *David Stringer*

Earnhardt at Las Vegas Motor Speedway

At Las Vegas Motor Speedway, which joined the Winston Cup circuit in 1998, Dale Earnhardt's performance at the desert track was vintage No. 3. Like other non-Ford drivers, Earnhardt struggled with the track's downforce requirements. The aerodynamic disadvantage never prevented solid performance from the Intimidator, however. Simply put, Earnhardt fashioned something from nothing in Vegas.

Qualifying at Las Vegas was disastrous for Earnhardt and his GM Goodwrench crew. In the track's first three Winston Cup races, Earnhardt was 38th in average start—finding himself taking the green flag, on average, in the 32nd starting position. Considering his poor qualifying and the everpresent danger of being lapped during the wide, smooth track's long green-flag runs, Earnhardt's ability to finish well at Las Vegas was awe-inspiring. Earnhardt was one of just four drivers to finish each of the track's first three races in the Top 10. His average finish of 7.7 was third best in that period, trailing only Jeff Burton and Mark Martin, the flagship teams of Vegas-dominating Roush Racing.

Dale Earnhardt Jr. conducts a press conference following the final race of 1999 in Atlanta, one of five Winston Cup races he participated in that season. Dale Jr. was one of the many highlights of the 2000 season when he won at Texas in just the seventh start of his first full season on the circuit. His father also won the seventh race of his first full Winston Cup season (at Bristol). Only Davey Allison won earlier, taking the sixth race he started during his 1987 rookie campaign. *David Stringer*

Las Vegas Record Book – All-Time
(min. 2 starts)

Category	Earnhardt's Total	Earnhardt's Rank	All-Time Track Leader*
Money Won	$270,750	8th	Jeff Burton – 898,365
Starts	3	T-1st	28 others with 3 starts
Total Points	435	3rd	Jeff Burton – 545
Avg. Start	32.3	38th	D. Jarrett, B. Labonte – 5.3
Avg. Finish	7.7	3rd	Jeff Burton – 1.3
Wins	0	—	Jeff Burton – 2
Winning Pct.	0.0	—	Jeff Burton – 66.7
Top 5s	0	—	Jeff Burton – 3
Top 10s	3	T-1st	(J. Burton, M. Martin – 3)
DNFs	0	—	Kenny Wallace – 2
Poles	0	—	Jarrett, B.Labonte, Rudd – 1
Front Row Starts	0	—	6 tied with 1 Front Row St.
Laps Led	1	21st	Jeff Burton – 204
Pct. Led	0.1	19th	Jeff Burton – 29.9
Races Led	1	5th	J. Burton, M. Martin – 3
Times Led	1	11th	Jeff Burton – 11
Times Led Most Laps	0	—	Jeff Burton – 2
Bonus Points	5	5th	Jeff Burton – 25
Laps Completed	682	T-1st	3 others with 682 Laps Comp.
Pct. of Laps Completed	100.0	T-1st	3 other at 100.0 percent
Points per Race	145	3rd	Jeff Burton – 181.7
Fin. on Lead Lap	3	T-1st	3 others with 3 Lead Lap Fin.

*2nd-place driver or co-leader listed in parentheses if Earnhardt is track leader.

Track Performance Chart

Las Vegas Motor Speedway

Las Vegas, Nevada, 1.5 miles, 12° banking

Year	Date	Race	St.	Fin.	Total Laps	Laps Completed	Laps Led	Condition	Money	Pts.	Bonus Pts.
1998	Mar 1	Las Vegas 400	26	8	267	267	1	Running	$84,500	147	5
1999	Mar 7	Las Vegas 400	38	7	267	267	0	Running	91,350	146	0
2000	Mar 5	Carsdirect.com 400	33	8	148	148	0	Running	94,900	142	0

Richard Childress Racing-built engines like this one powered Earnhardt to 67 wins, 17 poles and six Winston Cup championships. *Bill Burt*

Earnhardt at Lowe's Motor Speedway

Located just 15 miles south of Dale Earnhart's hometown of Kannapolis, the Lowe's Motor Speedway in Charlotte was the veteran's home track. Earnhardt raced in Winston Cup events at Charlotte four times before joining the series full time in 1979; when his career ended abruptly in 2001, he was sitting atop or near the top of most statistical categories in the track's record book. When his son, Dale Jr, decided to tackle the Winston Cup series, his debut came at Charlotte in the Coca-Cola 600—just like his dad 24 years before.

The problem with this touchy-feely story was the reality of Earnhardt's love-hate relationship with the track. Compared to North Wilkesboro or Bristol or Talladega or even Daytona, Charlotte largely resisted Earnhardt's considerable talents. The high-banked, D-shaped oval accounted for more of his finishes outside of the Top 10 than any other track (see chart).

In Earnhardt's first 30 Charlotte races, he finished 12th or worse 19 times. Though he broke through and swept the two Charlotte races in 1986, not until the early 1990s did he seem to find the right combination of luck, machinery and knowledge. Of course, while his ability to finish improved, his ability to find Victory Lane all but disappeared. Earnhardt's career ended with a seven-year, 15-race winless streak at Charlotte.

Memorable Charlotte Moments

1975 World 600. Driving the No. 8 Ed Negre Dodge, Earnhardt made his Winston Cup Grand National debut at Charlotte. Starting 33rd and finishing 22nd, 45 laps off the pace set by race winner Richard Petty, Earnhardt's first start was not overly impressive. Still, that race gave birth to a career that would span three decades, produce seven championships and generate 76 wins.

Most Earnhardt Finishes Outside of the Top 10
By Track

Track	No. of Finishes
Charlotte	26
Darlington	20
Martinsville	20
Pocono	19
Dover	19

Charlotte Record Book – The Modern Era
(min. 5 starts)

Category	Earnhardt's Total	Earnhardt's Rank	Modern Era Track Leader*
Money Won	$1,933,533	1st	(Jeff Gordon – 1,731,850)
Starts	48	3rd	Darrell Waltrip – 55
Total Points	6,093	2nd	Darrell Waltrip – 7,152.25
Avg. Start	17.3	32nd	David Pearson – 3.8
Avg. Finish	14.8	6th	Bobby Allison – 11.2
Wins	5	2nd	Darrell Waltrip – 6
Winning Pct.	10.4	8th	Jeff Gordon – 25.0
Top 5s	16	3rd	Darrell Waltrip – 19
Top 10s	22	3rd	Darrell Waltrip – 29
DNFs	11	17th	Dave Marcis – 30
Poles	0	—	David Pearson – 13
Front Row Starts	0	—	David Pearson – 16
Laps Led	1,522	2nd	Bobby Allison – 1,844
Pct. Led	8.6	7th	Bobby Allison – 16.3
Races Led	30	1st	(Darrell Waltrip – 25)
Times Led	120	1st	(Darrell Waltrip – 114)
Times Led Most Laps	5	2nd	Bobby Allison – 8
Bonus Points	175	1st	(Bobby Allison – 155)
Laps Completed	15,370	3rd	Darrell Waltrip – 18,239
Pct. of Laps Completed	87.3	28th	Ted Musgrave – 97.4
Points per Race	126.9	15th	Bobby Allison – 148.8
Fin. on Lead Lap	18	1st	(Elliott, Martin, Waltrip – 14)

*2nd-place driver listed in parentheses if Earnhardt is track leader.

Track Performance Chart

Lowe's Motor Speedway

Charlotte, N.C. – 1.5 miles – 24° banking

Year	Date	Race	St.	Fin.	Total Laps	Laps Completed	Laps Led	Condition	Money	Pts.	Bonus Pts.
1975	May 25	World 600	33	22	400	355	0	Running	$2,425	97	0
1976	May 30	World 600	25	31	400	156	0	DNF - Engine	1,725	70	0
1977	Oct 9	NAPA National 500	36	38	334	25	0	DNF - Rear End	1,375	49	0
1978	May 28	World 600	28	17	400	382	0	Running	3,415	112	0
1979	May 27	World 600	15	3	400	400	121	Running	27,100	170	5
	Oct 7	NAPA National 500	8	10	334	327	55	Running	14,515	139	5
1980	May 25	World 600	4	20	400	367	105	Running	13,690	108	5
	Oct 5	National 500	4	1	334	334	148	Running	49,050	185	10
1981	May 24	World 600	5	18	400	362	54	DNF - Engine	13,675	114	5
	Oct 11	National 500	24	25	334	220	2	DNF - Ignition	4,920	93	5
1982	May 30	World 600	15	30	400	279	122	DNF - Gasket	18,470	83	10
	Oct 10	National 500	15	25	334	237	0	DNF - Ball Joint	9,565	88	0
1983	May 29	World 600	3	5	400	399	55	Running	28,700	160	5
	Oct 9	Miler High Life 500	16	14	334	332	6	Running	11,650	126	5
1984	May 27	World 600	19	2	400	400	91	Running	49,625	175	5
	Oct 7	Miler High Life 500	16	39	334	74	0	DNF - Engine	8,010	46	0
1985	May 26	Coca-Cola World 600	5	4	400	399	97	Running	49,238	170	10
	Oct 6	Miler High Life 500	5	20	334	301	0	Running	12,050	103	0
1986	May 25	Coca-Cola 600	3	1	400	400	26	Running	98,150	180	5
	Oct 5	Oakwood Homes 500	3	1	334	334	80	Running	82,050	180	5
1987	May 24	Coca-Cola 600	3	20	400	305	0	Running	19,600	103	0
	Oct 11	Oakwood Homes 500	9	12	334	329	2	Running	16,440	132	5
1988	May 29	Coca-Cola 600	7	13	400	394	0	Running	19,205	124	0
	Oct 9	Oakwood Homes 500	11	17	334	328	83	Running	24,300	122	10
1989	May 28	Coca-Cola 600	14	38	400	223	2	DNF - Engine	10,750	54	5
	Oct 8	All Pro Auto Parts 500	12	42	334	13	0	DNF - Crankshaft	11,250	37	0
1990	Apr 8	Valleydale Meats 500	12	30	400	262	0	Running	13,950	73	0
	Oct 7	Mello Yello 500	15	25	334	320	0	Running	12,275	88	0
1991	May 26	Coca-Cola 600	14	3	400	400	26	Running	53,650	170	5
	Oct 6	Mello Yello 500	15	25	334	302	56	DNF - Valve	22,460	93	5
1992	May 24	Coca-Cola 600	13	1	400	400	54	Running	125,100	180	5
	Oct 22	Mello Yello 500	11	14	334	332	0	Running	19,050	121	0
1993	May 30	Coca-Cola 600	14	1	400	400	152	Running	156,650	185	10
	Oct 10	Mello Yello 500	9	3	334	334	3	Running	56,900	170	5
1994	May 29	Coca-Cola 600	24	9	400	397	0	Running	37,950	138	0
	Oct 9	Mello Yello 500	38	3	334	334	6	Running	66,000	170	5
1995	May 28	Coca-Cola 600	34	6	400	399	38	Running	52,500	155	5
	Oct 8	UAW-GM 500	43	2	334	334	2	Running	86,800	175	5
1996	May 26	Coca-Cola 600	20	2	400	400	7	Running	97,000	175	5
	Oct 6	UAW-GM 500	34	6	334	334	15	Running	44,700	155	5
1997	May 25	Coca-Cola 600	33	7	333	333	2	Running	54,400	151	5
	Oct 5	UAW-GM Quality 500	19	3	334	334	31	Running	85,650	170	5
1998	May 24	Coca-Cola 600	28	39	400	336	0	DNF - Crash	39,580	46	0
	Oct 4	UAW-GM Quality 500	33	29	334	278	0	Running	31,300	76	0
1999	May 30	Coca-Cola 600	15	6	400	400	0	Running	70,225	150	0
	Oct 10	UAW-GM Quality 500	17	12	334	332	0	Running	44,450	127	0
2000	May 28	Coca-Cola 600	15	3	400	400	23	Running	103,250	170	5
	Oct 8	UAW-GM Quality 500	37	11	334	334	58	Running	58,750	135	5

Earnhardt at Martinsville Speedway

Memorable Martinsville Moment – 1980 Old Dominion 500. In perhaps *the* defining win of his career, Dale Earnhardt somehow took the checkered flag in the 1980 fall race at tiny Martinsville Speedway and inched closer to his first Winston Cup championship. The victory extended Earnhardt's lead in the championship points race over hard-charging Cale Yarborough, the most feared driver on the circuit at the time. That first Martinsville win, perhaps even more than his first win at Bristol in 1979, revealed the competitiveness of the Winston Cup star.

The victory was so impressive because Martinsville proved to be incredibly difficult for Earnhardt to figure out, especially early in his career. He simply didn't have a good idea of how to get around the paper-clip-shaped track. In his first 12 Martinsville races, Earnhardt failed to finish on the lead lap in 11 of those races. He failed to finish at all in half of those races.

In the fall of 1980, Earnhardt defied the learning curve when he absolutely had to. At the time of the race, Earnhardt was engaged in a tight championship battle with NASCAR legends Richard Petty and Yarborough. Earnhardt, in just his second season on the Winston Cup circuit, was up against two of NASCAR's best, most experienced drivers: Petty was in his 23rd season, while Yarborough was competing in his 19th season.

Somehow during that 1980 race, he kept his car in contention and gave himself the opportunity to take advantage of Yarborough's late-race misfortune. Earnhardt avoided being part of the race's record 17 caution flags and hung around the leaders all day. He finally caught a break just 13 laps from the end of the race when leader Yarborough suffered a flat tire. Earnhardt assumed the lead and won by more than a second over Buddy Baker. Yarborough finished third.

The victory pushed Earnhardt ahead by 105 points. He needed every point he could get as Yarborough finished the season strong. Earnhardt won the Winston Cup title by just 19 points, the fifth-closest points finish in NASCAR history. Without question, the win at Martinsville—spurred by an amazing effort from the driver—propelled Earnhardt to his first championship.

On Winston Cup short tracks, Earnhardt won 27 times, including six times at Martinsville Speedway. His biggest win at the tiny Virginia track came in 1980 when he beat Cale Yarborough and padded his points lead. Earnhardt went on to outlast Yarborough by 19 points for the 1980 Winston Cup title, the first of his seven championships. *Bill Burt*

Martinsville Record Book – The Modern Era
(min. 5 starts)

Category	Earnhardt's Total	Earnhardt's Rank	Modern Era Track Leader*
Money Won	$1,211,455	1st	(Rusty Wallace – 1,172,695)
Starts	44	4th	Darrell Waltrip – 52
Total Points	5,984	2nd	Darrell Waltrip – 7,317
Avg. Start	12.2	21st	David Pearson – 4.9
Avg. Finish	11.9	10th	Cale Yarborough – 6.3
Wins	6	2nd	Darrell Waltrip – 11
Winning Pct.	13.6	5th	Cale Yarborough – 29.4
Top 5s	18	2nd	Darrell Waltrip – 27
Top 10s	24	3rd	Darrell Waltrip – 31
DNFs	11	8th	Dave Marcis – 16
Poles	0	—	Darrell Waltrip – 8
Front Row Starts	5	5th	Darrell Waltrip – 12
Laps Led	1,947	4th	Darrell Waltrip – 3,616
Pct. Led	8.9	7th	Cale Yarborough – 39.9
Races Led	22	3rd	Darrell Waltrip – 32
Times Led	59	3rd	Darrell Waltrip – 79
Times Led Most Laps	6	4th	R. Wallace, Yarborough – 9
Bonus Points	140	3rd	Darrell Waltrip – 195
Laps Completed	18,907	4th	Darrell Waltrip – 23,727
Pct. of Laps Completed	86.5	44th	Jeff Gordon – 98.6
Points per Race	136.0	9th	Jeff Gordon – 154.9
Fin. on Lead Lap	18	3rd	Darrell Waltrip – 25

*2nd-place driver or co-leader listed in parentheses if Earnhardt is track leader.

Track Performance Chart

Martinsville Speedway

Martinsville, Virginia .526 miles, 12° banking

Year	Date	Race	St.	Fin.	Total Laps	Laps Completed	Laps Led	Condition	Money	Pts.	Bonus Pts.
1979	Apr 22	Virginia 500	11	8	500	495	0	Running	$4,200	142	0
	Sep 23	Old Dominion 500	5	29	500	67	0	DNF - Crash	3,510	76	0
1980	Apr 27	Virginia 500	11	13	500	484	0	Running	5,400	124	0
	Sep 28	Old Dominion 500	7	1	500	500	176	Running	25,375	185	10
1981	Apr 26	Virginia 500	10	25	500	155	0	DNF - Engine	6,600	88	0
	Sep 27	Old Dominion 500	7	26	500	148	0	DNF - Engine	2,690	85	0
1982	Apr 25	Virginia National Bank 500	15	23	500	100	0	DNF - Overheating	7,170	94	0
	Oct 17	Old Dominion 500	12	27	500	118	0	DNF - Brakes	7,230	82	0
1983	Apr 24	Virginia National Bank 500	11	26	500	351	0	DNF - Crash	7,240	85	0
	Sep 25	Goody's 500	5	4	500	499	0	Running	11,200	160	0
1984	Apr 29	Sovran Bank 500	15	9	500	497	0	Running	7,345	138	0
	Sep 23	Goody's 500	11	12	500	489	0	Running	7,865	127	0
1985	Apr 28	Sovran Bank 500	4	25	500	345	1	DNF - Engine	8,975	93	5
	Sep 22	Goody's 500	11	1	500	500	58	Running	37,725	180	5
1986	Apr 27	Sovran Bank 500	3	21	500	347	102	DNF - Engine	9,915	105	5
	Sep 21	Goody's 500	2	12	500	494	56	Running	11,770	132	5
1987	Apr 26	Sovran Bank 500	4	1	500	500	156	Running	50,850	185	10
	Sep 27	Goody's 500	8	2	500	500	170	Running	29,875	180	10
1988	Apr 24	Pannill Sweatshirts 500	14	1	500	500	182	Running	53,550	185	10
	Sep 25	Goody's 500	10	8	500	498	0	Running	13,050	142	0
1989	Apr 23	Pannill Sweatshirts 500	7	2	500	500	103	Running	34,525	175	5
	Sep 24	Goody's 500	1	9	500	499	74	Running	15,950	143	5
1990	Apr 29	Hanes Activewear 500	2	5	500	499	21	Running	20,800	160	5
	Sep 23	Goody's 500	8	2	500	500	25	Running	30,550	175	5
1991	Apr 28	Hanes 500	10	1	500	500	251	Running	63,600	185	10
	Sep 22	Goody's 500	5	3	500	500	9	Running	30,350	170	5
1992	Apr 26	Hanes 500	2	9	500	497	167	Running	22,550	143	5
	Sep 28	Goody's 500	11	31	500	111	0	DNF - Engine	14,550	70	0
1993	Apr 25	Hanes 500	21	22	500	453	1	DNF - Engine	10,625	102	5
	Sep 26	Goody's 500	7	29	500	440	0	DNF - Axle	10,525	76	0
1994	Apr 24	Hanes 500	8	11	500	499	0	Running	21,060	130	0
	Sep 25	Goody's 500	20	2	500	500	10	Running	42,400	175	5
1995	Apr 23	Hanes 500	20	29	356	331	0	Running	27,515	76	0
	Sep 24	Goody's 500	2	1	500	500	253	Running	78,150	185	10
1996	Apr 21	Goody's 500	8	5	500	500	12	Running	35,195	160	5
	Sep 22	Hanes 500	19	15	500	498	0	Running	29,100	118	0
1997	Apr 20	Goody's 500	25	12	500	500	0	Running	28,400	127	0
	Sep 28	Hanes 500	13	2	500	500	0	Running	65,800	170	0
1998	Apr 19	Goody's 500	31	4	500	500	33	Running	49,475	165	5
	Sep 27	NAPA Autocare 500	33	22	500	495	0	Running	32,950	97	0
1999	Apr 18	Goody's 500	39	19	500	498	0	Running	39,150	106	0
	Oct 3	NAPA Autocare 500	38	2	500	500	45	Running	70,225	175	5
2000	Apr 9	Goody's 500	17	9	500	500	42	Running	48,550	143	5
	Oct 1	NAPA Autocare 500	12	2	500	500	0	Running	77,925	170	0

Earnhardt at Michigan International Speedway

Dale Earnhardt's less-than-inspiring career at the new California Speedway is not too surprising when his Michigan effort is factored in. Simply put, the semi-banked, 2-mile racetrack format was not an Earnhardt strength.

Both tracks, owned by Roger Penske, who owns the cars driven by Earnhardt rival Rusty Wallace, were stubborn with wins, strong finishes and, gulp, even with money during Earnhardt's career. Michigan is the only long-time Winston Cup track at which Earnhardt was not the NASCAR money leader. Among long-time Winston Cup tracks only Rockingham and Pocono have been intimidated less than Michigan (see chart).

Memorable Michigan Moment

1987 Miller American 400. In his 17th Michigan start, Earnhardt broke through with a victory on the 2-mile track and joined elite company at the same time. Earnhardt led 152 laps during the race, the fifth-highest single-race total in track history. The race was part of a dominant 1987 season for Earnhardt, during which he won 11 times.

Most Laps Led, Single Race
Michigan Speedway

Driver	Laps Led	Race
Rusty Wallace	162	1989 Champion Spark Plug 400
Geoffrey Bodine	160	1994 Goodwrench 400
Davey Allison	158	1992 Miller Genuine Draft 400
David Pearson	155	1972 Motor State 400
Dale Earnhardt	152	1987 Miller American 400

Old Tracks, Difficult Tracks
Earnhardt's least successful long-time Winston Cup tracks

Track	Starts	Wins	Win Pct.	Top 5s
Michigan	43	2	4.7	12
Pocono	41	2	4.9	10
Rockingham	44	3	6.8	13

Michigan Record Book – The Modern Era
(min. 5 starts)

Category	Earnhardt's Total	Earnhardt's Rank	Modern Era Track Leader*
Money Won	$1,151,680	3rd	Bill Elliott – 1,214,383
Starts	43	6th	Dave Marcis – 50
Total Points	5,663	3rd	Darrell Waltrip – 6,323
Avg. Start	14.7	24th	Davey Allison – 5.4
Avg. Finish	12.6	8th	Jeff Gordon – 7.1
Wins	2	10th	David Pearson – 8
Winning Pct.	4.7	13th	David Pearson – 33.3
Top 5s	12	7th	Cale Yarborough – 18
Top 10s	25	2nd	Bill Elliott – 27
DNFs	5	38th	Dave Marcis – 18
Poles	0	—	David Peason – 9
Front Row Starts	0	—	Bill Elliott – 11
Laps Led	597	7th	Cale Yarborough – 1,152
Pct. Led	6.9	10th	Cale Yarborough – 18.1
Races Led	19	6th	Darrell Waltrip – 33
Times Led	65	7th	Cale Yarborough – 128
Times Led Most Laps	2	10th	Cale Yarborough – 8
Bonus Points	105	8th	Darrell Waltrip – 190
Laps Completed	7,976	6th	Darrell Waltrip – 8,884
Pct. of Laps Completed	92.8	15th	Kenny Irwin – 98.7
Points per Race	131.7	19th	Jeff Gordon – 155.4
Fin. on Lead Lap	22	3rd	Bill Elliott – 24

*2nd-place driver or co-leader listed in parentheses if Earnhardt is track leader.

Earnhardt and Jeff Gordon battle for position during the 1998 Pepsi 400 at Michigan International Speedway. In 1995, Gordon outlasted Earnhardt in the points chase, winning by 34 points—the eighth closest championship battle in Winston Cup history. *Don Hamilton*

Track Performance Chart

Michigan Speedway

Brooklyn, Michigan, 2.0 miles, 18° banking

Year	Date	Race	St.	Fin.	Total Laps	Laps Completed	Laps Led	Condition	Money	Pts.	Bonus Pts.
1979	Jun 17	Gabriel 400	13	6	200	200	1	Running	$7,540	155	5
	Aug 19	Champion Spark Plug 400	Did Not Start due to Injury								
1980	Jun 15	Gabriel 400	3	12	200	197	55	Running	7,825	132	5
	Aug 17	Champion Spark Plug 400	8	35	200	79	1	DNF - Engine	6,410	63	5
1981	Jun 21	Gabriel 400	7	5	200	200	37	Running	11,925	160	5
	Aug 16	Champion Spark Plug 400	10	9	200	200	0	Running	7,955	138	0
1982	Jun 20	Gabriel 400	11	7	200	199	0	Running	13,550	146	0
	Aug 22	Champion Spark Plug 400	18	30	200	76	0	DNF - Brakes	8,750	73	0
1983	Jun 19	Gabriel 400	15	15	200	198	0	Running	10,125	118	0
	Aug 21	Champion Spark Plug 400	13	7	200	200	0	Running	12,140	146	0
1984	Jun 17	Miller High Life 400	15	2	200	200	0	Running	28,175	170	0
	Aug 12	Champion Spark Plug 400	14	7	200	199	0	Running	12,700	146	0
1985	Jun 16	Miller 400	14	5	200	200	19	Running	17,925	160	5
	Aug 11	Champion Spark Plug 400	12	22	200	191	0	Running	9,525	97	0
1986	Jun 15	Miller American 400	11	6	200	200	21	Running	17,650	155	5
	Aug 17	Champion Spark Plug 400	12	5	200	199	34	Running	18,750	160	5
1987	Jun 28	Miller American 400	5	1	200	200	152	Running	60,250	185	10
	Aug 16	Champion Spark Plug 400	8	2	200	200	63	Running	34,325	180	10
1988	Jun 26	Miller High Life 400	9	4	200	200	12	Running	26,175	165	5
	Aug 21	Champion Spark Plug 400	5	29	200	194	39	Running	14,315	81	5
1989	Jun 25	Miller High Life 400	6	17	200	198	0	Running	13,775	112	0
	Aug 20	Champion Spark Plug 400	15	17	200	198	0	Running	13,450	112	0
1990	Jun 24	Miller Genuine Draft 400	5	1	200	200	22	Running	72,950	180	5
	Aug 19	Champion Spark Plug 400	7	8	200	200	50	Running	19,400	147	5
1991	Jun 23	Miller Genuine Draft 400	6	4	200	200	14	Running	30,950	165	5
	Aug 18	Champion Spark Plug 400	26	24	200	194	0	Running	16,425	91	0
1992	Jun 21	Miller Genuine Draft 400	22	9	200	199	0	Running	23,110	138	0
	Aug 16	Champion Spark Plug 400	41	16	200	199	0	Running	19,665	115	0
1993	Jun 20	Miller Genuine Draft 400	6	14	200	199	27	Running	16,385	126	5
	Aug 15	Champion Spark Plug 400	7	9	200	200	0	Running	19,215	138	0
1994	Jun 19	Miller 400	24	2	200	200	18	Running	55,905	175	5
	Aug 21	Goodwrench 400	11	37	200	54	0	DNF - Crash	22,915	52	0
1995	Jun 18	Miller 400	7	35	200	127	2	DNF - Crash	29,945	63	5
	Aug 20	Goodwrench 400	8	35	200	87	0	DNF - Timing Belt	29,965	58	0
1996	Jun 23	Miller 400	11	9	200	200	0	Running	33,350	138	0
	Aug 18	Goodwrench 400	16	17	200	200	0	Running	32,865	112	0
1997	Jun 15	Miller 400	22	7	200	200	0	Running	41,375	146	0
	Aug 17	DeVilbiss 400	28	9	200	200	0	Running	37,940	138	0
1998	Jun 14	Miller Lite 400	25	15	200	199	0	Running	38,650	118	0
	Aug 16	Pepsi 400	37	18	200	198	3	Running	34,840	114	5
1999	Jun 13	Kmart 400	15	16	200	198	0	Running	39,825	115	0
	Aug 22	Pepsi 400	38	5	200	200	27	Running	51,005	160	5
2000	Jun 11	Kmart 400	9	2	194	194	0	Running	80,575	170	0
	Aug 20	Pepsi 400	37	6	200	200	0	Running	51,190	150	0

Earnhardt at Nashville Speedway

Like Bristol and North Wilkesboro, Nashville Speedway solidified Dale Earnhardt's reputation as a short-track genius. Before the track disappeared from the Winston Cup Grand National schedule in 1984, Earnhardt won twice and finished in the Top 10 nine times in just 12 starts.

Making this record more impressive are the circumstances surrounding it. When Earnhardt arrived on the Grand National scene, Nashville was under the spell of short-track wizards Cale Yarborough and Darrell Waltrip. Just as Jeff Gordon made road courses his personal playground in the late 1990s, the half-mile Nashville track was property of Waltrip and Yarborough. In 20 races between 1974 and 1984, Yarborough and Waltrip won a combined 15 times. Their dominance was nearly complete: the two drivers led an astonishing 5,606 of 8,400 laps. Eight times they led over 380 of a possible 420 circuits.

Earnhardt was one of only three drivers—the others: Richard Petty and Benny Parsons—who were able to crack the Waltrip-Yarborough oligopoly. Earnhardt did it in just his second season in the series, holding off Yarborough and leading the final 30 laps to win the 1980 Busch Nashville 420. Earnhardt later won the same event in 1983, this time more convincingly by leading 212 laps.

Depending on your point of view, Earnhardt was a short track genius or a bully who was not afraid to overuse his front bumper. Here, Earnhardt scoots by as Ted Musgrave (No. 16 Primestar) and Todd Bodine (No. 35 Tabasco) get tangled up in a wreck on the backstretch at Bristol. Though innocent in this situation, Earnhardt had a history of instigating incidents at Winston Cup short tracks. *Bill Burt*

Nashville Record Book – The Modern Era
(min. 5 starts)

Category	Earnhardt's Total	Earnhardt's Rank	Modern Era Track Leader
Money Won	$109,820	4th	Darrell Waltrip – 238,120
Career Starts	12	16th	R. Petty, D. Waltrip – 25
Total Points	1,733	14th	Darrell Waltrip – 3,622.75
Avg. Start	8.3	11th	Cale Yarborough – 2.5
Avg. Finish	8.9	6th	Cale Yarborough – 4.2
Wins	2	4th	Darrell Waltrip – 8
Winning Pct.	16.7	3rd	Cale Yarborough – 43.8
Top 5s	5	7th	Darrell Waltrip – 19
Top 10s	9	7th	Richard Petty – 20
DNFs	1	61st	Richard Childress – 11
Poles	0	—	Darrell Waltrip – 7
Front Row Starts	0	—	Darrell Waltrip – 9
Laps Led	375	8th	Cale Yarborough – 3,633
Pct. Led	7.4	8th	Cale Yarborough – 54.1
Races Led	4	6th	Darrell Waltrip – 20
Times Led	9	6th	Darrell Waltrip – 40
Times Led Most Laps	1	4th	Cale Yarborough – 11
Bonus Points	25	6th	D. Waltrip, C. Yarborough – 130
Laps Completed	4,810	14th	Richard Petty – 10,019
Pct. of Laps Completed	95.4	4th	Cale Yarborough – 96.7
Points per Race	144.4	3rd	Cale Yarborough – 153.4
Lead Lap Finishes	2	6th	Darrell Waltrip – 12

Track Performance Chart

Nashville Speedway USA

Nashville, Tenn. – .596 miles – 18° banking

Year	Date	Race	St.	Fin.	Total Laps	Laps Completed	Laps Led	Condition	Money	Pts.	Bonus Pts.
1979	May 12	Sun-Drop Music City USA 420	7	4	420	419	0	Running	$5,350	160	0
	Jul 14	Busch Nashville 420	3	3	420	417	0	Running	7,200	165	0
1980	May 10	Music City USA 420	7	6	420	418	27	Running	5,825	155	5
	Jul 12	Busch Nashville 420	7	1	420	420	103	Running	14,600	180	5
1981	May 9	Melling Tool 420	12	20	420	379	0	Running	6,500	103	0
	Jul 11	Busch Nashville 420	7	7	420	418	0	Running	7,375	146	0
1982	May 8	Cracker Barrel 420	12	10	420	415	0	Running	7,735	134	0
	Jul 10	Busch Nashville 420	13	9	420	417	0	Running	7,635	138	0
1983	May 7	Marty Robbins 420	7	24	420	258	0	DNF - Engine	6,450	91	0
	Jul 16	Busch Nashville 420	3	1	420	420	212	Running	23,125	185	10
1984	May 12	Coors 420	5	19	420	410	0	Running	7,250	106	0
	Jul 14	Pepsi 420	16	3	420	419	33	Running	10,775	170	5

Thanks to Dale Earnhardt's aggressive, sometimes controversial, driving style and frequent trips to Victory Lane, few fans are neutral in their feelings about the NASCAR legend. Many fans, like these two young Earnhardt loyalists, backed the No. 3 Goodwrench through thick and thin. *David Stringer*

Earnhardt at New Hampshire International Speedway

Let's just come right out and say it: Dale Earnhardt never liked NASCAR's new racetracks very much. Truth be told, he wasn't particularly good on them. For some reason, NASCAR's greatest driver could never get a handle on new pavement. At the six tracks added to the Winston Cup schedule during the 1990s, he won just one time in 32 races. Even more unEarnhardt-like, he had trouble getting to the front of the field, leading just 105 of 8,245 "new-track" laps during his career.

Foremost among the culprits was New Hampshire International Speedway, a flat, one-mile oval that began frustrating Earnhardt in 1993. While he produced two good runs at the New England track—second-place finishes in 1994 and 1997 —the hyper-competitive Earnhardt found New Hampshire to be a consistently fruitless patch of asphalt. Besides not winning, Earnhardt did not lead a lap at New Hampshire after leading the 1996 Jiffy Lube 300, and he couldn't crack the Top 5 after the spring race in 1997.

Earnhardt on the New Tracks

Track	Year Joined	No. of Starts	Wins	Winning Pct.	Laps Led
New Hampshire	1993	12	0	0.0	65
Indianapolis	1994	7	1	14.3	37
California	1997	4	0	0.0	2
Texas	1997	4	0	0.0	0
Las Vegas	1998	3	0	0.0	1
Homestead	1999	2	0	0.0	0
New Track Totals		**32**	**1**	**3.1**	**105**
Other Winston Cup Tracks		**644**	**75**	**11.6**	**25,608**

"The first time I was on the track with him was in Tokyo [in November 1998]. I searched for him during happy hour. I tried to get up close to him. It was cool just to be there."
—*Dale Earnhardt, Jr.*

New Hampshire Record Book – All-Time
(min. 5 starts)

Category	Earnhardt's Total	Earnhardt's Rank	All-Time Track Leader*
Money Won	$632,325	8th	Jeff Gordon – 1,119,890
Starts	12	T-1st	16 others with 12 Starts
Total Points	1,596	6th	Mark Martin – 1,717
Avg. Start	21.7	20th	Ken Schrader – 6.8
Avg. Finish	11.5	4th	Mark Martin – 7.8
Wins	0	—	Jeff Burton – 4
Winning Pct.	0.0	—	Jeff Burton – 33.3
Top 5s	2	7th	J.Burton, Gordon, Martin – 7
Top 10s	6	7th	Mark Martin – 10
DNFs	0	—	Andretti, T. Labonte – 5
Poles	0	—	5 tied with 2 Poles
Front Row Starts	0	—	Jeff Gordon – 4
Laps Led	65	13th	Jeff Burton – 593
Pct. Led	1.8	14th	Jeff Burton – 16.6
Races Led	3	12th	Jeff Gordon – 8
Times Led	6	10th	Jeff Gordon – 23
Times Led Most Laps	0	—	Jeff Burton, Jeff Gordon – 3
Bonus Points	15	13th	Jeff Gordon – 55
Laps Completed	3,565	1st	(Dale Jarrett – 3,561)
Pct. of Laps Completed	99.7	2nd	Johnny Benson – 99.8
Points per Race	133.0	6th	Mark Martin – 149.7
Fin. on Lead Lap	8	6th	Mark Martin – 10

*2nd-place driver or co-leader listed in parentheses if Earnhardt is track leader

Track Performance Chart
New Hampshire International Speedway
Louden, New Hampshire, 1.058 miles, 12° banking

Year	Date	Race	St.	Fin.	Total Laps	Laps Completed	Laps Led	Condition	Money	Pts.	Bonus Pts.
1993	Jul 11	Slick 50 300	24	26	300	296	0	Running	$15,300	85	0
1994	Jul 10	Slick 50 300	28	2	300	300	29	Running	68,000	175	5
1995	Jul 9	Slick 50 300	18	22	300	298	24	Running	43,350	102	5
1996	Jul 14	Jiffy Lube 300	5	12	300	300	12	Running	32,225	132	5
1997	Jul 13	Jiffy Lube 300	26	2	300	300	0	Running	82,950	170	0
	Sep 14	CMT 300	30	8	300	300	0	Running	49,025	142	0
1998	Jul 12	Jiffy Lube 300	20	18	300	299	0	Running	47,150	109	0
	Aug 30	Farm Aid on CMT 300	18	9	300	300	0	Running	50,550	138	0
1999	Jul 12	Jiffy Lube 300	14	8	300	300	0	Running	56,675	142	0
	Sep 19	Dura Lube/Kmart 300	16	13	300	300	0	Running	55,125	124	0
2000	Jul 9	Thatlook.com 300	24	6	273	273	0	Running	69,425	150	0
	Sep 17	Dura Lube 300	37	12	300	299	0	Running	62,550	127	0

Indianapolis was the last new track Earnhardt was able to win on. New Hampshire escaped his winning ways, as did California, Homestead, Las Vegas, and Texas. *Don Hamilton*

Earnhardt at North Carolina Speedway

When the "Why hasn't Dale won the 500 yet?" questions started in earnest in 1987, North Carolina Speedway—better known as Rockingham—was usually the first place Dale Earnhardt and the Winston Cup series visited after Speed Weeks at Daytona. Rockingham became Earnhardt's outlet, the place he released his Daytona frustrations—and launched his frequent championship runs.

Between 1987 and his Daytona 500 triumph in 1998, Rockingham was the first post-Daytona stop on the Winston Cup schedule eight times. In those eight races, Earnhardt excelled, winning twice and finishing in the Top 5 five times. Earnhardt emerged from Rockingham with the points lead three times. He ended up winning the championship in two of those years, 1990 and 1993.

But Rockingham's significance in Earnhardt's career extended well beyond its therapeutic value. Though clearly not his most successful track, it was a steady source of quality finishes. Between 1985 and 1996, Earnhardt enjoyed one of his best runs on any Winston Cup track. In 24 races during that time, he collected all three of his Rockingham wins and had 22 Top 10 finishes.

Of course, there was a flip side to the success. Like other tracks, Rockingham could not escape the hard times Earnhardt experienced during the late 1990s. In 1999, 'The Rock' was the site of Earnhardt's worst season ever at a Winston Cup track. Thanks to wrecks, he finished both 1999 races 40th or worse—40th in the spring race, 41st in the fall race. Earnhardt never experienced a worse season performance at a track before or after.

Earnhardt's Worst Average Finish in a Season
By Track

Track	Average Finish	Season
Rockingham	40.5	1999
Charlotte	40.0	1989
Pocono	39.0	1985
Charlotte	38.0	1977

Rockingham Record Book – The Modern Era
(min. 5 starts)

Category	Earnhardt's Total	Earnhardt's Rank	Modern Era Track Leader*
Money Won	$1,160,755	1st	(Kyle Petty – 1,081,956)
Career Starts	44	4th	Darrell Waltrip – 56
Total Points	6,016	2nd	Darrell Waltrip – 6,993.5
Avg. Start	14.2	23rd	Jeff Gordon – 6.3
Avg. Finish	11.4	2nd	Cale Yarborough – 10.8
Wins	3	7th	R. Petty, C. Yarborough – 6
Winning Pct.	6.8	16th	David Pearson – 26.7
Top 5s	13	5th	Darrell Waltrip – 19
Top 10s	28	2nd	Darrell Waltrip – 29
DNFs	7	26th	B. Baker, J.D. McDuffie – 18
Poles	0	—	M. Martin, K. Petty – 5
Front Row Starts	1	28th	Mark Martin – 8
Laps Led	1,415	7th	Cale Yarborough – 2,902
Pct. Led	6.9	14th	David Pearson – 23.1
Races Led	29	1st	(Darrell Waltrip – 25)
Times Led	87	2nd	Cale Yarborough – 93
Times Led Most Laps	2	10th	Cale Yarborough – 9
Bonus Points	155	1st	(Cale Yarborough – 150)
Laps Completed	19,150	3rd	Darrell Waltrip – 24,031
Pct. of Laps Completed	93.1	15th	Kenny Irwin – 99.1
Points per Race	136.7	8th	Cale Yarborough – 148.8
Lead Lap Finishes	16	1st	(Terry Labonte – 15)

*2nd-place driver or co-leader listed in parentheses if Earnhardt is track leader.

In 24 races at Rockingham from 1985 through 1996, Earnhardt enjoyed one of his best runs at any Winston Cup track. During that stretch, he won three times and had 22 Top 10 finishes. Here, Earnhardt lines up for the 2000 spring race with pole sitter Jeremy Mayfield (No. 12 Mobil 1), Ricky Rudd (No. 28 Havoline), Bobby Labonte (No. 18 Interstate Batteries), Matt Kenseth (No. 17 DeWalt), and Jeff Gordon (No. 24 Dupont). *Bill Burt*

Track Performance Chart

North Carolina Motor Speedway

Rockingham, North Carolina, 1.017 miles, 22-25° banking

Year	Date	Race	St.	Fin.	Total Laps	Laps Completed	Laps Led	Condition	Money	Pts.	Bonus Pts.
1979	Mar 4	Carolina 500	5	12	492	460	0	Running	$3,250	127	0
	Oct 21	American 500	10	5	492	488	0	Running	8,300	155	0
1980	Mar 9	Carolina 500	7	3	492	491	6	Running	14,420	170	5
	Oct 19	American 500	11	18	492	443	3	Running	6,650	114	5
1981	Mar 1	Carolina 500	11	26	492	285	0	DNF - Crash	8,250	85	0
	Nov 1	American 500	5	9	492	489	16	Running	7,360	143	5
1982	Mar 28	Warner W. Hodgdon Carolina 500	6	25	492	191	30	DNF - Overheating	8,660	93	5
	Oct 31	Warner W. Hodgdon American 500	8	14	492	445	52	DNF - Engine	9,300	126	5
1983	Mar 13	Warner W. Hodgdon Carolina 500	4	33	492	73	6	DNF - Crash	8,000	69	5
	Oct 30	Warner W. Hodgdon American 500	16	17	492	436	14	DNF - Engine	9,330	117	5
1984	Mar 4	Warner W. Hodgdon Carolina 500	8	14	492	470	0	Running	9,335	121	0
	Oct 21	Warner W. Hodgdon American 500	6	13	492	470	4	Running	8,710	129	5
1985	Mar 3	Carolina 500	11	10	492	491	13	Running	16,300	139	5
	Oct 20	Nationwise 500	15	8	492	489	32	Running	11,800	147	5
1986	Mar 2	Goodwrench 500	5	8	492	490	69	Running	19,510	147	5
	Oct 19	Nationwise 500	10	6	492	491	94	Running	15,750	155	5
1987	Mar 1	Goodwrench 500	14	1	492	492	319	Running	53,900	185	10
	Oct 25	AC-Delco 500	2	2	492	492	122	Running	38,915	175	5
1988	Mar 6	Goodwrench 500	22	5	492	492	22	Running	19,865	160	5
	Oct 23	AC-Delco 500	13	5	492	491	1	Running	27,965	160	5
1989	Mar 5	Goodwrench 500	19	3	492	492	0	Running	24,200	165	0
	Oct 22	AC-Delco 500	5	20	492	484	86	Running	13,775	108	5
1990	Mar 4	GM Goodwrench 500	4	10	492	489	0	Running	17,150	134	0
	Oct 21	AC-Delco 500	20	10	492	490	0	Running	19,750	134	0
1991	Mar 3	GM Goodwrench 500	13	8	492	489	0	Running	18,850	142	0
	Oct 20	AC-Delco 500	4	7	492	490	0	Running	19,250	146	0
1992	Mar 1	GM Goodwrench 500	8	24	492	469	0	Running	16,850	91	0
	Oct 25	AC-Delco 500	12	8	492	490	0	Running	22,350	142	0
1993	Feb 28	GM Goodwrench 500	7	2	492	492	133	Running	47,585	175	5
	Oct 24	AC-Delco 500	22	2	492	492	14	Running	49,550	175	5
1994	Feb 27	Goodwrench 500	19	7	492	491	17	Running	25,785	151	5
	Oct 23	AC-Delco 500	20	1	492	492	108	Running	60,600	185	10
1995	Feb 26	Goodwrench 500	23	3	492	492	72	Running	40,740	170	5
	Oct 22	AC-Delco 400	20	7	393	393	39	Running	34,050	151	5
1996	Feb 25	Goodwrench 400	18	1	393	393	95	Running	83,840	180	5
	Oct 20	AC-Delco 400	15	9	393	393	37	Running	30,700	143	5
1997	Feb 23	Goodwrench Service 400	27	11	393	393	0	Running	32,000	130	0
	Oct 27	AC-Delco 400	26	8	393	393	0	Running	32,800	142	0
1998	Feb 22	Goodwrench Service Plus 400	37	17	393	392	1	Running	32,100	117	5
	Nov 1	AC-Delco 400	29	9	393	393	8	Running	34,400	143	5
1999	Feb 21	Dura Lube/Big Kmart 400	18	41	393	275	0	DNF - Crash	36,725	40	0
	Oct 24	Pop Secret Popcorn 400	37	40	393	318	0	DNF - Crash	36,900	43	0
2000	Feb 27	Dura Lube/Kmart 400	4	2	393	393	1	Running	78,610	175	5
	Oct 22	Pop Secret Popcorn 400	27	17	393	393	1	Running	46,625	117	5

Earnhardt at North Wilkesboro Speedway

To say that Dale Earnhardt took a liking to North Wilkesboro Speedway is a monumental understatement. Earnhardt's career numbers at the Wilkes County, North Carolina, track are staggering. Consider:

- In 36 career starts, Earnhardt logged 32 Top 10s—an amazing 89 percent success rate;
- Illustrating his consistency another way, Earnhardt failed to finish just two of those 36 races;
- Earnhardt's 21 Top 5 finishes rank first in North Wilkesboro's modern era record book and third all-time;
- During one 10-race stretch from 1986 through 1990, he led 1,949 of 4,000 laps.

Explanations for such brilliance are not easy to generate. Perhaps the track's relative proximity to Earnhardt's hometown (Kannapolis) spurred his competitive drive (though he never enjoyed the same degree of success at the other nearby tracks—Charlotte and Rockingham). Perhaps the bullring characteristics of North Wilkesboro—a banked, .625-mile track—fit Earnhardt's style (he won 27 times on Winston Cup short tracks).

Whatever the answer, when the track shut down in September of 1996—a victim of NASCAR's growth spurt during the late 1980s and 1990s—Earnhardt lost one of his most trusted friends. Whenever the Winston Cup series stopped in Wilkes County, he could always count on a warm welcome and a friendly finish.

Memorable North Wilkesboro Moment

1989 Holly Farms 400. Locked in a tight points battle with Rusty Wallace, Earnhardt seemed poised to regain the championship lead with a dominating performance. He led 343 of 400 laps, but had to endure a final restart with two laps to go. On that restart, Ricky Rudd dipped underneath Earnhardt going into turn 1 of the final lap. Earnhardt and Rudd touched, spinning both cars and allowing the rest of the field to speed past. An irate Earnhardt finished in 10th place and had to be restrained in a post-race confrontation with Rudd (who finished ninth). Earnhardt's anger became more understandable as the season continued. Instead of taking an 12-point lead in the standings, Earnhardt fell two more points behind Wallace. With the momentum shift, Wallace went on to win his only Winston Cup title by 12 points over Earnhardt.

Earnhardt waits for his turn to qualify for the First Union 400 at North Wilkesboro in 1995. Earnhardt qualified fifth and went on to lead 227 laps en route to his fifth win at the now defunct track. *Bill Burt*

North Wilkesboro Record Book – The Modern Era
(min. 5 starts)

Category	Earnhardt's Total	Earnhardt's Rank	Modern Era Track Leader*
Money Won	$853,685	1st	(Darrell Waltrip – 693,565)
Career Starts	36	4th	Dave Marcis – 46
Total Points	5,630	2nd	Darrell Waltrip – 6,435.75
Avg. Start	9.8	8th	Cale Yarborough – 3.9
Avg. Finish	6.3	2nd	Cale Yarborough – 5.7
Wins	5	3rd	Darrell Waltrip – 10
Winning Pct.	13.9	4th	Cale Yarborough – 31.2
Top 5s	21	1st	(Richard Petty – 20)
Top 10s	32	1st	(Terry Labonte – 27)
DNFs	2	46th	J.D. McDuffie – 16
Poles	1	15th	Darrell Waltrip – 9
Front Row Starts	3	13th	Darrell Waltrip – 13
Laps Led	2,680	3rd	Darrell Waltrip – 2,923
Pct. Led	18.6	2nd	Cale Yarborough – 25.1
Races Led	24	T-1st	(Darrell Waltrip – 24)
Times Led	58	3rd	Darrell Waltrip – 65
Times Led Most Laps	7	2nd	R. Petty, D. Waltrip – 8
Bonus Points	155	2nd	Darrell Waltrip – 160
Laps Completed	13,974	4th	Darrell Waltrip – 17,370
Pct. of Laps Completed	97.0	8th	Ken Schrader – 99.2
Points per Race	156.4	1st	(Bobby Allison – 147.2)
Fin. on Lead Lap	22	1st	(Darrell Waltrip – 19)

*2nd-place driver or co-leader listed in parentheses if Earnhardt is track leader.

Track Performance Chart

North Wilkesboro Speedway

Wilkesboro, North Carolina, .625 miles, 36° banking

Year	Date	Race	St.	Fin.	Total Laps	Laps Completed	Laps Led	Condition	Money	Pts.	Bonus Pts.
1979	Mar 25	Northwestern Bank 400	5	4	400	400	9	Running	$4,275	165	5
	Oct 14	Holly Farms 400	1	4	400	398	12	Running	10,425	165	5
1980	Apr 20	Northwestern Bank 400	4	6	400	395	0	Running	6,525	150	0
	Sep 21	Holly Farms 400	8	5	400	399	0	Running	6,925	155	0
1981	Apr 5	Northwestern Bank 400	2	10	400	395	0	Running	8,800	134	0
	Oct 4	Holly Farms 400	10	4	400	399	0	Running	7,270	160	0
1982	Apr 18	Northwestern Bank 400	14	3	400	400	10	Running	12,425	170	5
	Oct 3	Holly Farms 400	15	20	400	365	0	DNF - Brakes	7,235	103	0
1983	Apr 17	Northwestern Bank 400	11	29	400	40	0	DNF - Engine	6,450	76	0
	Oct 2	Holly Farms 400	6	2	400	400	134	Running	15,500	175	5
1984	Apr 8	Northwestern Bank 400	10	8	400	399	0	Running	7,260	142	0
	Oct 14	Holly Farms 400	9	7	400	400	0	Running	8,150	146	0
1985	Apr 21	Northwestern Bank 400	8	8	400	398	1	Running	8,340	147	5
	Sep 29	Holly Farms 400	7	4	400	400	37	Running	10,960	165	5
1986	Apr 20	First Union 400	5	1	400	400	195	Running	38,550	185	10
	Sep 28	Holly Farms 400	14	9	400	398	24	Running	9,500	143	5
1987	Apr 5	First Union 400	3	1	400	400	319	Running	44,675	185	10
	Oct 4	Holly Farms 400	10	2	400	400	137	Running	26,950	175	5
1988	Apr 17	First Union 400	10	3	400	400	265	Running	22,115	175	10
	Oct 16	Holly Farms 400	22	6	400	400	107	Running	15,475	155	5
1989	Apr 16	First Union 400	3	1	400	400	296	Running	51,225	185	10
	Oct 15	Holly Farms 400	1	10	400	400	343	Running	15,155	144	10
1990	Apr 22	First Union 400	4	3	400	400	72	Running	21,775	170	5
	Sep 30	Tyson/Holly Farms 400	8	2	400	400	291	Running	32,075	180	10
1991	Apr 21	First Union 400	17	2	400	400	19	Running	35,225	175	5
	Sep 29	Tyson/Holly Farms 400	16	1	400	400	9	Running	69,350	180	5
1992	Apr 12	First Union 400	9	6	400	400	36	Running	32,540	155	5
	Oct 5	Tyson/Holly Farms 400	13	19	400	395	0	Running	15,350	106	0
1993	Apr 18	First Union 400	21	16	400	396	0	Running	13,130	115	0
	Oct 3	Tyson/Holly Farms 400	10	2	400	400	59	Running	46,285	175	5
1994	Apr 17	First Union 400	19	5	400	400	0	Running	26,740	155	0
	Oct 2	Tyson 400	3	7	400	398	38	Running	21,315	151	5
1995	Apr 9	First Union 400	5	1	400	400	227	Running	77,400	185	10
	Oct 1	Tyson 400	13	9	400	399	5	Running	27,850	143	5
1996	Apr 14	First Union 400	26	3	400	400	0	Running	38,525	165	0
	Sep 29	Tyson 400	11	2	400	400	35	Running	51,940	175	5

Earnhardt at Ontario Motor Speedway

Dale Earnhardt's experience at Ontario Motor Speedway was brief and his on-track performance was respectable. But few tracks could ever claim to be as lucrative for the Winston Cup legend as Ontario. Earnhardt raced at the California track just three times (once as a relief driver in 1978) before it disappeared from the Winston Cup schedule after the 1980 season. His visits in 1979 and 1980 capped significant accomplishments.

In his first Ontario start in 1979 as a rookie, Earnhardt used a ninth-place finish to solidify his hold on the Rookie of the Year award. Earnhardt beat Joe Millikan in the rookie standings, but actually trailed Millikan in the final Winston Cup standings (4,014 to 3,749). The difference was due to Earnhardt's missing four races due to injury earlier in the season.

Earnhardt's visit to Ontario the following season proved even more significant—and difficult. Earnhardt finished fifth in the 1980 Ontario race and claimed his first Winston Cup championship, but nearly lost it all to Cale Yarborough. Entering the race just 29 points behind Earnhardt in the standings, Yarborough did just about everything he had to, winning the won the pole, leading a lap and then nearly winning the race. Meanwhile, Earnhardt qualified second and used a fifth-place finish to preserve his championship by 19 points over Yarborough, the fifth closest points battle in Winston Cup history.

Ontario Record Book – All-Time
(min. 2 starts)

Category	Earnhardt's Total	Earnhardt's Rank	All-Time Track Leader*
Money Won	$18,335	13th	Bobby Allison – 99,655
Career Starts	2	47th	6 tied with 9 Career Starts
Total Points	303	40th	Bobby Allison – 1,248
Avg. Start	4.0	5th	A.J. Foyt – 2.4
Avg. Finish	7.0	4th	Cale Yarborough – 5.9
Wins	0	—	B. Allison, A.J. Foyt, B. Parsons – 2
Winning Pct.	0.0	—	A.J. Foyt – 40.0
Top 5s	1	10th	Buddy Baker – 7
Top 10s	2	13th	B. Allison, B. Baker – 7
DNFs	0	—	Chuck Bown – 6
Poles	0	—	Cale Yarborough – 3
Front Row Starts	1	6th	A.J. Foyt, C. Yarborough – 3
Laps Led	11	14th	A.J. Foyt – 289
Pct. Led	2.8	11th	A.J. Foyt – 28.9
Races Led	2	9th	Richard Petty – 8
Times Led	4	12th	Richard Petty – 43
Times Led Most Laps	0	—	A.J. Foyt – 2
Laps Completed	399	35th	James Hylton – 1,649
Pct. of Laps Completed	99.8	1st	(Joe Millikan – 99.5)
Points per Race	151.5	2nd	Cale Yarborough – 158.2
Lead Lap Finishes	1	9th	B. Allison, B. Baker, C. Yarborough – 5

*2nd-place driver or co-leader listed in parentheses if Earnhardt is track leader.

Track Performance Chart

Ontario Speedway
Ontario, California, 2.5 miles, 10° banking

Year	Date	Race	St.	Fin.	Total Laps	Laps Completed	Laps Led	Condition	Money	Pts.	Bonus Pts.
1979	Nov 18	Los Angeles Times 500	6	9	200	199	8	Running	$7,500	143	5
1980	Nov 15	Los Angeles Times 500	2	5	200	200	3	Running	10,835	160	5

Earnhardt at Phoenix International Raceway

With a win and nine Top 10s in 13 races, Phoenix International Raceway proved to be an immediately reliable track for Dale Earnhardt when it joined the Winston Cup series in 1988. The track became truly memorable for Earnhardt in 1990, however, when he delivered the best performance in track history—an effort that not only put him in the track's record books, but also propelled him to his fourth Winston Cup championship.

Earnhardt trailed Mark Martin in the 1990 championship chase by 45 points when the series arrived for its November race at Phoenix. Earnhardt needed something special to catch Martin. For five months, while getting close, he could never shake Martin from the top spot in the point standings. He got what he needed on lap 51 when he took the lead from polesitter Rusty Wallace and never gave it up. Earnhardt set a track record for laps led by fronting the remaining 262 laps. At precisely the right time, he won his first and only race on the 1-mile track. Martin, in many respects the best NASCAR driver ever at Phoenix, finished the race in 10th place and suddenly saw his five-month grip on the Winston Cup points lead vanish as Earnhardt took a six-point advantage. Earnhardt went on to win the 1990 title.

Similar to his performance in the fall race at Martinsville in 1980—a race Earnhardt won, boosting him to his first Winston Cup championship—the 1990 Phoenix race was yet more proof of Earnhardt's ability to generate a spectacular effort at precisely the right moment.

Phoenix Record Book – All-Time

(min. 5 starts)

Category	Earnhardt's Total	Earnhardt's Rank	Modern Era Track Leader*
Money Won	$494,480	2nd	Mark Martin – 603,460
Career Starts	13	T-1st	10 Others with 13
Total Points	1,840	2nd	Mark Martin – 1,982
Avg. Start	14.6	11th	Rusty Wallace – 5.0
Avg. Finish	9.5	3rd	Alan Kulwicki – 5.2
Wins	1	2nd	Davey Allison – 2
Winning Pct.	7.7	6th	Davey Allison – 40.0
Top 5s	5	3rd	Mark Martin – 7
Top 10s	9	2nd	Mark Martin – 11
DNFs	1	27th	Dick Trickle – 5
Poles	0	—	Rusty Wallace – 3
Front Row Starts	1	6th	Rusty Wallace – 5
Laps Led	337	4th	Rusty Wallace – 777
Pct. Led	8.4	6th	Rusty Wallace – 19.4
Races Led	5	3rd	M. Martin, R. Wallace – 9
Times Led	7	9th	M. Martin, R. Wallace – 20
Times Led Most Laps	1	3rd	Rusty Wallace – 3
Bonus Points	30	3rd	Rusty Wallace – 60
Laps Completed	3,777	8th	Terry Labonte – 3,995
Pct. of Laps Completed	94.4	21st	Alan Kulwicki – 100.0
Points per Race	141.5	3rd	Alan Kulwicki – 160.0
Lead Lap Finishes	9	2nd	Mark Martin – 11

*2nd-place driver or co-leader listed in parentheses if Earnhardt is track leader.

Track Performance Chart
Phoenix International Raceway

Phoenix, Arizona, 1.0 mile, 9-11° banking

Year	Date	Race	St.	Fin.	Total Laps	Laps Completed	Laps Led	Condition	Money	Pts.	Bonus Pts.
1988	Nov 6	Checker 500	13	11	312	311	0	Running	$15,100	130	0
1989	Nov 5	Autoworks 500	7	6	312	312	0	Running	16,995	150	0
1990	Nov 4	Checker 500	3	1	312	312	262	Running	72,100	185	10
1991	Nov 3	Pyroil 500	12	9	312	311	0	Running	18,200	138	0
1992	Nov 1	Pyroil 500K	19	10	312	311	0	Running	21,370	134	0
1993	Oct 31	Slick 50 500	11	4	312	312	2	Running	29,980	165	5
1994	Oct 30	Slick 50 300	8	40	312	91	0	DNF - Engine	19,575	43	0
1995	Oct 29	Dura-Lube 500K	2	3	312	312	71	Running	49,105	170	5
1996	Oct 27	Dura-Lube 500K	24	12	312	312	0	Running	29,055	127	0
1997	Nov 2	Dura-Lube 500	7	5	312	312	1	Running	39,300	160	5
1998	Oct 25	Dura Lube/Kmart 500	39	3	257	257	0	Running	57,175	165	0
1999	Nov 7	Checker/Dura Lube 500	14	11	312	312	0	Running	57,225	130	0
2000	Nov 5	Checker/DuraLube 500K	31	9	312	312	1	Running	69,300	143	5

Most Laps Led, Single Race*

Driver	Laps Led	Race
Dale Earnhardt	262	1990 Checker 500
Mark Martin	212	1993 Slick 50 500
Rusty Wallace	196	1998 Dura Lube 500
Ricky Rudd	183	1988 Checker 500
Davey Allison	162	1991 Pyroil 500

*Race length is 312 laps, except 1998 when rain shortened race to 257 laps

Earnhardt at Pocono Raceway

When he entered the Winston Cup Grand National world in 1979, Dale Earnhardt and Pocono Raceway never really hit it off. And their relationship never improved much over the course of Earnhardt's 22-year career.

Earnhardt's introduction to Pocono seemed friendly enough. In his first start at the uniquely shaped 2.5-mile track, the 28-year-old rookie qualified third and was working his way into the lead on lap 98 when he got caught up in one of the worst crashes of his career—a violent wreck that broke both collar bones and a leg. For the first and only time in his career, Earnhardt missed a race—four of them, to be precise, including the 1979 Southern 500 (which David Pearson ran in Earnhardt's place, and won). Foreshadowing the toughness that he would exhibit throughout his career, Earnhardt marked his return from the Pocono crash by winning the pole in his first two post-wreck qualifying efforts.

As for his relationship with Pocono, it took much longer to heal than the injuries he sustained in '79. The Pennsylvania track was never one of Earnhardt's favorites. In 41 starts, he won just twice and collected a relatively unimpressive 10 Top 5s, well off his career averages. To prove his mettle, Earnhardt returned the year after his wreck and finished fourth in the 1980 Coca-Cola 500. After that effort, however, his performance lacked the consistent excellence he demonstrated elsewhere.

Not until his 15th start was Earnhardt able to conquer Pocono. That win came during his championship season in 1987, when he won a career-high 11 races. His only other Pocono win came during another championship season, 1993.

Pocono Record Book – All-Time
(min. 5 starts)

Category	Earnhardt's Total	Earnhardt's Rank	All-Time Track Leader*
Money Won	$1,089,420	1st	(Jeff Gordon – 1,051,760)
Starts	41	3rd	Darrell Waltrip – 44
Total Points	5,230	2nd	Darrell Waltrip – 5,286
Avg. Start	11.6	12th	David Pearson – 4.7
Avg. Finish	14.1	11th	Jeff Gordon – 9.7
Wins	2	8th	Elliott, Richmond, R. Wallace, D. Waltrip – 4
Winning Pct.	4.9	17th	Tim Richmond – 28.6
Top 5s	10	6th	H. Gant, M. Martin – 14
Top 10s	22	1st	(Elliott, Martin, D.Waltrip – 20)
DNFs	9	9th	Dave Marcis – 15th
Poles	0	—	Ken Schrader – 5
Front Row Starts	0	—	Ken Schrader – 8
Laps Led	455	6th	Geoffrey Bodine – 809
Pct. Led	5.6	16th	David Pearson – 27.8
Races Led	24	1st	(Geoffrey Bodine – 23)
Times Led	60	5th	Darrell Waltrip – 106
Times Led Most Laps	2	7th	Geoffrey Bodine – 6
Bonus Points	130	2nd	Geoffrey Bodine – 145
Laps Completed	7,053	4th	Terry Labonte – 7,502
Pct. of Laps Completed	86.8	36th	Kevin Lepage – 99.8
Points per Race	127.6	9th	Jeff Gordon – 146.1
Fin. on Lead Lap	23	1st	(Mark Martin – 22)

*2nd-place driver or co-leader listed in parentheses if Earnhardt is track leader.

Memorable Pocono Moment
2000 Pocono 500. Earnhardt appeared headed to his third Pocono win and a step closer to points leader Bobby Labonte when Jeremy Mayfield decided to pull an 'Earnhardt.' Going into the race's final turn, Mayfield closed in on the back bumper of Earnhardt's car and, well, rattled his cage a little. Bumped out of the groove by Mayfield, Earnhardt saved his sliding car from hitting the wall, but not before slipping back to fourth place. Mayfield rolled to the win. The bump-and-run extended Earnhardt's Pocono winless streak to 13 races.

A common theme in the stories told by those who knew Earnhardt best was his ability to instill confidence in those he entrusted. In 1998, after Steve Park was injured in a wreck at Atlanta, Earnhardt tapped former rival Darrell Waltrip to pilot his No. 1 Pennzoil car. Waltrip responded with his best performances in years, including at Pocono where he led with just 11 laps remaining and finished sixth. Three years later, another Waltrip—Michael—was inspired by Earnhardt's trust; he won the 2001 Daytona 500, Earnhardt's last race. *Bill Burt*

Track Performance Chart

Pocono Raceway

Long Pond, Pennsylvania, 2.5 miles, 6-14° banking

Year	Date	Race	St.	Fin.	Total Laps	Laps Completed	Laps Led	Condition	Money	Pts.	Bonus Pts.
1979	Jul 30	Coca-Cola 500	3	29	200	98	43	DNF - Crash	$4,680	81	5
1980	Jul 27	Coca-Cola 500	11	4	200	200	6	Running	11,415	165	5
1981	Jul 26	Mountain Dew 500	8	11	200	198	4	Running	9,190	135	5
1982	Jul 6	Van Scoy Diamond Mine 500	4	34	200	45	8	DNF - Ball Joint	8,575	66	5
	Jul 25	Mountain Dew 500	7	25	200	134	9	DNF - Crash	9,700	93	5
1983	Jun 12	Van Scoy Diamond Mine 500	9	8	200	199	0	Running	11,200	142	0
	Jul 24	Like Cola 500	10	30	200	71	0	DNF - Engine	8,500	73	0
1984	Jun 10	Van Scoy Diamond Mine 500	8	8	200	199	34	Running	11,360	147	5
	Jul 22	Like Cola 500	5	10	200	198	9	Running	11,300	139	5
1985	Jun 9	Van Scoy Diamond Mine 500	4	39	200	3	0	DNF - Engine	8,700	46	0
	Jul 21	Summer 500	11	39	200	11	0	DNF - Engine	8,700	46	0
1986	Jun 8	Miller High Life 500	8	2	200	200	8	Running	29,750	175	5
	Jul 20	Summer 500	10	7	150	150	0	Running	14,655	146	0
1987	Jun 14	Miller High Life 500	7	5	200	200	56	Running	22,400	160	5
	Jul 19	Summer 500	16	1	200	200	85	Running	55,875	185	10
1988	Jun 19	Miller High Life 500	18	33	200	93	0	DNF - Engine	13,045	64	0
	Jul 24	AC Spark Plug 500	9	11	200	200	0	Running	15,025	130	0
1989	Jun 18	Miller High Life 500	7	3	200	200	12	Running	29,250	170	5
	Jul 23	AC Spark Plug 500	3	9	200	200	3	Running	14,275	143	5
1990	Jun 17	Miller Genuine Draft 500	6	13	200	200	3	Running	14,150	129	5
	Jul 22	AC Spark Plug 500	11	4	200	200	6	Running	22800	165	5
1991	Jun 16	Champion Spark Plug 500	21	2	200	200	28	Running	43,775	175	5
	Jul 21	Miller Genuine Draft 500	16	22	179	175	0	Running	15,350	97	0
1992	Jun 14	Champion Spark Plug 500	17	28	200	148	0	DNF - Engine	16,600	79	0
	Jul 19	Miller Genuine Draft 500	29	23	200	199	0	Running	16,540	94	0
1993	Jun 13	Champion Spark Plug 500	5	11	200	200	20	Running	14,815	135	5
	Jul 18	Miller Genuine Draft 500	11	1	200	200	71	Running	66,795	185	10
1994	Jun 12	UAW-GM 500	19	2	200	200	6	Running	46,425	175	5
	Jul 17	Miller 500	20	7	200	200	0	Running	26,210	146	0
1995	Jun 11	UAW-GM 500	24	8	200	200	0	Running	32,455	142	0
	Jul 16	Miller 500	5	20	200	199	0	Running	31,555	103	0
1996	Jun 16	UAW-GM 500	10	32	200	135	0	DNF - Engine	26,035	67	0
	Jul 21	Miller 500	8	14	200	199	0	Running	27,925	121	0
1997	Jun 8	Pocono 500	12	10	200	200	0	Running	34,025	134	0
	Jul 20	Pennsylvania 500	5	12	200	200	2	Running	29,490	132	5
1998	Jun 21	Pocono 500	11	8	200	200	1	Running	34,625	147	5
	Jul 26	Pennsylvania 500	9	7	200	200	14	Running	49,890	151	5
1999	Jun 20	Pocono 500	25	7	200	200	0	Running	57,190	146	5
	Jul 25	Pennsylvania 500	11	9	200	200	4	Running	48,765	143	5
2000	Jun 18	Pocono 500	16	4	200	200	17	Running	87,495	165	5
	Jul 23	Pennsylvania 500	25	25	200	199	6	Running	48,915	93	5

Earnhardt at Richmond International Raceway

Richmond International Raceway was an unwavering friend to Dale Earnhardt throughout his Winston Cup career. As a rookie, he took an immediate liking to the track and his affection grew nearly unabated thereafter.

In his second visit to the track in 1979, he won the pole and followed with his first Richmond Top 5, finishing fourth. In his first 25 trips to the Virginia track, Earnhardt scored 18 Top 5s and 22 Top 10s. During one amazing 14-race stretch from 1984 to 1991, Earnhardt collected all five of his Richmond wins and finished fourth or better 13 times. With 25 career Top 5s and 33 Top 10s, Richmond was one of Earnhardt's most consistent and productive tracks, equaled only by Atlanta.

Earnhardt experienced a brief falling-out with the track during the 1996, 1997, and 1998 seasons, during which his general problems extended to Richmond. In those three seasons, he failed to finish any better than 15th on the .75-mile track.

In the final years of his career, however, the spark seemed to return. Four consecutive Top 10s were capped in 2000 by a strong second place in the fall race, a Winston No Bull Million event that the eligible Earnhardt was hoping to collect. He was gaining on eventual winner Jeff Gordon when the checkered flag fell. Later, Gordon was penalized 100 points but was allowed to keep his win when NASCAR discovered an illegal intake manifold during post-race inspection.

Richmond Record Book – The Modern Era
(min. 5 starts)

Category	Earnhardt's Total	Earnhardt's Rank	Modern Era Track Leader*
Money Won	$1,272,235	1st	(Rusty Wallace – 1,060,515)
Starts	44	4th	Darrell Waltrip – 51
Total Points	6,546	2nd	Darrell Waltrip – 7,062
Avg. Start	13.2	18th	Benny Parsons – 5.2
Avg. Finish	8.3	2nd	Bobby Allison – 7.8
Wins	5	5th	B. Allison, R. Petty, R. Wallace, D. Waltrip – 6
Winning Pct.	11.4	8th	Bobby Allison – 20.0
Top 5s	25	1st	(Darrell Waltrip – 22)
Top 10s	33	T-1st	(Darrell Waltrip – 33)
DNFs	2	68th	J.D. McDuffie – 12
Poles	2	8th	Bobby Allison – 8
Front Row Starts	3	10	Darrell Waltrip – 14
Laps Led	1,976	5th	Richard Petty – 2,570
Pct. Led	11.3	7th	Bobby Allison – 20.5
Races Led	24	2nd	Darrell Waltrip – 27
Times Led	72	1st	(Rusty Wallace – 69)
Times Led Most Laps	5	4th	B. Allison, R. Wallace – 7
Bonus Points	145	2nd	Darrell Waltrip – 165
Laps Completed	16,808	3rd	Darrell Waltrip – 18,741
Pct. of Laps Completed	96.3	8th	Ted Musgrave – 99.4
Points per Race	148.8	2nd	Bobby Allison – 152.3
Lead Lap Finishes	25	1st	(Rusty Wallace – 23)

* 2nd-place driver or co-leader listed in parentheses if Earnhardt is track leader.

Earnhardt's Most Productive Tracks

Track	Top 5s	Top 10s	Points Earned
Atlanta	26	30	6,715
Richmond	25	33	6,546
Daytona	22	34	6,507
Bristol	20	30	6,303
Talladega	23	27	6,085

Earnhardt enjoyed a highly successful 2000 season as a car owner, getting three wins out of the teams he bankrolls. Steve Park, pictured, is one of Earnhardt's drivers, piloting the No. 1 Pennzoil team. *David Stringer*

Track Performance Chart

Richmond International Raceway

Richmond, Virginia, .750 miles, 14° banking

Year	Date	Race	St.	Fin.	Total Laps	Laps Completed	Laps Led	Condition	Money	Pts.	Bonus Pts.
1979	Mar 11	Richmond 400	4	13	400	390	0	Running	$2,015	124	0
	Sep 9	Capital City 400	1	4	400	399	19	Running	7,250	165	5
1980	Feb 24	Richmond 400	13	5	400	398	0	Running	6,550	155	0
	Sep 7	Capital City 400	5	4	400	399	39	Running	7,575	165	5
1981	Feb 22	Richmond 400	6	7	400	397	0	Running	7,550	146	0
	Sep 13	Wrangler Sanfor-Set 400	11	6	400	398	0	Running	6,270	150	0
1982	Feb 21	Richmond 400	8	4	250	250	1	Running	10,960	165	5
	Sep 12	Wrangler Sanfor-Set 400	6	27	400	158	0	DNF - Engine	7,105	82	0
1983	Feb 27	Richmond 400	8	2	400	400	81	Running	16,575	175	5
	Sep 11	Wrangler Sanfor-Set 400	9	22	400	181	0	DNF - Rear End	6,850	97	0
1984	Feb 26	Miller High Life 400	17	6	400	399	0	Running	8,675	150	0
	Sep 9	Wrangler Sanfor-Set 400	13	3	400	400	9	Running	13,450	170	5
1985	Feb 24	Miller High Life 400	4	1	400	400	95	Running	33,625	180	5
	Sep 8	Wrangler Sanfor-Set 400	9	4	400	400	24	Running	12,050	165	5
1986	Feb 23	Miller High Life 400	10	3	400	400	299	Running	19,310	175	10
	Sep 7	Wrangler Jeans Indigo 400	5	2	400	400	24	Running	24,525	175	5
1987	Mar 8	Miller High Life 400	3	1	400	400	235	Running	49,150	185	10
	Sep 13	Wrangler Jeans Indigo 400	8	1	400	400	220	Running	44,950	185	10
1988	Feb 21	Pontiac Excitement 400	2	10	400	399	151	Running	16,245	144	10
	Sep 11	Miller High Life 400	19	2	400	400	78	Running	29,625	175	5
1989	Mar 26	Pontiac Excitement 400	6	3	400	400	43	Running	30,900	170	5
	Sep 10	Miller High Life 400	8	2	400	400	135	Running	31,475	175	5
1990	Feb 25	Pontiac Excitement 400	4	2	400	400	41	Running	42,600	175	5
	Sep 9	Miller Genuine Draft 400	6	1	400	400	173	Running	59,225	185	10
1991	Feb 24	Pontiac Excitement 400	19	1	400	400	150	Running	67,950	180	5
	Sep 7	Miller Genuine Draft 400	16	11	400	398	5	Running	13,750	135	5
1992	Mar 8	Pontiac Excitement 400	29	11	400	399	0	Running	16,600	130	0
	Sep 12	Miller Genuine Draft 400	11	4	400	400	0	Running	29,655	160	0
1993	Mar 7	Pontiac Excitement 400	11	10	400	399	0	Running	17,000	134	0
	Sep 11	Miller Genuine Draft 400	8	3	400	400	0	Running	35,780	165	0
1994	Mar 6	Pontiac Excitement 400	9	4	400	400	10	Running	29,550	165	5
	Sep 10	Miller 400	12	3	400	400	41	Running	38,830	170	5
1995	Mar 5	Pontiac Excitement 400	26	2	400	400	11	Running	57,200	175	5
	Sep 9	Miller 400	1	3	400	400	73	Running	54,005	170	5
1996	Mar 3	Pontiac Excitement 400	9	31	400	393	0	Running	27,265	70	0
	Sep 7	Miller 400	23	20	400	398	0	Running	30,100	103	0
1997	Mar 26	Pontiac Excitement 400	4	25	400	397	0	Running	27,940	88	0
	Sep 6	Exide Batteries 400	22	15	400	398	0	Running	33,775	118	0
1998	Jun 6	Pontiac Excitement 400	38	21	400	398	0	Running	34,250	100	0
	Sep 12	Exide Batteries 400	34	38	400	260	0	Running	34,495	49	0
1999	May 15	Pontiac Excitement 400	37	8	400	400	0	Running	48,540	142	0
	Sep 11	Exide Batteries 400	33	6	400	400	0	Running	47,055	150	0
2000	May 6	Pontiac Excitement 400	31	10	400	400	19	Running	52,800	139	5
	Sep 9	Chevrolet Monte Carlo 400	22	2	400	400	0	Running	81,190	170	0

Earnhardt at Riverside International Raceway

For a kid growing up on the small-town bullrings of North Carolina, that first trip to Riverside, California, must have been something of a culture shock for young Dale Earnhardt. Sure, the care-free lifestyle of Southern California probably made an impression—but don't forget about the right turns.

For many years NASCAR's lone road course (visited twice a year, three times in 1981), Riverside offered Winston Cup drivers a chance to test their skills on something other than an oval.

Earnhardt was a quick learner, and his 1979 performance at Riverside was indicative of what the brash rookie had to offer. After a less-than-inspiring 21st-place finish in his first start in January of 1979, Earnhardt returned that summer and won the pole for the June race—the first pole of his Winston Cup career.

Soon after, the strong finishes began to accumulate. Though he never won at Riverside before it closed in 1988 (Earnhardt did not win on a road course until 1995 at Sears Point), Earnhardt compiled 13 Top 5 finishes at the track – a feat surpassed only by NASCAR giants Bobby Allison, Richard Petty and Benny Parsons.

Riverside Record Book – The Modern Era
(min. 5 starts)

Category	Earnhardt's Total	Earnhardt's Rank	Modern Era Track Leader*
Money Won	$255,165	5th	Bobby Allison – 390,350
Career Starts	20	10th	B. Allison, R. Petty – 34
Total Points	2,793	10th	Bobby Allison – 4,975.75
Avg. Start	6.8	6th	Cale Yarborough – 3.8
Avg. Finish	10.7	5th	Cale Yarborough – 7.4
Wins	0	—	B. Allison, D. Waltrip – 5
Winning Pct.	0.0	—	Tim Richmond – 28.6
Top 5s	13	3rd	Bobby Allison – 15
Top 10s	14	5th	Richard Petty – 23
DNFs	3	55th	Hershel McGriff – 19
Poles	1	7th	Darrell Waltrip – 9
Front Row Starts	2	10th	Darrell Waltrip – 15
Laps Led	58	13th	Bobby Allison – 820
Pct. Led	2.7	13th	Cale Yarborough – 35.6
Races Led	9	6th	Bobby Allison – 22
Times Led	15	9th	Bobby Allison – 69
Times Led Most Laps	0	—	Bobby Allison – 8
Bonus Points	45	8th	Bobby Allison – 150
Laps Completed	1,903	12th	Bobby Allison – 3,754
Pct. of Laps Completed	88.9	10th	Jody Ridley – 97.8
Points per Race	139.7	8th	David Pearson – 153.5
Lead Lap Finishes	15	3rd	Bobby Allison – 18

* 2nd-place driver or co-leader listed in parentheses if Earnhardt is track leader.

Most Top 5 Finishes at Riverside
All-Time

Driver	No. of Top 5s
Bobby Allison	19
Benny Parsons	15
Richard Petty	15
Dale Earnhardt	13
David Pearson	11
Cale Yarborough	11

"[Earnhardt is] a pure driver. He might have won three hundred races if he'd come along when I did."
—*Richard Petty*

Track Performance Chart

Riverside International Raceway

Riverside, California, 2.62 miles, Road Course

Year	Date	Race	St.	Fin.	Total Laps	Laps Completed	Laps Led	Condition	Money	Pts.	Bonus Pts.
1979	Jan 14	Winston Western 500	10	21	119	103	0	Running	$2,230	100	0
	Jun 10	NAPA Riverside 400	1	13	95	87	2	Running	7,250	129	5
1980	Jan 19	Winston Western 500	5	2	119	119	0	Running	19,400	170	0
	Jun 8	Warner W. Hodgdon 400	5	5	95	95	21	Running	9,100	160	5
1981	Jan 11	Winston Western 500	6	3	119	119	0	Running	16,325	165	0
	Jun 14	Warner W. Hodgdon 400	2	2	95	95	11	Running	18,725	175	5
	Nov 22	Winston Western 500	3	4	119	119	0	Running	10,560	160	0
1982	Jun 13	Budweiser 400	5	4	95	95	5	Running	11,935	165	5
	Nov 21	Winston Western 500	7	42	119	8	0	DNF - Oil Leak	8,125	37	0
1983	Jun 5	Budweiser 400	15	4	95	95	0	Running	11,475	160	0
	Nov 20	Winston Western 500	9	4	119	119	4	Running	13,725	165	5
1984	Jun 3	Budweiser 400	3	5	95	95	0	Running	10,950	155	0
	Nov 18	Winston Western 500	4	11	119	119	0	Running	9,000	130	0
1985	Jun 2	Budweiser 400	13	40	95	19	0	DNF - Engine	8,240	43	0
	Nov 17	Winston Western 500	7	5	119	119	6	Running	13,175	160	5
1986	Jun 1	Budweiser 400	10	5	95	95	0	Running	14,125	155	0
	Nov 16	Winston Western 500	8	2	119	119	1	Running	26,750	175	5
1987	Jun 21	Budweiser 400	8	7	95	95	0	Running	13,500	146	0
	Nov 8	Winston Western 500	8	30	119	93	1	DNF - Engine	11,975	78	5
1988	Jun 12	Budweiser 400	6	4	95	95	7	Running	18,600	165	5

The "Dream Team" that never was, Earnhardt and crew chief Larry McReynolds never found the success they expected when they teamed in 1997. In their 45 races together, Earnhardt's average start was 22nd and his average finish was 14th. Though they won just one race together, it was a huge victory: the 1998 Daytona 500. *Bill Burt*

Earnhardt at Sears Point Raceway

He really didn't need it, but Dale Earnhardt added an important bullet point to his resume in 1995 when he won at Sears Point Raceway. The victory—his first on a road course—came in his 36th attempt to conquer right turns.

Similar to his quest for a Daytona 500 win, Earnhardt had done just about everything there is to do on a Winston Cup road course before finally getting that first win. In those 36 attempts at Riverside, Watkins Glen and Sears Point, he had won poles (four), led laps (174) and accumulated Top-5 (18) and Top-10 (26) finishes at an impressive rate. But not until he passed Mark Martin in the hairpin turn 12 at Sears Point with just two laps to go in 1995 had he ever finished first on a road course.

In true Earnhardt fashion, when wins were not forthcoming, he turned to unyielding consistency. From 1991 through 2000, Earnhardt was the only driver to complete all 854 competitive laps run on the winding Sonoma, Calif., track. Only Martin, a road-course master, has more Top 10s at Sears Point (10 to Earnhardt's 9). Though a late-career tendency to qualify poorly hit Earnhardt hard at Sears Point (he averaged a 25th starting spot after 1996), the ability to finish well also marked Earnhardt's efforts (he averaged a ninth-place finish during the same span).

Sears Point Record Book – All-Time
(min. 5 starts)

Category	Earnhardt's Total	Earnhardt's Rank	All-Time Track Leader*
Money Won	$450,205	5th	Jeff Gordon – 607,465
Starts	12	T-1st	10 others with 12 Starts
Total Points	1,737	2nd	Mark Martin – 1,758
Avg. Start	11.9	7th	Jeff Gordon – 5.3
Avg. Finish	8.6	2nd	Jeff Gordon – 7.8
Wins	1	4th	Jeff Gordon – 3
Winning Pct.	8.3	6th	Jeff Gordon – 37.5
Top 5s	4	5th	Martin, Rudd, R. Wallace – 7
Top 10s	9	2nd	Mark Martin – 10
DNFs	0	—	Hershel McGriff
Poles	1	4th	Ricky Rudd – 4
Front Row Starts	1	7th	Ricky Rudd – 6
Laps Led	45	6th	Jeff Gordon – 183
Pct. Led	4.5	7th	Jeff Gordon – 25.9
Races Led	4	3rd	Rusty Wallace – 8
Times Led	6	6th	Rusty Wallace – 15
Times Led Most Laps	1	4th	J. Gordon, R. Wallace – 3
Bonus Points	25	5th	Rusty Wallace – 55
Laps Completed	993	2nd	Michael Waltrip – 996
Pct. of Laps Completed	99.1	6th	Johnny Benson – 100.0
Points per Race	144.8	3rd	Jeff Gordon – 153.4
Lead Lap Finishes	11	1st	4 tied with 10 Lead Lap Fin.

* 2nd-place driver or co-leader listed in parentheses if Earnhardt is track leader.

"I caught Earnhardt and I really thought I might have had a shot at passing him, but you know, his bumper gets mighty wide there at the end."
—*Rick Mast, after finishing second to Earnhardt in the 1994 AC-Delco 500*

Track Performance Chart
Sears Point Raceway
Sonoma, Caliornia, 1.949 miles, Road Course

Year	Date	Race	St.	Fin.	Total Laps	Laps Completed	Laps Led	Condition	Money	Pts.	Bonus Pts.
1989	Jun 11	Banquet Frozen Foods 300	10	4	74	74	0	Running	$20,350	160	0
1990	Jun 10	Banquet Frozen Foods 300	3	34	74	65	0	Running	12,650	61	0
1991	Jun 9	Banquet Frozen Foods 300	3	7	74	74	0	Running	19,800	146	0
1992	Jun 7	Save Mart 300K	12	6	74	74	0	Running	21,910	150	0
1993	May 16	Save Mart Supermarkets 300K	1	6	74	74	33	Running	27,790	160	10
1994	May 15	Save Mart 300	4	3	74	74	3	Running	37,825	170	5
1995	May 7	Save Mart 300	4	1	74	74	2	Running	74,860	180	5
1996	May 5	Save Mart 300	5	4	74	74	7	Running	39,160	165	5
1997	May 5	Save Mart Supermarkets 300	32	12	74	74	0	Running	39,580	127	0
1998	Jun 28	Save Mart/Kragen 300K	17	11	112	112	0	Running	44,950	130	0
1999	Jun 27	Save Mart Supermarkets 300	23	9	112	112	0	Running	46,165	138	0
2000	Jun 25	Save Mart/Kragen 300	29	6	112	112	0	Running	65,165	150	0

Starting in 1998, Earnhardt became a full-time Winston Cup car owner, fielding the No. 1 Pennzoil Chevy with driver Steve Park. In 2000, Earnhardt added the No. 8 Budweiser Chevy piloted by his son, Dale Jr. A third car will be added to the stable in 2001 when the Michael Waltrip-driven NAPA Auto Parts Chevy takes the track. *Bill Burt*

Earnhardt at Talladega SuperSpeedway

According to legend, Dale Earnhardt could "see the air" during Winston Cup restrictor plate races. It's hard to question that myth at Talladega, the longest and fastest of NASCAR's tracks. Earnhardt won more than twice as many races (10) as the next most prolific winners at the Alabama track (Buddy Baker and Darrell Waltrip). He piled up the most Top 5 finishes in track history and easily the largest pot of cash.

In recent years, Earnhardt only added to his Talladega legend. His performances dropped the jaws of fan and critic alike. In 1999, Earnhardt swept both races, including the memorable Winston 500 during which he climbed from his 27th starting spot into the Top 5 within seven laps. In 2000, he added another win in a remarkable finish in the DieHard 500.

As every driver knows, however, Talladega can bite back. Earnhardt's triumphs at the track were tempered by near tragedies. In 1996, the 2.66-mile D-shaped oval was the site of one of Earnhardt's most violent crashes. In 1998, he suffered second-degree burns to his face in a front stretch crash that was nearly a replay of the 1996 wreck.

Memorable Talladega Moments

2000 Winston 500. Called by many fans "the greatest race of all time," Earnhardt climbed from 22nd place to the lead in the final 10 laps to claim his 10th Talladega victory. Seemingly out of contention, Earnhardt called on his drafting skills and passed 21 cars in eight laps to take the lead with two laps to go. After that, it was no contest.

1996 DieHard 500. In one of the scariest wrecks of his career, Earnhardt became a pinball on the frontstretch of Talladega SuperSpeedway on lap 117. The victim of contact between Ernie Irvan and Sterling Marlin, Earnhardt slammed into the outside retaining wall, flipped on his side in the way of oncoming traffic and was plowed into by three cars, including a hard hit to the roof of the car. He suffered a broken sternum and left collarbone – and a 28th-place finish. Amazingly, he maintained his consecutive starts streak at the Brickyard 400 six days later and won the pole at Watkins Glen 14 days later.

Talladega Point Record Book – The Modern Era
(min. 5 starts)

Category	Earnhardt's Total	Earnhardt's Rank	Modern Era Track Leader*
Money Won	$3,081,045[1]	1st	(Dale Jarrett – 1,992,280)
Starts	44	5th	Dave Marcis – 56
Total Points	6,085	2nd	Darrell Waltrip – 6,297.25
Avg. Start	10.2	5th	Bobby Isaac – 5.2
Avg. Finish	12.4	1st	(Davey Allison – 12.6)
Wins	10	1st	(B. Baker, D. Waltrip – 4)
Winning Pct.	22.7	1st	(Davey Allison – 20.0)
Top 5s	23	1st	(Darrell Waltrip – 14)
Top 10s	27	1st	(B. Elliott, T. Labonte – 22)
DNFs	11	18th	Darrell Waltrip – 23
Poles	3	4th	Bill Elliott – 8
Front Row Starts	6	5th	Bill Elliott – 13
Laps Led	1,377	1st	(Buddy Baker – 1,007)
Pct. Led	16.8	1st	(Davey Allison – 16.7)
Races Led	38	1st	(Darrell Waltrip – 28)
Times Led	203	1st	(Buddy Baker – 199)
Times Led Most Laps	12	1st	(Buddy Baker – 9)
Bonus Points	250	1st	(Buddy Baker – 170)
Laps Completed	7,199	5th	Dave Marcis – 8,993
Pct. of Laps Completed	87.8	28th	Robert Pressley – 96.4
Points per Race	138.3	3rd	Donnie Allison – 142.5
Lead Lap Finishes	27	1st	(Bill Elliott – 23)

*2nd-place driver or co-leader listed in parentheses if Earnhardt is track leader.
[1] Money total includes 2000 No Bull Million bonus.

With 10 wins and more than $3 million in prize winnings, Talladega Superspeedway was Dale Earnhardt's most successful track. No other driver has more than four wins in the track's history. *Bill Burt*

Track Performance Chart

Talladega Superspeedway

Talladega, Alabama, 2.66 miles, 33° banking

Year	Date	Race	St.	Fin.	Total Laps	Laps Completed	Laps Led	Condition	Money	Pts.	Bonus Pts.
1978	Aug 6	Talladega 500	27	12	188	180	0	Running	$2,740	127	0
1979	May 6	Winston 500	14	36	188	4	0	DNF - Crash	5,075	55	0
	Aug 5	Talladega 500	Did Not Start due to Injury								
1980	May 4	Winston 500	4	2	188	188	55	Running	28,700	175	5
	Aug 3	Talladega 500	16	3	188	188	3	Running	16,975	170	5
1981	May 3	Winston 500	4	8	188	183	5	Running	14,775	147	5
	Aug 2	Talladega 500	3	29	188	83	5	DNF - Transmission	9,375	81	5
1982	May 2	Winston 500	20	8	188	186	3	Running	14,850	147	5
	Aug 1	Talladega 500	18	35	188	29	0	DNF - Crash	9,290	58	0
1983	May 1	Winston 500	17	24	188	120	1	DNF - Brakes	10,035	96	5
	Jul 31	Talladega 500	4	1	188	188	41	Running	46,950	185	10
1984	May 6	Winston 500	5	27	188	149	3	Running	10,475	87	5
	Jul 29	Talladega 500	3	1	188	188	40	Running	47,100	180	5
1985	May 5	Winston 500	13	21	188	155	12	DNF - Engine	11,410	105	5
	Jul 28	Talladega 500	14	24	188	156	8	Running	11,080	96	5
1986	May 4	Winston 500	14	2	188	188	18	Running	53,900	175	5
	Jul 27	Talladega 500	2	26	188	153	54	DNF - Engine	15,355	95	10
1987	May 3	Winston 500	5	4	178	178	10	Running	31,350	165	5
	Jul 26	Talladega 500	2	3	188	188	8	Running	35,050	170	5
1988	May 1	Winston 500	16	9	188	188	0	Running	21,500	138	0
	Jul 31	Talladega DieHard 500	6	3	188	188	37	Running	37,775	170	5
1989	May 7	Winston 500	17	8	188	188	2	Running	20,450	147	5
	Jul 30	Talladega DieHard 500	9	11	188	188	0	Running	15,020	130	0
1990	May 6	Winston 500	5	1	188	188	107	Running	98,975	185	10
	Jul 19	DieHard 500	1	1	188	188	134	Running	152,975	185	10
1991	May 6	Winston 500	8	3	188	188	112	Running	56,100	175	10
	Jul 28	DieHard 500	4	1	188	188	101	Running	88,670	185	10
1992	May 3	Winston 500	10	3	188	188	10	Running	46,970	170	5
	Jul 26	DieHard 500	30	40	188	52	0	DNF - Engine	18,140	43	0
1993	May 2	Winston 500	1	4	188	188	102	Running	39,870	170	10
	Jul 25	DieHard 500	11	1	188	188	59	Running	87,315	185	10
1994	May 1	Winston 500	4	1	188	188	64	Running	94,865	180	5
	Jul 24	DieHard 500	1	34	188	80	41	DNF - Engine	30,725	66	5
1995	Apr 30	Winston 500	16	21	188	188	6	Running	34,735	105	5
	Jul 23	DieHard 500	5	3	188	188	20	Running	57,105	170	5
1996	Apr 28	Winston Select 500	16	3	188	188	26	Running	64,620	170	5
	Jul 28	DieHard 500	4	28	129	117	40	DNF - Crash	31,020	89	10
1997	May 10	Winston 500	3	2	188	188	76	Running	85,445	180	10
	Oct 12	DieHard 500	12	29	188	167	25	Running	48,500	81	5
1998	Apr 26	DieHard 500	2	36	188	144	10	DNF - Crash	38,250	60	5
	Oct 11	Winston 500	14	32	188	175	12	DNF - Rear End	40,920	72	5
1999	Apr 25	DieHard 500	17	1	188	188	70	Running	147,795	185	10
	Oct 17	Winston 500	27	1	188	188	18	Running	120,290	180	5
2000	Apr 16	DieHard 500	4	3	188	188	5	Running	92,630	170	5
	Oct 15	Winston 500	20	1	188	188	34	Running	1,135,900	180	5

Earnhardt at Texas Motor Speedway

Dale Earnhardt never needed a lesson in racing economics (Lesson 1: Winning = Big Paycheck) during his career, and certainly not from his son. But that's what he got at Texas Motor Speedway. After four pretty solid years of racing at the new Texas track, Earnhardt direct deposited $373,925 in earnings. Despite that impressive amount, he was still No. 2 among drivers named Dale Earnhardt in Texas winnings after the 2000 season. Earnhardt's son, Dale Jr., out-earned his dad at the track in just one race.

Junior scored his first career Winston Cup win at the Texas track in 2000, a Sunday drive worth more than $374,000. Besides being lucrative, Junior's win was historic. The 25-year-old driver matched his dad with a victory in just the seventh race of his rookie season. The elder Earnhardt won his seventh race in 1979 at Bristol.

Being overshadowed at a Winston Cup track is rare for Dale Sr., but the eclipse was made possible by Texas' newness and Earnhardt's inability to win consistently later in his career – Earnhardt had just six victories in his final 134 races. Earnhardt's pattern at Texas reflected his pattern elsewhere: poor qualifying gave way to strong finishes. His average starting position (26th) is 33rd in track history. His average finish (14th) was ninth best. Surely, Earnhardt would have tried to adopt his son's pattern in 2001: qualify well, then finish even better.

Texas Record Book – All-Time
(min. 2 starts)

Category	Earnhardt's Total	Earnhardt's Rank	All-Time Track Leader*
Money Won	$373,925	9th	Jeff Burton – 785,675
Starts	4	T-1st	25 others with 4 Starts
Total Points	496	8th	B. Labonte, T. Labonte – 652
Avg. Start	26.0	33rd	Steve Park – 4.5
Avg. Finish	14.0	9th	Bobby Labonte – 4.3
Wins	0	—	J. Burton, T. Labonte, Martin, Earnhardt, Jr. – 1
Winning Pct.	0.0	—	Earnhardt, Jr. – 100.0
Top 5s	0	—	Bobby Labonte – 3
Top 10s	3	3rd	B. Labonte, T. Labonte – 4
DNFs	0	—	Ernie Irvan – 3
Poles	0	—	Irwin, Jarrett, Mayfield, T. Labonte – 1
Front Row Starts	0	—	8 tied with 1 Front Row Start
Laps Led	0	—	Terry Labonte – 231
Pct. Led	0.0	—	Terry Labonte – 17.3
Races Led	0	—	Dale Jarrett – 4
Times Led	0	—	Mark Martin – 13
Times Led Most Laps	0	—	Terry Labonte – 2
Bonus Points	0	—	Terry Labonte – 25
Laps Completed	1,207	14th	B. Labonte, T. Labonte – 1,336
Pct. of Laps Completed	90.3	23rd	B. Labonte, T. Labonte, Stewart – 100.0
Points per Race	124.0	10th	B. Labonte, T. Labonte – 163.0
Lead Lap Finishes	3	3rd	B. Labonte, T. Labonte – 4

*2nd-place driver or co-leader listed in parentheses if Earnhardt is track leader.

Track Performance Chart
Texas Motor Speedway
Fort Worth, Texas, 1.5 miles, 24° banking

Year	Date	Race	St.	Fin.	Total Laps	Laps Completed	Laps Led	Condition	Money	Pts.	Bonus Pts.
1997	Apr 6	Interstate Batteries 500	15	6	334	334	0	Running	$111,700	150	0
1998	Apr 5	Texas 500	34	35	334	205	0	Running	55,700	58	0
1999	Mar 28	Primestar 500	38	8	334	334	0	Running	97,775	142	0
2000	Apr 2	DirecTV 500	17	7	334	334	0	Running	108,750	146	0

During the 1990s, Earnhardt and Jeff Gordon were NASCAR's perennial frontrunners. The two won 7 of the decade's 10 championships and combined for 87 wins. *Bill Burt*

Texas World Record Book – All-Time
(min. 3 starts)

Category	Earnhardt's Total	Earnhardt's Rank	All-Time Track Leader*
Money Won	$33,850	9th	Richard Petty – 94,755
Career Starts	3	32nd	B. Allison, C. Gordon, J. Hylton, B. Parsons, R. Petty – 8
Total Points	455	36th	Richard Petty – 1,526
Avg. Start	4.3	3rd	Buddy Baker – 1.8
Avg. Finish	7.7	3rd	Buddy Baker – 4.0
Wins	0	—	Richard Petty – 3
Winning Pct.	0.0	—	Richard Petty – 37.5
Top 5s	1	9th	B. Allison, R. Petty – 6
Top 10s	2	11th	Richard Petty – 7
DNFs	1	37th	Ed Negre, D.K. Ulrich – 4
Poles	0	—	Buddy Baker – 3
Front Row Starts	0	—	Buddy Baker – 4
Laps Led	191	3rd	Buddy Baker – 506
Pct. Led	31.8	2nd	Buddy Baker – 42.2
Races Led	3	4th	Buddy Baker – 5
Times Led	24	3rd	B. Baker, R. Petty – 39
Times Led Most Laps	1	3rd	Buddy Baker – 3
Laps Completed	580	29th	Richard Petty – 1,785
Pct. of Laps Completed	96.7	2nd	Buddy Baker – 97.7
Points per Race	151.7	5th	Cale Yarborough – 172.5
Lead Lap Finishes	1	3rd	Richard Petty – 4

*2nd-place driver or co-leader listed in parentheses if Earnhardt is track leader.

Earnhardt at Texas World Speedway

Dale Earnhardt probably wished the new Texas Motor Speedway had been junked and the old Texas World Speedway revived. He struggled on the new Texas Motor Speedway, which joined the Winston Cup schedule in 1997. At the new track, Earnhardt was not Earnhardt: he never won and never led a lap.

The state of Texas used to be more hospitable to the NASCAR legend, however. Back when stock cars rumbled on the two-mile oval in College Station, Texas—the Winston Cup Grand Nationals raced at the troubled track just eight times before it disappeared in 1981—Earnhardt was a Lone Star force. In each of his three Texas World races, Earnhardt was a contender. He was in front of the field for significant portions of each race, leading 191 of 600 possible laps in his three starts.

In his first Texas race in 1979, Earnhardt seemed to have eventual race winner Darrell Waltrip covered when a cut tire sent Earnhardt into the wall and out of contention. He finished 12th, 11 laps off the pace. In 1980, Earnhardt's challenge to Cale Yarborough ended when his car experienced late-race engine problems. Finally, in his best chance to win in 1981, tire problems allowed Benny Parsons to overtake Earnhardt with just four laps remaining. Earnhardt settled for second place.

Track Performance Chart
Texas World Superspeedway
College Station, Texas, 2.0 miles

Year	Date	Race	St.	Fin.	Total Laps	Laps Completed	Laps Led	Condition	Money	Pts.	Bonus Pts.
1979	Jun 3	Texas 400	3	12	200	189	41	DNF - Crash	$6,400	132	5
1980	Jun 1	NASCAR 400	7	9	200	191	54	Running	8,800	143	5
1981	Jun 7	Budweiser NASCAR 400	3	2	200	200	96	Running	18,650	180	10

No modern-era driver was better on NASCAR's superspeedways (tracks two miles long or longer). His 18 victories were equaled only by legends Richard Petty and David Pearson, but no one can match Earnhardt's career totals in Top 5s, Top 10s, or laps led. *Sean Stringer*

Earnhardt at Watkins Glen International

Road courses were not particularly cooperative in Dale Earnhardt's quest for victories during his 23-year career. The master of oval-track racing had just one victory in 47 road-course starts. Watkins Glen, like Riverside, never contributed to Earnhardt's win total. In his 15 starts at the upstate New York track, his career-best finish was third.

Still, any study of Earnhardt's performance on road courses necessarily produces a healthy respect for his ability to make right turns. For instance, while Earnhardt accumulated a modest 22 poles in his career, only Atlanta Motor Speedway accounts for more career poles than the three he won at Watkins Glen (see chart). Finishing wasn't much of a problem for Earnhardt at Watkins Glen, either. His 11.5 average finish is fourth in track history, trailing only noted road-course drivers Mark Martin, Jeff Gordon and Wally Dallenbach.

Memorable Watkins Glen Moment

1996 The Bud at the Glen. In one of the most stirring performances of his career, Earnhardt shrugged off the excruciating pain of a broken sternum and claimed his third career pole on Watkins Glen's 2.54-mile road course. Just two weeks after a violent wreck at Talladega left him nursing a broken sternum and a fractured collarbone, Earnhardt set a track qualifying record (since broken). He then defied medical opinion by driving the entire race – during which he led a race-high 54 laps—instead of yielding to a relief driver. Earnhardt finished sixth in the race, but once again established his reputation as the toughest driver on the track.

Earnhardt's Career Poles
By Track

Track	No. of Poles
Atlanta	5
Watkins Glen	3
Daytona	3
Talladega	3

Q: How do children learn to count in North Carolina?
A: 1-2-Earnhardt-4-5.
—Joke told in Winston Cup garages

Watkins Glen Record Book – All-Time
(min. 5 starts)

Category	Earnhardt's Total	Earnhardt's Rank	All-Time Track Leader*
Money Won	$449,515	4th	Mark Martin – 734,715
Starts	15	T-1st	5 others with 15 Starts
Total Points	2,023	2nd	Mark Martin – 2,093
Avg. Start	8.2	5th	Jeff Gordon – 5.9
Avg. Finish	11.5	4th	Mark Martin – 5.2
Wins	0	—	J. Gordon, M. Martin – 3
Winning Pct.	0.0	—	Jeff Gordon – 37.5
Top 5s	3	5th	Mark Martin – 11
Top 10s	8	3rd	Mark Martin – 12
DNFs	0	—	Derrike Cope – 6
Poles	3	T-1st	(Mark Martin – 3)
Front Row Starts	3	2nd	Mark Martin – 4
Laps Led	134	4th	Mark Martin – 204
Pct. Led	10.2	4th	Jeff Gordon – 20.3
Races Led	8	2nd	Rusty Wallace – 9
Times Led	12	3rd	M. Martin, R. Wallace – 16
Times Led Most Laps	1	5th	J. Gordon, M. Martin – 3
Bonus Points	45	2nd	Rusty Wallace – 55
Laps Completed	1,310	1st	(Geoffrey Bodine – 1,279)
Pct. of Laps Completed	99.9	2nd	Darrell Waltrip – 100.0
Points per Race	134.9	4th	Mark Martin – 161.0
Lead Lap Finishes	14	T-1st	(Darrell Waltrip – 14)

*2nd-place driver or co-leader listed in parentheses if Earnhardt is track leader.

Track Performance Chart

Watkins Glen International

Watkins Glen, New York, 2.454 miles, Road Course

Year	Date	Race	St.	Fin.	Total Laps	Laps Completed	Laps Led	Condition	Money	Pts.	Bonus Pts.
1986	Aug 10	The Budweiser at the Glen	10	3	90	90	0	Running	$25,250	165	0
1987	Aug 10	The Budweiser at the Glen	11	8	90	90	6	Running	17,005	147	5
1988	Aug 14	The Budweiser at the Glen	19	6	90	90	0	Running	18,530	150	0
1989	Aug 13	The Budweiser at the Glen	4	3	90	90	21	Running	38,140	170	5
1990	Aug 12	The Budweiser at the Glen	1	7	90	90	11	Running	22,380	151	5
1991	Aug 11	The Budweiser at the Glen	8	15	90	90	1	Running	16,180	123	5
1992	Aug 9	The Budweiser at the Glen	1	9	51	51	10	Running	22,430	143	5
1993	Aug 8	The Budweiser at the Glen	5	18	90	90	26	Running	13,510	114	5
1994	Aug 14	The Bud at the Glen	6	3	90	90	5	Running	39,605	170	5
1995	Aug 13	The Bud at the Glen	15	23	90	89	0	Running	30,890	94	0
1996	Aug 11	The Bud at the Glen	1	6	90	90	54	Running	52,960	160	10
1997	Aug 10	The Bud at the Glen	3	16	90	90	0	Running	29,575	115	0
1998	Aug 9	The Bud at the Glen	22	11	90	90	0	Running	36,355	130	0
1999	Aug 15	Frontier at the Glen	14	20	90	90	0	Running	41,525	103	0
2000	Aug 13	Global Crossing @ the Glen	3	25	90	90	0	Running	45,180	88	0

Earnhardt's most impressive characteristic was his ability to lead the pack. He clawed his way to the lead 1,398 times during his career, a modern-era record, outdistancing his rival Darrell Waltrip, who took the lead 1,227 times. *Bill Burt*

Dale Earnhardt's Performance in the Biggest Events

On the Winston Cup schedule, there are races, and then there are events. In the NASCAR world, the biggest events are the season-opening Dayona 500, the Memorial Day Coca-Cola 600 and the Labor Day Southern 500. While other races are popular or important to the Winston Cup schedule—races such as the Brickyard 400, the Bristol night race and the Talladega races—none has yet reached the prestige of the Big Three.

This section details Earnhardt's career in the Major Races, listing career statistics, season-by-season totals and individual race performances. For each of Earnhardt's starts, the following details are listed: year, date, start, finish, total laps, laps completed, laps led, race-ending condition, series championship points and bonus points. For each season, total points, final standing and money earned are listed.

Dale Earnhardt's ability to use the draft to his advantage at Talladega was legendary. Earnhardt won three of the four races at the track in 1999 and 2000. He holds the track record for victories (10) and laps led (1,377). Pictured, Earnhardt takes the high line against, from left, Jimmy Spencer (No. 26 Kmart), Michael Waltrip (No. 7 Nations Rent), Scott Pruett (No. 32 Tide), Ricky Rudd (No. 28 Havoline), Johnny Benson (No. 10 Lycos) and John Andretti (No. 43 STP). *Bill Burt*

Earnhardt in the Daytona 500

Dale Earnhardt's death in the Daytona 500 is so fraught with irony, that many journalists interviewed after the race admitted that they could scarcely grasp the event's meaning and all of the story's angles. The track and the race—the Daytona 500 – never seemed to return the respect Earnhardt unfailingly showed them. Earnhardt professed a deep desire to win at Daytona, in particular the 500; the track mostly repaid him with heartbreak. Cut tires, empty gas tanks, violent wrecks and plain bad luck were Earnhardt's reward. He never gave up on the track, of course. Each year, he returned for more, and often seemed to give as well as he got. No driver dominated Speed Weeks or the 500 like Earnhardt. In fact, by most statistical categories, the contest for greatest Daytona driver isn't even close. For the writers and the fans who followed Earnhardt's career, who knew his love for the track and his history on it, grasping the fact that his death occurred there, just a half mile from the finish line of the sport's biggest event, is nearly unbearable. But when attention returns to the celebrations in Earnhardt's life, Daytona will again emerge as the site of his greatest triumph, the 1998 Daytona 500.

Daytona 500 Performance Chart

Year	Date	St.	Fin.	Laps	Laps Completed	Laps Led	Condition	Money	Pts.	Bonus Pts.
1979	Feb 18	10	8	200	199	10	Running	$22,845	147	5
1980	Feb 18	32	4	200	199	10	Running	36,350	165	5
1981	Feb 15	7	5	200	200	4	Running	37,365	160	5
1982	Feb 14	10	36	200	44	6	DNF - Engine	14,700	60	5
1983	Feb 20	3	35	200	63	2	DNF - Engine	37,011	63	5
1984	Feb 19	29	2	200	200	19	Running	81,825	175	5
1985	Feb 17	18	32	200	84	0	DNF - Engine	17,150	67	0
1986	Feb 16	4	14	200	197	34	DNF - Engine	61,655	126	5
1987	Feb 15	13	5	200	200	16	Running	64,925	160	5
1988	Feb 14	6	10	200	200	2	Running	52,540	139	5
1989	Feb 19	8	3	200	200	3	Running	95,550	170	5
1990	Feb 18	2	5	200	200	155	Running	109,325	165	10
1991	Feb 17	4	5	200	200	46	Running	113,850	160	5
1992	Feb 16	3	9	200	199	0	Running	87,000	138	0
1993	Feb 14	4	2	200	200	107	Running	181,825	180	10
1994	Feb 20	2	7	200	200	45	Running	110,340	151	5
1995	Feb 19	2	2	200	200	23	Running	269,750	175	5
1996	Feb 18	1	2	200	200	32	Running	215,065	175	5
1997	Feb 16	4	31	200	195	48	Running	72,545	75	5
1998	Feb 15	4	1	200	200	107	Running	1,059,105	185	10
1999	Feb 14	4	2	200	200	0	Running	613,659	170	0
2000	Feb 20	21	21	200	200	0	Running	116,075	100	0
2001	Feb 18	7	12	200	199	16	DNF - Crash	194,111	132	5

Daytona 500 Record Book – The Modern Era
(min. 5 starts)

Category	Earnhardt's Total	Earnhardt's Rank	Modern Era Event Leader*
Money Won	$3,664,556	1st	(Jeff Gordon – 3,367,128)
Starts	23	4th	D. Marcis, D. Waltrip: 28
Total Points	3,238	1st	(Darrell Waltrip – 3,106)
Avg. Start	8.6	4th	Mike Skinner – 5.8
Avg. Finish	11.0	2nd	Jody Ridley – 9.7
Wins	1	8th	Richard Petty – 4
Winning Pct.	4.3	17th	Dale Jarrett – 23.1
Top 5s	12	1st	(Bill Elliott – 9)
Top 10s	16	1st	(Bill Elliott – 14)
DNFs	5	23rd	A.J. Foyt – 13
Poles	1	7th	Bill Elliott – 4
Front Row Starts	4	2nd	Bill Elliott – 5
Laps Led	685	1st	(Buddy Baker – 573)
Pct. Led	14.9	2nd	Buddy Baker – 15.9
Races Led	19	1st	(Richard Petty – 14)
Times Led	91	1st	(Cale Yarborough – 69)
Times Led Most Laps	3	T-1st	(B. Allison, B. Baker – 3)
Bonus Points	110	1st	(B. Elliott, R. Petty – 75)
Laps Completed	4,179	4th	Darrell Waltrip – 4,726
Pct. of Laps Completed	90.8	15th	Rick Mast – 99.1
Points per Race	140.7	1st	(Jody Ridley – 135.5)
Lead Lap Finishes	14	1st	(Bill Elliott – 12)

*2nd-place driver or co-leader listed in parentheses if Earnhardt is event leader.

Though he won the race just one time, no driver dominated the Daytona 500 like Earnhardt. He is the only modern-era driver to lead over 100 laps in the 500 three times. His 12 Top 5s and 16 Top 10s are also modern-era records. *Bill Burt*

Earnhardt in the Coca-Cola 600

Perhaps no rookie driver has ever been better prepared for the Coca-Cola 600 in his rookie season than Dale Earnhardt. When he took to the Charlotte track for the 600 as an official newcomer in 1979, Earnhardt had already competed in three previous 600s. The preparation worked as Earnhardt led 121 laps. His success continued throughout his career. Only legend Darrell Waltrip earned more Top 5s and Top 10s in the 600 than Earnhardt during the modern era. Earnhardt accomplished this despite horrific qualifying: His last Top 10 start in the 600 came in 1988.

Coca-Cola 600 Performance Chart

Year	Date	St.	Fin.	Total Laps	Laps Completed	Laps Led	Condition	Money	Pts.	Bonus Pts.
1975	May 25	33	22	400	355	0	Running	$2,425	97	0
1976	May 30	25	31	400	156	0	DNF - Engine	1,725	70	0
1978	May 28	28	17	400	382	0	Running	3,415	112	0
1979	May 27	15	3	400	400	121	Running	27,100	170	5
1980	May 27	4	20	400	367	105	Running	13,690	108	5
1981	May 24	5	18	400	362	54	DNF - Engine	13,675	114	5
1982	May 30	15	30	400	279	122	DNF - Gasket	18,470	83	10
1983	May 29	3	5	400	399	55	Running	28,700	160	5
1984	May 27	19	2	400	400	91	Running	49,625	175	5
1985	May 26	5	4	400	399	97	Running	49,238	170	10
1986	May 25	3	1	400	400	26	Running	98,150	180	5
1987	May 24	3	20	400	305	0	Running	19,600	103	0
1988	May 29	7	13	400	394	0	Running	19,205	124	0
1989	May 28	14	38	400	223	2	DNF - Engine	10,750	54	5
1990	May 27	12	30	400	262	0	Running	13,950	73	0
1991	May 26	14	3	400	400	26	Running	53,650	170	5
1992	May 24	13	1	400	400	54	Running	125,100	180	5
1993	May 30	14	1	400	400	152	Running	156,650	185	10
1994	May 29	24	9	400	397	0	Running	37,950	138	0
1995	May 28	34	6	400	399	38	Running	52,500	155	5
1996	May 26	20	2	400	400	7	Running	97,000	175	5
1997	May 25	33	7	333	333	2	Running	54,400	151	5
1998	May 24	28	39	400	336	0	DNF - Crash	39,580	46	0
1999	May 30	15	6	400	400	0	Running	70,225	150	0
2000	May 28	15	3	400	400	23	Running	103,250	170	5

Coca-Cola 600 Record Book – The Modern Era
(min. 5 starts)

Category	Earnhardt's Total	Earnhardt's Rank	Modern Era Event Leader*
Starts	25	2nd	Darrell Waltrip – 28
Total Points	3,313	2nd	Darrell Waltrip – 3,751.25
Avg. Start	16.0	24th	David Pearson – 2.8
Avg. Finish	13.2	6th	Bobby Labonte – 10.5
Wins	3	2nd	Darrell Waltrip – 5
Winning Pct.	12.0	9th	Jeff Gordon – 37.5
Top 5s	10	2nd	Darrell Waltrip – 11
Top 10s	14	2nd	Darrell Waltrip – 15
DNFs	5	18th	Dave Marcis – 15
Poles	0	—	David Pearson – 6
Front Row Starts	0	—	David Pearson – 9
Laps Led	975	1st	(Bobby Allison – 861)
Pct. Led	9.8	6th	Davey Allison – 15.2
Races Led	16	1st	4 tied with 11 Races Led
Times Led	72	1st	(Darrell Waltrip – 71)
Times Led Most Laps	3	2nd	Bobby Allison – 4
Bonus Points	95	1st	(Bobby Allison – 75)
Laps Completed	8,948	2nd	Darrell Waltrip – 10,317
Pct. of Laps Completed	90.1	18th	Ernie Irvan – 97.5
Points per Race	132.5	12th	David Pearson – 146.9
Lead Lap Finishes	10	1st	(D. Jarrett, D. Waltrip – 7)

*2nd-place driver or co-leader listed in parentheses if Earnhardt is event leader.

The first race of Earnhardt's career was the 1975 World 600 at Charlotte (renamed the Coca-Cola 600 in 1986). In fact, he ran in three 600s before joining the Winston Cup series full time in 1979. Despite the early experience, Earnhardt didn't win his first 600 until 1986. *Don Hamilton*

Earnhardt in the Southern 500

The first time Dale Earnhardt's car won the Southern 500, NASCAR's oldest event, he wasn't driving it. Still nursing injuries from a crash at Pocono a month earlier, Earnhardt missed the race. Instead, stock car legend David Pearson climbed into Rod Osterlund's No. 2 Pontiac and drove to his third Southern 500 win. For Earnhardt, he would have to wait until 1987 for his first Labor Day win at Darlington. He followed up with two more Southern 500 wins in the next three seasons. After ceding to Pearson reluctantly in 1979, Earnhardt conducted himself admirably in Darlington's major event, finishing in the Top 10 on 14 occassions in 22 starts.

Southern 500 Performance Chart

Year	Date	St.	Fin.	Total Laps	Laps Completed	Laps Led	Condition	Money	Pts.	Bonus Pts.
1978	Sep 4	14	16	367	313	0	Running	$3,100	115	0
1979	Sep 3	Did Not Start due to Injury								
1980	Sep 3	8	7	367	366	27	Running	11,125	151	5
1981	Sep 7	10	6	367	366	0	Running	10,695	150	0
1982	Sep 6	5	3	367	367	36	Running	21,225	170	5
1983	Sep 5	17	11	367	363	0	Running	11,855	130	0
1984	Sep 2	20	38	367	57	0	DNF – Engine	7,860	49	0
1985	Sep 1	5	19	367	349	147	DNF – Engine	12,835	116	10
1986	Aug 31	21	9	367	366	17	Running	15,735	143	5
1987	Sep 6	5	1	202	202	109	Running	64,650	185	10
1988	Sep 4	2	3	367	367	85	Running	31,375	170	5
1989	Sep 3	10	1	367	367	153	Running	71,150	185	10
1990	Sep 2	1	1	367	367	99	Running	210,350	185	10
1991	Sep 1	3	8	367	365	22	Running	20,470	147	5
1992	Sep 6	13	29	298	241	0	Running	16,555	76	0
1993	Sep 5	6	4	351	351	101	Running	31,090	165	5
1994	Sep 4	27	2	367	367	87	Running	45,030	175	5
1995	Sep 3	3	2	367	367	208	Running	62,155	180	10
1996	Sep 1	12	12	367	365	0	Running	30,545	127	0
1997	Aug 31	36	30	367	282	0	Running	30,925	73	0
1998	Sep 6	18	4	367	367	0	Running	64,465	160	0
1999	Sep 5	25	22	270	268	0	Running	42,470	97	0
2000	Sep 3	6	3	328	328	47	Running	82,745	170	5

Southern 500 Record Book – The Modern Era

(min. 5 starts)

Category	Earnhardt's Total	Earnhardt's Rank	Modern Era Event Leader*
Starts	22	6th	Darrell Waltrip – 27
Total Points	3,119	3rd	Bill Elliott – 3,326
Avg. Start	12.1	16th	David Pearson – 4.7
Avg. Finish	10.5	4th	Jeff Gordon – 6.1
Wins	3	3rd	J. Gordon, C. Yarborough – 4
Winning Pct.	13.6	7th	Jeff Gordon – 50.0
Top 5s	10	T-1st	(Bill Elliott – 10)
Top 10s	14	3rd	Bill Elliott – 16
DNFs	2	59th	H.B. Bailey, B. Baker – 9
Poles	1	8th	David Pearson – 5
Front Row Starts	2	7th	B. Elliott, D. Pearson – 6
Laps Led	1,138	1st	(Cale Yarborough – 907)
Pct. Led	14.8	4th	Cale Yarborough – 17.0
Races Led	13	3rd	Bill Elliott – 17
Times Led	55	2nd	Darrell Waltrip – 56
Times Led Most Laps	5	1st	(Cale Yarborough – 4)
Bonus Points	90	3rd	B. Elliott, D. Waltrip – 95
Laps Completed	7,151	6th	Darrell Waltrip – 8,252
Pct. of Laps Completed	93.0	12th	Jeff Gordon – 99.8
Points per Race	141.8	6th	Jeff Gordon – 153.8
Lead Lap Finishes	10	2nd	Bill Elliott – 12

*2nd-place driver or co-leader listed in parentheses if Earnhardt is event leader.

The Southern 500 was the scene of another unusual event in Earnhardt's career in 1997. On the opening lap of the race, he blacked out and hit the wall in Turn 3. He returned the car to the pits but had to be relieved by Mike Dillon. Even though Earnhardt had medical tests done the following week, no cause for the incident was ever found. *Bill Burt*

Dale Earnhardt's Performance in All-Star and Qualifying Events

Adding spice to the Winston Cup schedule is a collection of non-points races that, despite having no direct effect on the championship, are nevertheless run with an unbridled urgency sometimes missing from regular point-paying events. Two of the three non-points races currently on the schedule—the Budweiser Shootout and the Winston—are all-star races; the third, the Twin 125 qualifying races, determines the driver's starting spot in the series' most important event, the Daytona 500.

This section details Earnhardt's career performance in these races. For each event, Earnhardt's effort is broken down via a performance chart and summarized in 12 statistical categories. The performance chart lists the year, date, race name, along with Earnhardt's start, finish, total laps, laps completed, laps led, race-ending condition and money earned.

Bud Shootout
Daytona International Speedway

Year	Date	Race	St.	Fin.	Total Laps	Laps Completed	Laps Led	Condition	Money
1980	Feb 10	Busch Clash	5	1	20	20	1	Running	$50,000
1983	Feb 14	Busch Clash	3	12	20	18	0	DNF - Crash	10,000
1986	Feb 9	Busch Clash	4	1	20	20	15	Running	75,000
1987	Feb 8	Busch Clash	4	4	20	20	0	Running	13,000
1988	Feb 7	Busch Clash	2	1	20	20	14	Running	75,000
1991	Feb 10	Busch Clash	6	1	20	20	18	Running	60,000
1993	Feb 7	Busch Clash	13	1	20	20	10	Running	60,000
1994	Feb 13	Busch Clash	3	3	20	20	8	Running	45,000
1995	Feb 12	Busch Clash	2	1	20	20	18	Running	45,000
1996	Feb 11	Busch Clash	16	3	20	20	3	Running	24,000
1997	Feb 9	Busch Clash	9	3	20	20	0	Running	29,000
2001	Feb 11	Budweiser Shootout	2	2	70	70	11	Running	102,722

Earnhardt in the Bud Shootout

Races Run	12
Victories	6
Winning Pct.	50
Total Winnings	$588,722
Top 5s	11
Top 10s	11
DNF's	1
Average Start	5.75
Average Finish	2.8
Races Led	9
Laps Led (Pct.)	98 (33.8)
Laps Completed (Pct.)	288 (99.3)

Crew members and NASCAR officials push the No. 3 Chevy Monte Carlo into position before the 1997 Busch Clash at Daytona. Since renamed the "Budweiser Shootout" and reformatted as a 70-laps race, Earnhardt won the event six times in 11 starts. *David Stringer*

The Goodwrench crew members gather on pit road and send their driver off before the 1997 Busch Clash. Earnhardt, flanked by Ted Musgrave (Primestar), earned a spot in the race by winning poles at Daytona and Watkins Glen during the 1996 season. The Watkins Glen pole, won just 13 days after his horrific crash at Talladega, was the 22nd and last pole of Earnhardt's career. *David Stringer*

Earnhardt in the Twin 125s

Races Run	23
Victories	12
Winning Pct.	52.2
Total Winnings	$505,123
Poles	4
Top 5s	18
Top 10s	20
DNF's	2
Average Start	4.6
Average Finish	5.1
Races Led	14
Laps Led (Pct.)	402 (35)
Laps Completed (Pct.)	1,078 (93.7)

Earnhardt in The Winston

Races Run	16
Victories	3
Winning Pct.	18.8
Total Winnings	$1,285,410
Poles	1
Top 5s	9
Top 10s	12
DNF's	4
Average Start	5.6
Average Finish	7.1
Races Led	11
Laps Led (Pct.)	145 (10.9)
Laps Completed (Pct.)	1,235 (93)

Twin 125s
Daytona International Speedway

Year	Date	Race	St.	Fin.	Total Laps	Laps Completed	Laps Led	Condition	Money
1979	Feb 15	Twin 125 - No. 2	8	4	50	50	0	Running	$2,525
1980	Feb 14	Twin 125 - No. 1	3	31	50	7	1	DNF - Engine	0
1981	Feb 12	Twin 125 - No. 1	6	4	50	50	0	Running	2,275
1982	Feb 11	Twin 125 - No. 2	11	4	50	50	1	Running	3,850
1983	Feb 17	Twin 125 - No. 1	9	1	50	50	—	Running	18,000
1984	Feb 16	Twin 125 - No. 2	4	27	50	21	0	DNF	1,150
1985	Feb 14	Twin 125 - No. 2	5	9	50	50	—	Running	3,500
1986	Feb 13	Twin 125 - No. 2	2	1	50	50	—	Running	22,000
1987	Feb 12	Twin 125 - No. 1	3	7	50	50	—	Running	3,800
1988	Feb 11	Twin 125 - No. 2	5	2	50	50	0	Running	13,000
1989	Feb 16	Twin 125 - No. 2	2	3	50	50	42	Running	12,000
1990	Feb 15	Twin 125 - No. 2	1	1	50	50	24	Running	34,000
1991	Feb 14	Twin 125 - No. 2	3	1	50	50	50	Running	35,000
1992	Feb 13	Twin 125 - No. 1	4	1	50	50	23	Running	35,400
1993	Feb 11	Twin 125 - No. 2	4	1	50	50	34	Running	35,200
1994	Feb 17	Twin 125 - No. 2	1	1	50	50	34	Running	35,200
1995	Feb 16	Twin 125 - No. 2	1	1	50	50	28	Running	35,000
1996	Feb 15	Twin 125 - No. 1	1	1	50	50	21	Running	35,990
1997	Feb 13	Twin 125 - No. 2	5	1	50	50	32	Running	40,589
1998	Feb 12	Twin 125 - No. 2	2	1	50	50	50	Running	42,005
1999	Feb 11	Twin 125 - No. 2	3	1	50	50	43	Running	46,409
2000	Feb 17	Twin 125 - No. 2	9	11	50	50	0	Running	15,346

Among Earnhardt's records, none is more impressive than his 10 consecutive Twin 125 victories from 1990 to 1999 at Daytona. That he built such a streak in a short race (50 laps) on a restrictor-plate track—where leaders are regularly shuffled deep into the field, especially late in the race—is remarkable. As unbreakable as Joe DiMaggio's 56, the streak will live long in the memories of NASCAR fans. *Bill Burt*

Though absent from Victory Lane since 1993, Earnhardt had a memorable career in The Winston—NASCAR's all-star race. His most dominant performance came in 1990 when he started from the pole, led all 70 laps, and won the race. *Bill Burt*

The Winston

Charlotte Motor Speedway†

Year	Date	Race	St.	Fin.	Total Laps	Laps Completed	Laps Led	Condition	Money
1985	May 25	The Winston	7	10	70	70	0	Running	$11,500
1986	May 11	The Winston	3	2	83	83	1	Running	75,000
1987	May 17	The Winston	4	1	135	135	10	Running	200,000
1988	May 22	The Winston	3	7	135	135	17	Running	27,000
1989	May 21	The Winston	2	3	135	135	7	Running	70,000
1990	May 20	The Winston	1	1	70	70	70	Running	325,000
1991	May 19	The Winston	4	10	70	70	0	Running	21,000
1992	May 16	The Winston	8	14	70	69	6	DNF - Crash	25,500
1993	May 22	The Winston	3	1	70	70	2	Running	222,500
1994	May 21	The Winston	11	18	70	49	0	DNF - Crash	18,000
1995	May 20	The Winston	4	14	70	60	4	DNF - Crash	25,500
1996	May 18	The Winston	2	3	70	70	15	Running	100,000
1997	May 17	The Winston	2	4	70	70	11	Running	55,000
1998	May 17	The Winston	19	19	70	9	0	DNF - Crash	18,000
1999	May 22	The Winston	5	4	70	70	2	Running	30,000
2000	May 20	The Winston	12	3	70	70	0	Running	61,410

†Note: 1986 race held at Atlanta International Raceway

Chapter 7

Dale Earnhardt's Performance in the International Race of Champions Series

For 25 years, the International Race of Champions (IROC) has been staged as an exhibition series. Designed to pit the champions of various series together in identically prepared cars, the series attempts to isolate driver talent by removing any mechanical advantage and thereby determine which driver from which series is truly the best.

This section details Earnhardt's IROC career, listing career statistics, season-by-season totals and individual race performances. For each of Earnhardt's races, the following details are listed: year, date, start, finish, total laps, laps completed, laps led, race-ending condition, series championship points and bonus points. For each season, total points, final standing and money earned are listed.

Career IROC Results

Year	Date	Track	St.	Fin.	Laps	Laps Completed	Laps Led	Condition	Pts.	Bonus Pts.		
1984	Jun 16	Michigan Speedway	2	7	50	50	4	Running	8	0	Total Points	31
	Jul 7	Burke Lakefront Airport (Cleveland)	6	10	30	30	0	Running	5	0	Final Standing	9th
	Jul 28	Talladega Superspeedway	3	3	38	38	0	Running	14	0	Prize Winnings	$21,000
	Aug 11	Michigan International Speedway	7	11	50	46	0	Running	4	0		
1987	Feb 13	Daytona International Speedway	8	2	40	40	0	Running	17	0	Total Points	30
	Jun 6	Mid-Ohio Sports Car Course	11	11	29	29	0	Running	4	0	Final Standing	10th
	Aug 1	Michigan International Speedway	6	12	50	12	0	DNF - Crash	3	0	Prize Winnings	$30,000
	Aug 8	Watkins Glen International	8	9	30	30	0	Running	6	0		
1988	Feb 12	Daytona International Speedway	6	2	40	40	0	Running	17	0	Total Points	45
	Jun 11	Riverside International Raceway	11	12	30	10	0	DNF - Crash	3	0	Final Standing	5th
	Aug 6	Michigan International Speedway	6	2	50	50	0	Running	17	0	Prize Winnings	$51,000
	Aug 13	Watkins Glen International	5	7	30	30	0	Running	8	0		
1989	Feb 17	Daytona International Speedway	7	3	40	40	20	Running	19	5	Total Points	57
	Apr 29	Pennsylvania Int. Raceway (Nazareth)	8	7	75	74	0	Running	8	0	Final Standing	4th
	Aug 5	Michigan International Speedway	10	2	50	50	9	Running	20	3	Prize Winnings	$58,900
	Aug 12	Watkins Glen International	3	5	30	30	0	Running	10	0		
1990	May 5	Talladega Superspeedway	9	1	38	38	10	Running	24	3	Total Points	60
	Jul 13	Burke Lakefront Airport (Cleveland)	12	5	30	30	0	Running	10	0	Final Standing	1st
	Aug 4	Michigan International Speedway	2	1	50	50	25	Running	26	5	Prize Winnings	$175,000
1991	Feb 15	Daytona International Speedway	2	12	40	13	4	DNF - Crash	3	0	Total Points	27
	May 4	Talladega Superspeedway	1	9	38	36	2	Running	6	0	Final Standing	9th
	Aug 3	Michigan International Speedway	1	9	50	50	1	Running	6	0	Prize Winnings	$40,000
	Aug 10	Watkins Glen International	9	4	30	30	0	Running	12	0		
1992	Feb 14	Daytona International Speedway	7	1	40	40	12	Running	24	3	Total Points	63
	May 2	Talladega Superspeedway	11	2	38	38	9	Running	19	2	Final Standing	2nd
	Aug 1	Michigan International Speedway	11	5	50	50	0	Running	10	0	Prize Winnings	$65,000
	Aug 15	Michigan International Speedway	11	5	50	50	0	Running	10	0		
1993[1]	May 1	Talladega Superspeedway	5	3	38	38	8	Running	17	3	Total Points[1]	32
	Jul 31	Michigan International Speedway	7	5	50	50	36	Running	15	5		
1994	Feb 18	Daytona International Speedway	1	1	40	40	7	Running	21	0	Total Points	56
	Mar 26	Darlington Raceway	12	4	46	46	0	Running	12	0	Final Standing	4th
	Apr 30	Talladega Superspeedway	11	8	38	38	4	Running	9	2	Prize Winnings	$50,000
	Jul 30	Michigan International Speedway	11	4	50	50	8	Running	14	2		
1995	Feb 17	Daytona International Speedway	2	1	40	40	9	Running	24	3	Total Points	61
	Mar 25	Darlington Raceway	11	8	60	20	0	DNF - Crash	7	0	Final Standing	1st
	Apr 29	Talladega Superspeedway	10	1	38	38	17	Running	26	5	Prize Winnings	$225,000
	Jul 29	Michigan International Speedway	11	11	50	7	0	DNF - Mechanical	4	0		

Year	Date	Track											
1996	Feb 16	Daytona International Speedway	6	1	40	40	3	Running	23	2	Total Points	39
	Apr 27	Talladega Superspeedway	12	9	38	5	0	DNF - Crash	6	0	Final Standing	8th
	May 17	Charlotte Motor Speedway	10	10	67	8	0	DNF - Crash	5	0	Prize Winnings	$40,000
	Aug 17	Michigan Speedway [2]	8	10	50	50	0	Running	5	0		
1997	Feb 14	Daytona International Speedway	2	3	40	40	2	Running	14	0	Total Points	35
	May 16	Charlotte Motor Speedway	9	8	67	67	0	Running	7	0	Final Standing	7th
	Jun 21	California Speedway	8	9	50	50	0	Running	6	0	Prize Winnings	$40,000
	Jul 27	Michigan Speedway	6	7	50	50	0	Running	8	0		
1998	Feb 13	Daytona International Speedway	5	4	30	30	2	Running	12	0	Total Points	36
	May 2	California Speedway	9	10	50	50	0	Running	5	0	Final Standing	7th
	Jun 13	Michigan Speedway	7	4	50	50	0	Running	12	0	Prize Winnings	$40,000
	Jul 31	Indianapolis Motor Speedway	8	8	40	40	0	Running	7	0		
1999	Feb 12	Daytona International Speedway	6	1	40	40	1	Running	21	0	Total Points	75
	Apr 24	Talladega Superspeedway	12	1	38	38	1	Running	21	0	Final Standing	1st
	Jun 11	Michigan Speedway	12	1	50	50	24	Running	26	5	Prize Winnings	$225,000
	Aug 6	Indianapolis Motor Speedway	11	8	40	40	0	Running	7	0		
2000	Feb 18	Daytona International Speedway	1	1	40	40	17	Running	26	5	Total Points	74
	Apr 15	Talladega Superspeedway	12	3	38	38	0	Running	14	0	Final Standing	1st
	Jun 10	Michigan Speedway	12	3	50	50	15	Running	17	3	Prize Winnings	$225,000
	Jul 27	Indianapolis Motor Speedway	12	2	40	40	0	Running	17	0		
2001	Feb 16	Daytona International Speedway	1	7	40	40	15	Running	13	5		
	Apr 15	Talladega Superspeedway										
	Jun 10	Michigan Speedway										
	Jul 27	Indianapolis Motor Speedway										

[1] Earnhardt drove for the late Alan Kulwicki. Points were credited to Kulwicki.

[2] Ricky Rudd drove for the injured Earnhardt. Points were credited to Earnhardt.

Earnhardt's IROC Career

Championships	4
Victories	11
Races Run	57
Winning Pct.	19
Total Winnings	$1,285,900
Top 5's	33
DNF's	7
Average Finish	5.4
Races Led	26
Laps Led (Pct.)	265 (10.5)
Laps Completed (Pct.)	2,197 (89.16)
Total Points	702
Points per Race	12.3
Total Bonus Points	61

Earnhardt's success in racing extended to the International Race of Champions (IROC) series. He competed in the series 14 times, winning 11 races and a record-tying 4 championships. The series was created 25 years ago to pit top drivers from various racing series against each other in identically prepared cars. *David Stringer*

Appendix

Sources and References

Charlotte Observer. 1989-1993.

Fielden, Greg. *Forty Years of Stock Car Racing: Big Bucks and Boycotts, 1965-1971*. Vol. 3. Surfside Beach, S.C.: The Galfield Press.

——. *Forty Years of Stock Car Racing: Forty Plus Four, 1990-1993*. Surfside Beach, S.C.: The Galfield Press, 1994.

——. *Forty Years of Stock Car Racing: The Modern Era, 1972-1989*. Vol. 4. Surfside Beach, S.C.: The Galfield Press, 1990.

Fielden, Greg and Peter Golenbock. *The Stock Car Racing Encyclopedia*. New York: MacMillan, Inc., 1997

Vehorn, Frank. *The Intimidator*. Asheboro, N.C.: Down Home Press, rev. 1999.

Winston Cup Scene, 1992-2000

www.country.com

www.Thatsracin.com

INDEX